D0442127

# Holding Court

## Reflections on the Game I Love

Dick Vitale
with
Dick Weiss

A Division of Howard W. Sams & Company

Published by Masters Press (A Division of Howard W. Sams)
2647 Waterfront Pkwy E. Dr, Suite 300,
Indianapolis, IN 46214



Printed in the United States of America.



**Library of Congress Cataloging-in-Publication Data**

Vitale, Dick.
Holding court: reflections on the game I love / Dick Vitale with Dick Weiss.
p. cm.
ISBN: 1-57028-037-1
1. Basketball--United States. I. Weiss, Dick. II. Title.
GV885.7.V58 1995 95-38479
796.323'0973--dc20 CIP

10 9 8 7 6 5 4 3 2 1

# Table of Contents

Credits:

Edited by Mark Montieth
Cover design by Suzanne Lincoln
Text design by Leah Marckel
Editorial Assistance provided by Kim Heusel and Pat Brady
Cover photos by Jeffrey Camp, Brian Spurlock and Allen Einstein
Interior photos provided by Dick Vitale, with the exception of the photos on pages 49, 68, 85, 96, 108, 113, 135, 231, 241, 246 and 253 © Brian Spurlock, page 76 © Allen Einstein, page 112 by Robert Crawford, page 174 by John Guolielmi of *The New Castle Courier Times*, and page 160 by Robert Smith of *The Leaf Chronicle*

# Acknowledgments

I would first like to thank Dick Vitale, his wife Lorraine and his daughters Sherri and Terri for all their cooperation and patience during this project. It's nice to know there's still room for nice guys at the top. Joan Williamson for reading the manuscript. Tom Bast, Steve Carroll and Mark Montieth of Masters Press for getting the project underway. Peter Goldberg and every one at IMG for their help along the way. Kevin Whitmer, Barry Werner, Cindy Boren, John Temple, Steve Miller, Dave Kaplan, Ian O'Connor, D.L. Cummings, Anthony Rieber, Will Pakutka, Delores Thompson, Wayne Coffey and Adam Berkowitz of the *Daily News* for their constant encouragement and enthusiasm. My parents Dick and Barbara Weiss and my brother Roger. Bob Ryan, Lesley Visser, Larry Donald, Mike Sheridan, Norb Garrett, John Roach, Malcolm Moran, Ivan Maisel, Mark Blaudschun, Tom Luicci, Joe Calabrese,John Rowe, Bill Brill, Rick Bozich, Skip Myslenski, Steve Richardson, Gene Wojciechowski, Tony Kornheiser, Ray Didinger, Steve Wieberg, Howard Garfinkel, Harvey Araton, Bill Benner, John Feinstein, Alex Wolff, Kenny Denlinger, Chet Coppock, Mike Kern, Dick Jerardi, Diane Weiss, Joe Cassidy, Sam Albano, Paul Finebaum, Fran Fraschilla, David Little, Rick Pitino, Mary Flannery, Jerry McLaughlin, Len Shapiro, Tony Barnhart, Tom Shatel, Andy Katz, Joe Biddle, Kevin Scarbinsky, Chris Weiler, Jersey Red Ford, Mike Flynn and Jen Dorfmeister of Blue Star, Rick Troncelliti, Frank Morgan, all the folks at WFAN and the Guys for their friendship and support. — D.W.

# Dedication

I'd like to dedicate this book to all the athletes I had the privilege to coach on the high school level in East Rutherford, N.J. They helped me grow professionally by playing their hearts out and winning back-to-back state championships in 1969 and 1970; to my assistant coaches Bob Stolarz, Al D'Amato, Lou Ravettine and to the administration, faculty and fans of East Rutherford High.

— D.V.

I'd like to dedicate this book to my wife Joan, who should have been a newspaper person, and to all the college basketball writers in America who love the sport as much as I do.

— D.W.

# Holding Court

Reflections on the Game I Love

# Introduction: Greetings, Mr. President

When my ESPN broadcasting partner, Brad Nessler, and I walked into the USAir Arena in Landover, Md., we thought it was going to be just another night at the office — an office with thousands of screaming fans and television cameras all over the place, sure, but hey, that's where I work. Somebody's got to do it.

Then we saw all these security types, with walkie-talkies and firearms.

"Hey, what's going on?" we asked.

"The Prez is coming out here tonight."

"You can't be serious!"

We knew then there was only one thing for us to do: Get the president on the air with us.

At first the security people said no, there was no way. But when we found out he was sitting right behind us, we said, "Look, we just want to talk some hoops."

Bill Clinton is a big hoops fan. He really follows Arkansas, the biggest school in his home state. He took his daughter Chelsea to see George Washington play Massachusetts early in the 1994-95 season, when UMass was numero uno. He even suggested George Washington start the game in a zone. GW coach Mike Jarvis is a man-to-man guy, but he did it. And I'll tell you what, the Prez outcoached Calipari and GW got a big W. C'mon John, baby, I can't understand it. You can't beat the

Prez but you have all these NBA teams knocking on your door? Maybe President Clinton will have a job waiting for him on the sidelines after he leaves the White House.

Anyway, after Nessler and I had settled into our seats, we started hearing some whispers. Something was going on. And before long someone tells us, "You're going to have the president at halftime."

I had never had a chance to talk to a president — THE president — in my life. I was close one time, though. I was at a rally in New Jersey for J.F.K. I didn't get a chance to meet him, but I was close — me and about a million other people.

So, we got President Clinton. Me and Nessler, two-on-one with the Prez. I tell you, we were in our glory. It was amazing the basketball that he knew. Brad asked him a couple of questions about the game and he had insightful answers.

I pointed out a "Clinton-Vitale 96" banner over by the Georgetown pep band. "Hey," I said, "I want to run with you. Think we got a shot?"

"That may be Al Gore's idea," he said.

Then we told him we wanted to go visit him at the White House. Brad said he wanted to jog with him. I said I wanted to shoot some hoops with him in the Rose Garden.

He said, "Let's do it. Get back to me."

I want to go one-on-one with the president. I want to take him to the rack, use a little change of direction, show off my great vertical rise and wham, bam, jam on him! It's going to be Seton Hall against the Hogs. Or maybe Seton Hall against the Hoyas. Clinton's a Hoya, too. That's where he went to college as an undergrad before going on to law school at Yale.

The president's heart belongs to Arkansas, though. He's the No. 1 Hog. He became friends with Eddie Sutton when he was governor of Arkansas and Sutton was coaching the Razorbacks, and he really supports Nolan Richardson's program. He was in Charlotte the night the Hogs won the national title in 1994. They call him The Boss Hog down in

Fayetteville. I'm always teasing him on the air: "The Razorbacks are winning! The Hogs! Woo, Pig Sooie! I can see it now. The Prez is doing a high five with Hillary, baby!"

It was a thrilling moment to get to interview him. We got a picture, which he autographed. I mean, the president! Say anything you want, it's a special moment. It's a great high, sitting there talking to the Prez about playing hoops in the White House. Brad and I were in seventh heaven. We went out afterward and watched the replays over at the hotel. If my buddies in Jersey could see me now.

I couldn't wait to call my daughters at Notre Dame, to tell them to get down there and watch *SportsCenter*. "Your father's gone big time. It's the president and Dickie V. Hello America, here we are!"

I tell you, sometimes I sit back and pinch myself. Me, Dick Vitale, the son of a couple of second-generation Italian immigrants, John and Mae Vitale... a kid from Passaic, N.J. ... the product of a working class family ... a certified bald, one-eyed wacko ... getting to meet the President of the United States!

And it's all because of college basketball. I tell you, it's the greatest game going. I know I'm prejudiced, but no game produces the passion and enthusiasm of college hoops. There's just nothing like it, with the student and alumni support, the pageantry, the bands, the cheerleaders ... all the rah-rah stuff that goes into making college basketball a real happening. There are no strikes, no walkouts, no holdouts, just a bunch of kids playing their hearts out for their schools. There's just so much to love about it. But there are problems, too, there's no doubt about that. There are a lot of things we need to take a look at, a lot of improvements we can make.

So let me hold court with you, and have some fun along the way.

Are you listening, Mr. President?

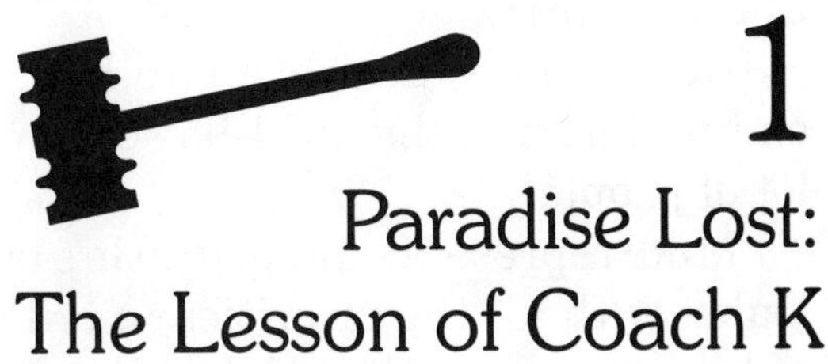

# 1 Paradise Lost: The Lesson of Coach K

Pinch me. Shake me. I couldn't believe it. I was looking at the pairings for the NCAA Tournament on Selection Sunday and I couldn't find the name "Duke."

If there has been one stable force in college basketball over the past decade or so, it has been the Duke Blue Devils. But the 1994-95 season was a wacky year. Duke finished the season with a 13-18 record, 2-14 in the ACC. The 18 losses matched the school record for a season, and the league mark was easily the worst in school history. It was also the first time since the 1985-86 season that Duke fell out of the AP rankings.

Not coincidentally, Duke coach Mike Krzyzewski wasn't on the sidelines for most of it.

If Robert Montgomery Knight of Indiana is a Five-Star General, then Michael K, who played for Knight in college, is approaching Four-Star status. He's led his team to so much success, including seven trips to the Final Four and back-to-back national titles in 1991 and '92. Hey, where do I enlist, baby?

Mike Krzyzewski. I call him the 5-C Man: Character, Communicator, Commitment, Class. And he's Clean. He's created one of the model programs in college basketball.

Mike has it all. He works at a prestigious school that doesn't cheat and he has a chance to recruit the best student-athletes in the country.

But it finally caught up to him. And what Krzyzewski endured during the 1994-95 season served as a lesson to a lot of people.

Mike represents integrity. He's built a model program at Duke, with all the priorities in order. In 1991, when three of his seniors — Alaa Abdelnaby, Robert Brickey and Phil Henderson — didn't graduate, he refused to hang the Final Four banner in Cameron Indoor Stadium until they received their degrees. In the spring of '94 he cancelled a trip to Australia because he was fed up with the poor academic performance of some of his players.

Coach K has taken a lot from Bobby Knight. Mike tells the story about how, when he was at West Point and his father died, Knight went to Chicago and spent time with him and the family. I think Bobby helped instill in Mike a lot of the qualities I admire — especially integrity, loyalty and the importance of being more than just a jump shooter.

*Duke fans are among the most loyal in the country. Here a fan puts his feelings in writing, where everybody can read it.*

Everywhere I go, I hear people talk about emulating Duke.

You should hear the fans: "Why can't we do it the Duke way? Graduate players; have a great basketball environment; win." It's a lot easier said than done, though. The bottom line is, only a limited number of high school players combine both the great academics and the super skills on the basketball court. And Duke has nearly cornered the market on them.

In an age when there is so much scrutiny of college basketball programs around America — from the media, university presidents, and fans — the Duke program rates at the top.

Not only have the Blue Devils won, big-time, they have an outstanding program, in all aspects. They also have Cameron Indoor Stadium, which provides the best atmosphere in all of college basketball. It belongs to the students. They get the best seats, and they sit down front and go bananas. I'm telling you, the place makes your eardrums scream for mercy. And it's the envy of so many fans around the country.

I get a lot of letters from fans saying things like, "Come to our arena and see what it's like. We're just like the Dookies, man." "Wait 'til you come to Stillwater and find out what it's like in Gallagher-Iba." "Wait 'til you come to Missouri and find out what it's like in Tigerland." People always use Duke and the program there as the reference point. Let me share this. I have great respect for so many of the guys working in the trenches across America. But if I had a son, and he was skilled both academically and in shooting the J, you'd better believe I would be proud to see him wear the blue and white of the Dookies. In fact, as a kid growing up, and being an avid follower of college hoops, Dick Groat, the former Dookie and former major-league baseball star, was one of my favorites. I always dreamt of pitching for the Yankees or stroking the jumper wearing a Duke uniform. Yes, Dick Groat had the best of both worlds. He was a star in both sports.

I get a big kick now seeing Dick in my travels. He's the color commentator for the University of Pittsburgh basketball games.

Duke goes back a long way in my mind as being one of the class programs in America. It's only gotten better and better under the guidance of Mike Krzyzewski.

And Coach K has been right in the middle of it all.

A lot of people don't realize Krzyzewski wasn't an established coach when he took over at Duke. It took a lot of courage to hire him, and I have to lay all the credit on Tom Butters, Duke's athletic director. Butters pitched for the Pittsburgh Pirates in the early 1960s. He didn't have a distinguished career, going 2-3 over four seasons, but he's become one of the truly outstanding administrators in college athletics. In fact, he would make a great commissioner for baseball. You look at baseball, and it seems all the owners want is a commissioner who says yes, yes, yes. Butters would be great for the game. Are you listening, owners?

Think about what Butters did when he hired Krzyzewski. He had the guts and the foresight to see beyond the won-lost record, beyond the limited resumé, beyond the lack of name recognition.

Do you know how many qualified coaches wanted the Duke job when it opened up in 1980? Duke wasn't exactly at the bottom of the barrel at the time. They had Gene Banks, Mike Gminski and some other great players. They had reached the Final Four in 1978 and the Final Eight in 1980. This was a program with great tradition, a great reputation.

So Butters goes out and hires a guy who was coming off a losing season at Army. Most athletic directors don't have the guts to do something like that. They want the hottest coach at the moment. They say, "Hey, this guy won 20 games this year; he must be super," rather than looking at the big picture. You see this happen all the time. Georgia hired

Tubby Smith in the spring of 1995. His teams at Tulsa had reached the Sweet Sixteen twice, and he was hot. Dick Bennett got Wisconsin-Green Bay into the tournament in '95 and nearly knocked off Big Ten champion Purdue. The job opens up at Wisconsin and they hire him, after turning him down in the past.

These coaches probably will do a great job, but Butters took a different approach. He studied. He analyzed. He talked to people. He talked to Bob Knight, who was unbelievable in his praise of Krzyzewski. People don't realize the impact Knight had on Coach K getting the job. He did a great job selling Butters, convincing him that Mike fit the Duke puzzle perfectly. "Mike Krzyzewski is Duke," Knight told Butters. Knight was right, and I know Mike is indebted to him.

After Krzyzewski took over, the Coach K Show started. And it's had a great run, last season notwithstanding. He took what he liked from various coaches, including Knight, and applied it in his own style. And it's helped him build a national power that can compete with Dean Smith and North Carolina, Duke's natural rival, down on Tobacco Road.

That's saying something. My guy, the late Jimmy Valvano, used to tell a great story on the banquet circuit about Dean Smith. It may not be 100 percent true, but it gets the point across. It seems a North Carolina State fan was getting a haircut one day, and the barber says, "Boy, Carolina's got a great team."

"Yeah," says the guy, "but look at N.C. State and Norm Sloan. They've got David Thompson. They're 27-0."

And the barber stops and says, "Yeah, but just think what Dean would have done with that team."

That's what Krzyzewski was up against when he started at Duke. Dean Smith had set the standard on Tobacco Road. I call him Michelangelo because he's been the architect of one of college basketball's all-time great programs. He's like an artist at work. He's taken Carolina to two national championships and 10 Final Fours since starting there in 1962. And he's like a fine wine, getting better and better with age.

But Mike has never worked in awe or fear of Dean. A lot of coaches wouldn't have acknowledged North Carolina's success, or they would have been jealous. But Mike said, "I respect what they've done down there. They've done it the right way. But we're going in feeling we're on equal ground. We have to feel we're as good as they are. If we don't feel that way, we won't get the job done."

Now Mike is regarded as Dean's equal. In 1993, when North Carolina beat Duke in the Smith Center, breaking a long Duke winning streak, you should have seen the Carolina fans celebrating, pouring onto the court, jumping with joy. It was Jubilation City, players being hoisted, the whole bit. That was something you never used to see during the regular season. In the past, it was like, "Hey, we're not going to act like that.

Beating Duke is no big deal to us."

Now it's a big deal, for Carolina or anybody else, because of all of Duke's success.

Mike Krzyzewski, 48 years old, was at the absolute top of his profession when the season began in October 1994. But he found out the hard way he wasn't Superman.

Krzyzewski underwent surgery for a ruptured disc on October 21, but rushed back to work within a week. I'm not a doctor, but I knew he came back too quickly. He was back in the gymnasium trying to coach, working late at night. That's the only way he knows how to do things. He's a doer, a worker, an achiever. But along the way he forgot about the most important thing — his health.

Even though he was sitting in a special chair during practice, he was thinking about basketball, not rehabilitation. I heard he stood up all the way on a flight to Hawaii when Duke played in the Rainbow Classic over

Christmas. Here's a guy who was recovering from back surgery, and instead of taking a few months to recover he's flying to Hawaii, coaching, sitting up and watching film.

His hasty return led to exhaustion and finally forced him out of coaching for the rest of the season. Doctors told him on January 4 that he had to concentrate solely on rehabilitating his back. That meant total rest and cutting ties with a basketball program he had built into a giant over the past 15 seasons.

Krzyzewski finally came out of hibernation in March 1995 to meet with the media. After undergoing two months of intensive rehabilitation, he looked relaxed and appeared to be in good spirits. He said he wanted to coach in the ACC Tournament. He said he felt like he *could* coach. But he knew fatigue would set in. This time, common sense prevailed.

Mike knows he can no longer juggle the responsibilities of coaching, a family, and numerous charities with his work with international basketball, the NCAA rules committee, and the National Association of Basketball Coaches. Not if he wants to do his best job for the players.

If confession is good for the soul, Mike did himself a big favor that day when he admitted he tried to come back too early after the operation. "I thought I could get it done in a couple of days," he said. "I was thinking in terms of days instead of weeks, which was foolish on my part. I thought one good week and I'd be back. I'd never had surgery before. It was stupid, and I admit it."

Then, like any good Catholic, he flashed the sign of the cross.

"I could never balance the rehabilitation, the rest and coaching my team," he said. "Finally, my back wasn't getting any better and I was completely exhausted to a point where I couldn't get any sleep. I've never had that feeling before in my life, and you can be damn sure I won't again. It's revealing to me. It shows you have limits no matter who the hell you think you are.

"And there's always somebody there who knows more than you do.

"I've learned that."

When Mike was out, all kinds of crazy rumors started circulating. He had cancer. He was going through a divorce. His wife had given him an ultimatum. He was battling with the school president.

There was no way his wife Mickie was going to leave him.

But she wanted to give him a little jolt, to understand it was time to start thinking about Mike Krzyzewski, time to start thinking more about his wife and family and less about everyone else. A similar thing happened to Bill McCartney, who stepped down as Colorado's football coach after leading the Buffaloes to a Fiesta Bowl victory over Notre Dame in 1995 because he needed to spend more time with his family. I can relate to what the families of coaches have to endure, because I remember what my wife and daughters had to go through when I coached. Think about it. It's Christmas and it's supposed to be a joyous occasion. But my team's getting ready to play in the Motor City Classic, a four-team holiday tournament with Michigan, Eastern Michigan and Western Michigan. Naturally, I scheduled us against what I thought was the easiest opponent, the Hurons of Eastern Michigan. Michigan was to play Western Michigan, and of course I'm figuring we'll play Michigan for the championship with Callihan Hall rockin' and rollin'. In fact, I went out and got a sponsor and bought wrist watches for the winning team. Then I showed them to my players and said, "This is what we're going to be wearing after we win this thing."

But you know what they say about the best-laid plans.

Eastern Michigan beat us in the preliminary game, then Michigan beat us in the consolation. Who suffered the most over the losses? Poor ol' Dickie V? No, my wife and daughters had one of the worst Christmases you could imagine, because I was pouting over the losses. All I wanted to do was get back in the gym and practice and study film so I could relieve the burden I felt. If the guy next door is an accountant, people don't know if he had a bad day at the office or not. But when you're a coach, the wins and losses are all in the newspaper and everybody knows. I really believe coaches' wives are special people because of the pressure they endure. It's amazing how a coach can get wrapped up in his everyday chores and let the family be pushed to the background.

Krzyzewski laid all the rumors to rest, and he dispelled the burnout theory. But the back surgery and the physical and emotional fatigue that came afterward caught up with him. He just had nothing left. It was a valuable lesson for a guy who was trying to do too much, a humbling reminder that you have to keep your priorities in order, that you can't be on top all of the time.

His players wound up having to learn the same lesson.

Duke was 9-3 when Krzyzewski took his leave of absence, and it was obvious how much the players missed him. There are only a relatively few coaches who have built up the special stature and credibility over the years that Krzyzewski has. It's not just about X's and O's or substituting. It's the intangibles they bring to the game. It's about a kid looking into a coach's eyes and realizing he's playing for one of the best. When the game is close and time is running down, it means a lot if a kid can look up at his coach and think, "He'll do the right thing." But now suddenly Duke's players never even got to see their coach, and it had to be tough for them.

When Brent Musburger and I broadcast Duke's game against Virginia for ABC, you could see that the Duke kids were well prepared. They did a fantastic job executing and were up 40-19 at the half. But they lost in double overtime after Virginia's point guard, Cory Alexander, took over.

It was nice to see Virginia's coach, Jeff Jones, do such a good job, but my heart bled for Pete Gaudet, Duke's interim coach. I got into the car after the game and I said to

Musburger, "Wow, can you think what it must be like for him to have to walk into the press conference?" It must have been torture.

Gaudet is so thorough, so precise. He knows the Duke system as well as anybody, next to Krzyzewski. He's also one of the nicest people you'll find in the coaching fraternity, not to mention hard-working and knowledgeable. He's always been one of my sources, a guy I'd call whenever I needed information about a team in theACC or one of Duke's opponents. I could count on him for as good a scouting report as anybody could give.

But he came in and lost a couple of close games early and suddenly the players' confidence began to erode. They started to play as a scared team, not an aggressive team. It just multiplied and multiplied and multiplied. They never were able to get over the hump. They played ACC rivals like North Carolina, Wake Forest, Virginia and Maryland tough, but lost seven games to ranked teams by an average of seven points.

Their most heartbreaking loss had to be against North Carolina at Cameron. I did that game for ESPN, and it doesn't get any better than it was that night. Two schools eight miles apart.

Two of the elite programs in America — forget about Duke's record at the time — going head-to-head in a 102-100 double-overtime game with 9,000 ranting and raving Duke fans pouring their hearts out.

I've been at Cameron when the fans were rocking, but never like this. They were trying to will their team to a W. They were truly the sixth man, a real factor in the game. And I've seen plenty of close, exciting games, even double-overtime games that went down to the final buzzer. But in that game you had a team that was 0-7 in ACC games playing without its head coach, going against its biggest rival, a team that had a great chance to reach the Final Four.

We were broadcasting from way up in the rafters, sitting on a cement block, because Raycom also was televising the game and had courtside priority. But I would have sat on the roof for that game. A lot of the great names in the media were up there with me. It was like a who's who of college basketball media, with sportswriters from all the major newspapers from New York to California.

The game was a shocker in a lot of ways. Carolina could not have played more perfectly at the beginning, jumping out to a 26-9 lead. I was saying to my ESPN partner, Mike Patrick, "Let's get out the filler material." No way did I ever believe Duke would come back and play them to the buzzer in double OT.

I couldn't believe all the great plays. When Jerry Stackhouse made a reverse, one-handed jam, I got so excited I jumped out of my seat and banged my head on a rafter. Patrick started laughing like crazy. "Maybe you'll grow some hair now!" he said.

You had Rasheed Wallace dunking. You had Duke coming back with jumpers by Cherokee Parks, showing the pro scouts what he could do. You had Jeff Capel making a 40-footer at the buzzer to send it into double OT. It went on and on. Patrick and I were screaming by this time. I had a 6 a.m. flight, but as long as I made that, I wanted them to keep playing all night long, just like Lionel Richie once sang. All night long, baby!

I watched my wife during the game. She was sitting along the baseline. She's not a basketball expert — and a lot of critics say her husband's not one, either — but she's a fan who appreciates effort. She said to me later, "Gawd, the sweat, and listening to them talk to one another!" She didn't believe the things the players were saying, the typical basketball chatter: "Bring it in the lane, it's coming back in your face," that kind of thing.

Carolina finally took control of the game when Jeff McInnis scored on a layup and then scored off a steal of the inbounds pass. Duke had one last chance to force a third overtime when freshman Steve Wojciechowski put up a 10-footer just before the buzzer, but the shot bounced off the rim.

At the end of the game, you could see the respect between the two teams. It was Aretha Franklin time, baby. R-E-S-P-E-C-T.

The hugs. The squeezes. Stackhouse with Parks. Wallace and Parks. Wallace and Capel. It was great to see.

I caught the 6 a.m. flight to L.A. the next morning. When I arrived, I put in a call to Dean Smith. I had to tell him I thought it was such a special, special game and to congratulate his players on hanging in there and getting that W. He said, "In all my years of college basketball, in the regular season, that was the best I've ever been involved in."

That's saying something, coming from a guy who's sat through a lot of memorable games. Smith said this, too: "They may be 0-8 in the league, but they have been the toughest team we have played all year long."

The craziest thing about Duke's season, though, was that Gaudet — a veteran coach who was working like mad to keep the team together in Krzyzewski's absence — was making all of $16,000 for his trouble. Total.

Pete filed a suit in Durham in 1994, claiming the NCAA had put a ceiling on his salary: $12,000 in base pay and $4,000 for working Duke's summer camp. The suit was thrown out of federal court. But during the spring, three coaches, including Peter Hermann, the former head coach at the Naval Academy who later became an assistant at Virginia, won a class action suit in California. Now schools can pay part-time assistants a decent salary.

But it's too late for Gaudet, who has left the profession. He simply couldn't make ends meet financially. He's now teaching physical education at Duke, conducting clinics and working for Coach K's private corporation.

I think it was absurd that the NCAA stipulated what a guy can make. Coaches should be like everyone else, earning what the market will bear, whatever a school wants to pay. I find it mind-boggling that in America, in the 1990s, we have salary caps for assistant coaches. Hey, we're supposed to be living in a free enterprise society. It made no sense, when you consider all the money that college basketball generates, for assistant coaches to be making $16,000 a year.

I saw Pete at the Final Four in Seattle. He might as well have been staying at Heartbreak Hotel that week. The pain and disappointment he felt was obvious. A coach's self-esteem gets a little shattered after the kind of season he had been through. I would simply tell Peter that he did the best he could, and that all the people who know basketball respect his knowledge and work habits. Unfortunately, too many fans judge coaches only on their wins and losses, and that's sad.

As long as Pete Gaudet can look in the mirror and say he did everything he could do, he can hold his head high. He ran the same plays Mike did, basically. He kept the system intact. The ball just didn't bounce his way at times. He can feel good about his effort and that his players never quit.

Pete should remember that not everybody has to be a great head coach to be successful. You can take a lot of pride in being a good assistant, too. I think too many coaches, in all sports, get caught up in having to be the boss. Take the case of the Miami Dolphins in 1972. They were undefeated and won the Super Bowl that season, and suddenly everybody wanted to hire Don Shula's assistant coaches.

Hey, just because Shula's team won every game that season doesn't mean his assistants were necessarily cut out to be head coaches. That's what coaches — and the people who hire them — have to learn. In the real world, you have to know your strengths and your weaknesses. Some people make great assistant coaches, but don't make good head coaches, just like some people who make good captains aren't fit to be generals. We see it all the time — guys getting their big break and taking a head coaching job, but failing and going back to being an assistant, or getting out of coaching altogether. It takes a certain kind of personality to be a successful head coach, and you either have it or you don't. You can't buy it, borrow it or steal it.

As for Gaudet, he wasn't working with a typical Duke team, either. Past Duke rosters have been filled with high first-round NBA draft picks such as Danny Ferry, Christian Laettner, Bobby Hurley and Grant Hill. The team Gaudet coached was in somewhat of a rebuilding mode and had only one "star" player: Cherokee Parks.

Parks had a solid season, but he struggled with the losing. He told me at Duke's shoot-around before the Blue Devils were blown out by UCLA in February, "You know, there's nothing like winning. All the numbers, all the stats don't mean anything. I'm just going to keep playing hard."

Parks wound up being the 12th player picked in the NBA draft, by Dallas. Some people might have been surprised by that, but he deserved it. He can post you inside and he's got a velvet touch from outside for a 6-foot-11 player. I'm telling you, he can tinkle the twine all the way out to three-point range. I think he'll make a very good NBA player because anybody who can combine size with shooting touch in the NBA will be a force. When you can shoot the rock, you can hide all sorts of deficiencies.

Duke's troubles really got to some of the younger players.

Guard Chris Collins, son of new Pistons coach Doug Collins, told me he just couldn't get into the groove. The year before, when he was playing with Grant Hill, he could run and hide and knock down threes. Last season, I don't think he ever recovered from a stress fracture he suffered during the off-season. I think he came back too early and he never got his timing down.

Duke also had to play without a creator at point guard, somebody who could break down defenses. Most of Krzyzewski's teams have been able to use dribble penetration to break down defenses, to attack gaps. Last season's club didn't have that ability. Jeff Capel, their sophomore point guard, was brilliant at times, but he had lulls, too.

Capel's struggles exemplified what coaching is all about, why Krzyzewski missed it and why he was missed. After a heartbreaking two-point loss to Maryland, Capel called Krzyzewski late that night. "He said he was down, so I told him to come over to the house," Krzyzewski said. "He brought over some food and we talked the way a coach and player should talk. I missed that.

It's not about wins and losses. It's about relationships. And I think I was getting away from that."

A good relationship takes a lot of hard work — on both sides. Krzyzewski has always demanded a lot from his players, both on and off the court, and he has always demanded a lot from himself. It's paid off because he's one of the few coaches who has been able to keep his players in school for four years. The only one who even thought about leaving early was Danny Ferry.

"A lot of guys play hard," Krzyzewski has said. "They give a great effort. But that's not how you build a winner. How you build a winner is to get a TEAM to play hard. And when a team plays hard, you've got a chance."

That's one thing Krzyzewski hopes to do when he returns.

But what kind of team will he have when he comes back?

Mike's absence had to affect Duke's recruiting because one thing that is always a factor in recruiting — and it's always bothered me — is the negative talk that goes on behind the scenes. It's sad in a way. Another coach could be shaking your hand, but at the same time, because of his desire to win, he sticks it to you behind your back. He does it in little subtle ways, like saying to a prospect: "By the way, son, I understand you're thinking about going to Duke. That's a fine school. Mike is a great guy. Mike's one of the best. But you know, Mike may not be coaching at Duke two or three years from now. He's a little unhappy with the university president. He might go to the NBA, like P.J. Carlesimo."

Sometimes the methods aren't so subtle. When I was recruiting at Detroit, there was an article in one national news magazine that labeled Detroit the 'Murder Capital of the Country.' All of a sudden the players we were recruiting were getting copies of that article. That's the kind of stuff that goes on behind the scenes. Mike should be able to overcome this because he's recruiting a different kind of kid. Most kids choose a school because of the coach, they really do, if everything else, such as geography, is equal. I think Mike can sell Duke University and what it stands for despite his temporary absence. I don't think his absence will hurt his recruiting much at all in the long run.

While he was away from coaching, Mike made it a point to get to know his family again. He's working on those relationships, too. He said he realized he had a problem when his mother called up and said, "Gee, Mike, I really hate to bother you right now. I know you're busy, but I wanted to tell you this ...".

Mike said, "Wow, what is it getting to when my mother hated to bother me on the phone? My mother is 83. I want her to take all my time. She gave me all her time. The people who are closest to you are the most sensitive to who you are as a person."

Mike rediscovered the importance of family during his year off. "It's great to feel loved by people and have enough time to allow people who love you to actually show that to you," Mike said. "That's probably as good a remedy as you can have."

I know where he's coming from because I've dealt with the same thing. When I was coaching I used to say, "Dad, I've got to go now. I've got to run to the airport." And later I'd think, 'Wow, that's my father. I shouldn't do that.'

My father has been struggling lately. He's in his 80s. He's had a heart attack and a small stroke, and he can't walk. He was a big, strong, hard-nosed guy, and now he can't get around on his own. Let me tell you, don't take your family for granted. That's the lesson Mike learned, and we all learn — even if it's too late.

Mike Krzyzewski has a heart as big as the triangle down in Raleigh-Durham, and he never learned how to say no to many of the people who were after him. He helped all kinds of charities, attended so many functions. He's involved in a big way with the Jimmy V Fund, the fund-raising charity for cancer in memory of Jim Valvano, the former North Carolina State coach.

I'll always remember the night Mike and I had to help Jimmy to the stage during the ESPY Awards. Jimmy and his family flew up from Raleigh with the Krzyzewskis. According to Mike, Jimmy was throwing up on the plane and had to be placed in a wheelchair at the hotel. But that night he responded like a true champ. Jimmy V gave a speech that was the most electrifying I had ever heard.

*I realize people sometimes think I'm reaching when I make a point. Here I do it literally while talking with (from left) Bob Ley, Mike Krzyzewski and Jim Valvano during the 1991 NCAA Tournament.*

Jimmy said there were three things he made it a point to do every day: think, laugh and cry. As Jimmy said so eloquently, "Cancer can take away my physical ability, but it can't touch my heart, my soul or my spirit." Jimmy was a special guy, and that night I learned Mike was, too. He's more than a super coach, he's a warm and compassionate person.

I shared some time with Lon Kruger of Florida during the Great Eight Tournament in Detroit at the start of the 1994-95 season. Kruger's team had been in the Final Four in 1994, but was struggling the following season to regain its intensity. He came over to Mike and said, "I don't think we're doing a very good job of handling being in the Final Four. Can you give me some advice on how I can help my players deal with the expectations?"

Mike always has time for everybody. Mike told Lon his players had to realize this was a new season, with new goals and new objectives, and the players had to attack them by giving the same effort they had last season. You can't live on your memories or accomplishments from the previous season, but you can build on your success.

*I love a good game of tennis, especially with people like Krzyzewski, N.C. State coach Les Robinson and Charles Barkley.*

But now Mike has learned to make time for himself. There are a lot of pressures and demands on coaches, not just with the games, but with public speaking, fund-raising, public relations and recruiting. You get into a rut of thinking you have to say yes to everyone, that you can't say no to anything, that you can't be outworked by the other coaches.

I was guilty of it as a coach and I'm guilty of it now as a broadcaster, in a way. But I can't complain. If I don't want to go out and do a speaking engagement, I can simply say no. That's harder for a coach to do because it's important for him to get out with the public and be with the alumni and fans. After all, they're the ones who support the program, the ones who pay the coach's salary. But a coach who makes too many public appearances detracts from his performance in the gym. This is happening more and more. As the money increases, a coach has more demands on his time. Nobody gives you cash for doing nothing. If a company signs you to endorse a product, they want you to come and shake hands with their employees and clients. Everything has its price. Coaches today have to be careful not to be distracted by all the outside influences and maintain a balance.

That's what I love about my job now, the balance. This year, for example, I've been to see Billy Joel, Jon Secada, Natalie Cole, Tina Turner and Jimmy Buffet in concert. When I was coaching at the University of Detroit and with the Detroit Pistons, I never would have done that. It was basketball, basketball, basketball, from the minute I got up until the time I went to sleep late at night. I could never sit at a ballpark and enjoy a spring training game. I would be thinking, 'Oh my God, Michigan's on the phone with a kid now. I've got to get to a phone right now. I've got to find out what this recruit's thinking. I want to have the winning edge. How can I have the winning edge if I'm sitting here and I'm not working?'

Coaches are always worried that they're being outworked. I tell coaches to try to strike a balance between the gymnasium, the outside interests and the family. And always remember that your family comes first. Everything else has to come second because coaching is such an unstable profession today. If you lose your job, you need to be able to fall back on your family.

If you don't have a strong family at a time like that, you're in big trouble. I know that when I got fired by the Pistons, I couldn't have made it without the support of my family.

But it's tough to convince a coach of that when he's got the student body, the alumni and the local talk shows screaming for his head. Today, with the exception of a choice few who are well-established, it's "what have you done for me today?"

Modern coaches face major challenges, as we've seen all over America. Not only did we have the Mike Krzyzewski situation, we had Tim Grgurich at UNLV. He's one of the great assistant coaches of all time, and had been a major reason for Jerry Tarkanian's success there. But when he took over as the head coach at UNLV after the start of the 1994-95 season, he couldn't handle it. He felt like he had to work 24 hours a day to catch up.

All the expectations, the pressure to win, the scrutiny — it just wears on you. It's a 12-month cycle with the academic pressures and recruiting. Then if you do get to the top of the mountain, like a Mike Krzyzewski, a Nolan Richardson or a Jim Harrick, you have to play by a new set of rules.

The same is true for players. Take Michael Jordan. I was watching one of his games after he returned to the Chicago Bulls, and the analysts were saying how he had lost a step, how he couldn't get to the goal, how he had become a jump shooter. This is the type of scrutiny that goes on every night. Here's a guy getting 25 points every night, but it wasn't good enough. Nothing you do is ever good enough.

That same mentality exists in college basketball, and it wears on the coaches. They're human beings, with everyday problems like the rest of us. People don't understand that.

People who are in the limelight have the same problems as everyone else — illnesses, family concerns, the day-to-day challenges of life — and then they have to pick up the paper or listen to the radio or television and have their every move analyzed.

That's why I believe coaches deserve the money they make.

They have to sacrifice a lot to get where they are. The wear and tear of coaching is unbelievable. I don't think I could survive as a coach today, and my wife agrees. I would be a dead man, and I mean that literally. I'd have had a heart attack by now. The hours and the pressure, combined with my personality, would have destroyed my body.

If one of my players didn't graduate or had a problem off the court, I would take it personally. I would be all over kids for not keeping up academically. But then you get accused of using kids, just wanting them to stay eligible so you can play them and win games. And if a kid doesn't get his degree, you get accused of using them and not caring about their lives outside of basketball. You can't win.

No, I couldn't handle it. That's why I believe the best thing that ever happened to me was getting fired by the Pistons early in my second season with the team. It didn't seem like it at the time. I was 38 years old and thought my life was over. I went into a major depression for awhile. But it turned out to be the best thing for me. Yes, Bill Davidson, the Pistons' owner, did me a huge favor by giving me the ziggy.

My heart goes out to the guys today in the high-profile programs where everything they do or say gets written about and discussed. I was reading an article the other day about Arkansas, about what a disappointing year Nolan Richardson's team had. I mean, what are they talking about? Are they serious? Arkansas won 32 games and went to the final game of the tournament. But because they returned five starters from the 1994 NCAA championship team and finished "only" second in '95, some people considered them a failure. Give me a break!

Is there anything that can be done about this situation?

Not really.

We're all guilty. As a member of the media, I'm guilty of it, too. You have newspapers and magazines. You have ESPN, CNN and the other networks. You have radio talk shows. You even have the Internet, with computer bulletin boards where fans write in and rip athletes and coaches all the time for not winning more often.

Everything gets magnified today, and it affects the outlook of the fans. We seem to live in a neurotic age, where people would rather complain about someone else's lack of perfection than work to become better themselves.

I try to be understanding of the coaches because I know what they're going through. But then I get ripped sometimes for being too nice to them. So it's a no-win situation.

You're not going to see as many coaches survive for years at the same school like you used to. I don't think you'll see many guys who last 30 to 40 years at one school. The Dean Smiths, the Bobby Knights, the John Thompsons: they're still at the same schools because they're giants and they can survive a bad year now and then. But the majority of coaches today can't.

Billy Tubbs of TCU said it best when he suggested on ESPN that coaches switch jobs every six years or so. "You've got to pack your bags and go somewhere else if you want to last in this racket. Six years and out," he said.

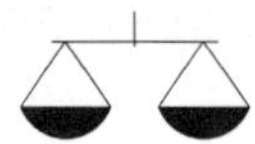

Mike Krzyzewski is joining the ranks of the legends who can survive at one place for as long as they want. He's synonymous with Duke. From talking with Mike over the years, I know he loves everything that Duke stands for. I have asked him many times to share some time with kids who might be interested in becoming students at Duke; not athletes, but everyday students who are friends of my family. Mike lights up with pride when he talks about Duke to these kids. He's Mr. Public Relations for the university, because he sincerely believes it's such a special place.

For that reason, I don't think he'll ever coach anywhere but Duke. The NBA intrigues him, the challenge of instilling the team concept within the superstars of the sport, but I don't think he'll ever do it.

Let's face reality. The college game is dominated by the coaches and the NBA is a player's league. It's wacky. The players there want to run the entire show. Take a look at Portland, where P.J. Carlesimo, the former Seton Hall coach, found out immediately that unless the players agree with everything you say, they'll blast you in the local media. Case in point: Rod Strickland. Then again, with Strickland, what else is new?

I really believe that when Mike studies how crazy the relationship is between the coaches and the players in the pros, he'll decide to remain on the college level. He'll realize what a great situation he has at Duke and not give it up.

Coach K will be back on the sideline. But he'll be back the right way: strong physically, emotionally and mentally. He'll come back rejuvenated. He'll have priorities in order. He'll learn to say no now and then to people who want his time.

But I know he can't wait for next season's tipoff.

# 2
# In Search of Michael Jordan

William Gates and Arthur Agee each had his 15 minutes of fame. They were celluloid heroes, stars of *Hoop Dreams*. The documentary should have been nominated for an Academy Award even though it didn't have a happy ending.

This was no Disney production. The three-hour movie following two inner-city Chicago kids from their early playground days until they entered college should be required viewing for every kid chasing the dream of playing professional basketball.

Gates and Agee both planned to play in the NBA when they were recruited by St. Joseph's of Westchester, a suburban Chicago Catholic school that Isiah Thomas had attended. Arthur even stenciled "Tuss" — Isiah's old nickname — on the back of his sneakers. But each discovered there are no guarantees.

Gates, who is from the Cabrini Green projects, one of the most difficult places in America in which a kid can grow up, had been rated as one of the top sophomores in the country. He received more than 300 letters from colleges. He felt invincible. But he developed knee problems before his junior year in high school and became a backup player at Marquette. He's married now and the father of two. One baby was born the day before Marquette played Virginia Tech in the NIT finals. Gates flew home for the birth and then returned for the final game of his career.

At least he has his head together and understands he's not a kid any more. William is scheduled to graduate with a degree in communications in December 1995. He wants to be a sports reporter on TV and he'll work for the Hoop Dreams Foundation, which awards scholarships to kids like him.

Agee went through tougher times. His father used drugs and his mother struggled to bring the family out of welfare by earning a nurse's aide degree. In the middle of his sophomore year, Arthur transferred to Marshall High near his home because his parents could not afford the tuition on his partial scholarship at St. Joseph's. Eventually, he helped lead his team to an upset victory over Rashard Griffith and King High School in the Chicago Public League title game. He earned a scholarship to Mineral Area Junior College in Flat River, Missouri.

Agee eventually surfaced at Arkansas State, where he averaged 8.3 points and 3.8 assists his senior year. His parents have since reconciled. His father is off drugs. His mother has a good job. But his half-brother was killed. In the spring of 1994, he signed a contract to play for the Florida Sharks of the United States Basketball League.

For him, the dream ended in May when the Sharks' Eric Musselman — yes, the son of Bill Musselman, who's returning to the college ranks at South Alabama — gave him the ziggy.

A lot of kids have dreams like Gates and Agee did. That's great, but too many kids become one-dimensional. They work harder on their jump shot than on their schoolwork, and it comes back to haunt them. Kids need to keep in mind Arthur Ashe's beautiful message: "Get to the library. Get knowledge. When you have knowledge, that gives you options. Read, read and read. Store that knowledge away." That's what too many kids don't understand. They can't play hoops all their lives. Most of them don't get to play beyond high school, and very, very few — less than one percent — make it to the NBA.

It's sad to see so many kids banking on basketball and not investing in their academics. They watch TV and imagine themselves becoming the next Michael Jordan. They go to sleep at night dreaming of playing in the NBA. *Hoop Dreams* brought some of that reality home and showed America that this is crazy, to a certain degree.

I always talk about a boy, a ball and a dream. It's wonderful to have a dream, to pursue a goal, to devote yourself to a great challenge. But you have to have other options. Basketball has to be used in a positive way. Kids can have so many great experiences in basketball without making their living at it. If you never make it past high school competition, or college, so be it. Enjoy that moment. But always try to be the best person you can be, because basketball can open doors in your life that can lead you to great opportunities.

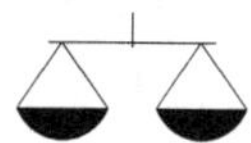

I wish more people stressed that. Maybe more dreams would come true then.

Half the basketball world wants to be the next Michael Jordan. The other half is looking for him. If there's one part of coaching I don't miss, it's recruiting. The pressure to sign the great players is enormous, and it never leaves. Everybody talks about the pressure on the kids, but what about the pressure on a coach who has to make a living? If a college coach can sign one superstar he can change the prospects of the entire team. That's what's unique about basketball. One truly great player, surrounded by decent talent, can take a team a long way.

One of the hottest recruits of recent vintage is Stephon Marbury, a guard out of Lincoln High in Brooklyn who led his team to the big prize, the New York State Federation Championship.

I watched Marbury at the ABCD camp in the summer of '94, and the kid is flat-out for real. He's got the jumper and the ability to penetrate. He's explosive. Just ask 'Garf' — Howard Garfinkel, who has run the grandfather of all summer basketball camps, the Five-Star Camp in Pennsylvania, for the past 30 years. "You can quote me," Garf said. "I've had them all at Five-Star — from Isiah (Thomas) to Kenny (Anderson) — and Stephon Marbury has been the best perimeter player at the high school level to come through our camp."

One NBA scout even suggested if everyone had been eligible for the NBA draft that June, Marbury would have been the first point guard taken.

As soon as Jerry Tarkanian resurfaced as the head coach at Fresno State in late March, he set off an earthquake in college basketball circles. Boom! Speculation that measured 7.0 on the Richter scale arose that Marbury, who had verbally committed to Georgia Tech, had changed his mind and would sign with Fresno State because Tark was going to offer Stephon's brother a job as an assistant coach.

When that story broke out of New York right after the Final Four, Bobby Cremins, the Georgia Tech coach, freaked out. He flew up to New York just to make sure Marbury hadn't changed his mind.

Marbury really had become a big fan of Tark's over the winter. Tark went out to see him play in a holiday tournament in Vegas and then again over Christmas in a game at San Diego. He built up a relationship with the family. People can say what they want, but Tark has a great reputation with his former players. Show me one of them who rips him publicly.

Don't think that wasn't passed on to the Stephon Marburys of the world. "Tark's coming back!" "Big-time winner." "Tark will turn it around." "Tark's great with kids who need direction." The kid may have made a comment or two about how much he liked Tark. And Stephon's father was quoted as saying how much his son always liked Tark and would love to play for Tark.

So then it all got magnified. Tark never spoke to the brother about a job. I know that. That was blown out of proportion. He did speak to the father. Tark's argument is that he wanted to recruit the best kids possible, but that he never had a chance to talk to the kid because he wasn't a head coach when Marbury verbally committed.

The rumors weren't true, though. Bobby Harstein, Marbury's high school coach, told me the kid wasn't thinking in any way, shape or form of going to Fresno State.

Stephon was invited to play in the Magic Johnson Roundball Classic at The Palace of Auburn Hills, and we had some fun at the banquet the night before the game. The place was packed with about 700 people and a lot of writers. I got up to the podium and I said, "Stephon's a little bit nervous now. He asked me if I would intervene on his behalf and share with you this story. As you know, he orally committed to Georgia Tech, but he wants to enjoy the rest of the evening and asked if I would make this announcement. He has changed his mind. He is going to Fresno State."

The place went nuts. Writers were running out the back door to use the phones. I had to shout: "Wait a minute! We're only joking! We're only joking!"

I pulled it off pretty good. I just wanted to have some fun, and we did.

Marbury eventually signed with Tech. His decision didn't really surprise me, when you look at Bobby Cremins and the success he's had with point guards. In fact, Georgia Tech should be renamed Point Guard University.

Think about it. First there was Mark Price, then Kenny Anderson and now Travis Best. Price was the first player taken in the second round of the 1986 draft and has had a great career with the Cleveland Cavaliers. Anderson was a lottery pick with the New Jersey Nets in 1991. And Best was the 23rd player chosen in the first round of the 1995 draft, by the Indiana Pacers.

Cremins gets those types of players because he just turns them loose. Gives them a green light. Kids like his personality, and Atlanta is a booming city with the Olympics coming in. I heard Marbury was nearly a lock for Syracuse until he went to Atlanta to visit Tech. He just fell in love with the environment. I heard his dad and mom still wanted him to go to Syracuse, but at least the kid made his own decision. That's good to hear. A kid should have a chance to go where he wants to go because it's his life and he has to live with the decision.

No one can ever live up to the expectations that are laid out for the supers coming in. No matter what Marbury does, he'll be a target. He turns the ball over several times, misses an important jumper or takes a bad shot, and the critics will come out of nowhere.

I like the kid, I really do. For all the publicity and the notoriety he's received, it's amazing how he carries himself. He just has so much talent. The only thing I worry about — and I see this with a lot of kids who are really gifted — is that he tries to play to the crowd at times. He tries to make the spectacular pass or take the jump shot from 25 feet instead of working for a better shot because he wants to get the fans out of their seats. I watched Marbury for two days and I knew he could take his defender to the goal at will almost any time he wanted. But sometimes he tried to impress everybody by making a play that was basically impossible.

Marbury has been canonized before he's ever played a college game, the same as guys like Kevin Garnett of Farragut High in Chicago; Vince Carter of Daytona Beach, Florida; ShareefAbdul-Rahim of Marietta, Georgia; and Ron Mercer of Oak Hill Academy in Mouth of Wilson, Virginia.

Garnett eventually declared for the '95 NBA draft and was the fifth player selected, by the Minnesota Timberwolves. Carter signed with North Carolina. Adbul-Rahim signed with California. Mercer signed with Kentucky.

Then there's Robert Traylor, known as Tractor Traylor.

Traylor, who scored 22 points in Magic's game in Detroit, is a 6-foot-8, 300-pound Mr. Basketball out of Murray-Wright High School in Detroit who put the finishing touches on another great recruiting year by Michigan. He's going to be a special player. He's agile, mobile and has a great touch. I remember when Charles Barkley, the Round Mound of Rebound, was playing at Auburn. Traylor has the potential to be another Barkley, but it's going to be up to him. He's going to work with a personal trainer and with the training staff at Michigan and try to lose 25 to 30 pounds. He'll dominate if he develops the work ethic that's needed to succeed at the major college level.

The Wolverines also signed Louis Bullock, a 6-3 guard out of Laurel Baptist in Maryland, who scored 40 points in the Capitol Classic, and 6-5 Albert White, another high school All-America from Inkster, Michigan. They've had three Top Five recruiting classes in five years now, setting off another flurry of excitement among their fans. Could this be another Fab Five-type class?

People wonder how Steve Fisher does it. After all, he doesn't come across as the most dynamic guy in the world. But Michigan has one of the hottest programs in America. Their souvenir sales are through the roof. You see kids everywhere wearing their colors. The Fab Five really kicked off a trend, with the baggy shorts and the black shoes and black socks, and kids have been jumping on the bandwagon ever since. It seems like everybody wants to be part of the fashion show in Ann Arbor.

Fisher's got a lot more than image going for him, though. Michigan has great visibility, with a tremendous national alumni corps, and a great reputation academically. Any kid who goes to Michigan is immediately part of something big. Believe me, it has become a recruiter's dream. Fisher sells the school spirit, the sense of pride in wearing the Maize and Blue and the social life on campus. Yes, Ann Arbor is a college town that ranks with the best in the land, and Michigan's coaching staff does a great job of marketing all of its advantages.

But with all this comes the responsibility of evaluating talent and making certain they select the right people to wear their uniform. Over-recruiting can become a nightmare. Like anything else in life, too much of a good thing can turn into a bad thing, and Michigan is already getting a taste of that. Jerod Ward, who was rated as the best high school player in the country coming out of high school in 1994, didn't get many minutes as a freshman. And over the summer Makhtar Ndiaye, who had started several games at center for the Wolverines, said bye-bye because he was worried about his future playing time and transferred to North Carolina.

It's very simple. Everybody wants to play, and when you have a host of high school All-Americas it's difficult to keep them all happy. Believe me, it won't be all peaches and cream for Mr. Fisher. His coaching staff will have to work diligently to keep the players excited about wearing the uniform when they don't get a lot of P.T. Playing time, baby, that's what kids want.

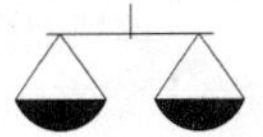

*Steve Fisher is one of the most successful recruiters in the country. His challenge will be figuring out how to keep everyone happy.*

---

Everybody talked about the Big Ten being down in the 1994-95 season, but just think if the Fab Five had remained intact and if Glenn Robinson had stayed for his senior season at Purdue. It would have been the dominant conference in college basketball.

It still wasn't a lock Michigan would have won the national championship even with the Fab Five. That's the thing about the tournament. One bad night and the party's over. Chris Webber, Juwan Howard, Jalen Rose, Jimmy King and Ray Jackson were such a unique group. They fit together perfectly — a small forward, power forward, center, point guard and shooting guard. They also had a certain toughness, a confident attitude that placed them above most kids who come into college basketball.

The Fab Five did something that will never, ever be duplicated in college basketball. Five kids come out of high school and, in less than 12 months, they're marching toward the Final Four and playing for the NCAA championship. That was absolutely awesome. And they did it two years in a row. Rather than be criticized, I think they should be saluted. Steve Fisher did a great job with them.

I could never understand what former UCLA star and NBC analyst Bill Walton was talking about when he said they were the biggest underachievers in the history of the sport. Maybe Bill's standards are different because he was the best post player of his era at UCLA and won two national championships. But not every team can cut down the nets. Michigan lost to Duke, and then to North Carolina. There was no shame in that.

People tried to build Michigan's 1994 recruiting class into the second coming of the Fab Five. Jerod Ward, Maurice Taylor, Willie Mitchell, Travis Conlan and Maceo Baston are all good players and are going to have fine college careers. But if they played the Fab Five it would be an NCer — no contest. Name the score, the Fab Five would dominate.

The Fab Five had to undergo a lot of scrutiny right away, and some blue chippers don't want that. They want to blend in with older players and not have to be "the man" right away. That's what happened with Ron Mercer out of Tennessee.

Kentucky and Tennessee had a real battle over Mercer, who was one of the top three high school prospects in the country. Miami was in there, too. Mercer, like a lot of high school kids, had a lot of adults, including fans and coaches, squirming on pins and needles while he made up his mind. Kentucky fans became concerned when Mercer was supposed to attend Kentucky's final home game, Senior Day, and didn't show up. A lot of people thought Rick Pitino had gone down for the count on that one.

But you couldn't tell that to Pitino. He keeps getting back up. He finally got Mercer into his home and brought out the lasagna and the rigatoni, not to mention the charisma, and got back into the hunt.

Not only did he get back into the hunt, he bagged the big prize. On April 18, 1995 the phone rang at the home of Kevin O'Neill, Tennessee's coach, in Knoxville. It was Ron Mercer. And it wasn't a pleasant conversation. Mr. Mercer told Kevin, "Sorry, but I'm not going to be coming to Tennessee, coach. I've decided on Kentucky."

It wasn't bad enough that he wasn't going to Tennessee. Now he was going to Kentucky, a conference rival, where O'Neill would have to play against him.

Kevin handled his disappointment in a classy way. He said, "Rick did a great job in the home, and he said the kid was very honest about why. He said the kid told him, 'I don't want to come and be a savior. I don't want that kind of pressure. I want to enjoy myself and just be part of a team. When I look at Tennessee, I know it's my home state; but Kentucky offers me a chance to be part of the puzzle.' "

When I talked to Rick that day I could tell, by his tone of voice, that he knew he had signed a kid who could help him to the winner's circle five extra times during the course of a season. Mercer's the kind of player who can make a coach look like a genius.

Billy Packer, the CBS analyst — wow, I'm giving some press to my competition! C'mon, Packer, give me some press! — constantly states that the media overhypes these young players who come in with big reputations. I don't think we do. We just report the facts. Are you kidding me? A kid scores more than 2,000 points, gets all kinds of notoriety from the scouting services, becomes a legend in his hometown ... how can we avoid letting people know about him? You don't have to be a genius to know some kids have instant stardom written all over them after you watch them play in one of the postseason all-star games.

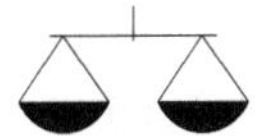

When I was an assistant at Rutgers, and later the head coach at the University of Detroit, a coach could be a workaholic because there were no restrictions placed on you by the NCAA. You could see a kid as many times as you wanted. After awhile you became obsessed with recruiting. I was "guilty" of that. If you went after a kid, you'd just spend hours and hours developing a relationship with him, his family, his coaches, his teachers, even his friends. You could simply outwork people. While the other coaches were at the beach, I'd be writing letters or going to a summer camp somewhere.

That's how my boss at Rutgers, Dick Lloyd, and I got Phil Sellers out of Thomas Jefferson High School in Brooklyn. Sellers was one of the premier high school players in America. He had been named the MVP of the Dapper Dan Roundball Classic and was being recruited by big-time programs all over the country. I can't tell you how many times I drove to Brooklyn to hang around Sellers' school and develop a relationship with him and the people around him.

The rules today favor the established programs by limiting how many times you can have contact with a player. You couldn't get a Phil Sellers to go to a Rutgers today unless you had a unique connection of some kind.

By the way, here's some great trivia: Who reached the Final Four in 1976? Yes, there was Indiana, when the General had the greatest team ever to win the NCAA Tournament. Oh, I can hear them screaming out at UCLA, but I have to go with Indiana. Who else was there? Yes, Michigan and UCLA. The fourth team? Little ol' Rutgers, with Mr. Sellers. Rutgers never would have been a part of the Big Dance that year if today's rules were in effect then, because we never would have been able to persuade him to go to Rutgers if we hadn't courted him so hard.

Today, coaches can see a recruit play five times, and they have only a three-week observation period during the summer. The good side of this is that they can have more time at home with their families, and it enables their assistant coaches to do more than recruit and establish reputations as coaches, too. It's also good for the kids, who don't get hassled as much. The downside is that it makes it much more difficult to evaluate talent, which is an inexact science to begin with, and a lot of kids get overlooked.

The way the rules are written today, the elite schools prosper even more because they don't need additional time to excite a prospect. The rich get richer, because a hot recruit is going to get excited if the phone rings and it's Dean Smith from North Carolina. But when Dickie V from the University of Detroit calls, it's not such a big deal. I would need 30 visits to get the kid to look up off the ground. I would need 30 visits to build up a relationship and get the kid interested in me and my school. That's how I got Phil Sellers to get excited about Rutgers. How can I walk in and sell my program when the Michigans and the North Carolinas and the Kentuckys and the UCLAs have been banging on the door, and he has only a limited time to visit with each of us?

Today's rules don't allow a coach to really get to know the youngsters, to find out about their personal lives and their families. Whenever you go to a high school, everybody there tells you he's the greatest kid in the world; he's a superstar; he's a beautiful person. So you don't know a kid until he arrives on your campus, and then you find out about all the little problems.

In the past, you could really tell who the best recruiters were because everything was equal. We all could go out as many times as we wanted. Maybe you were restricted budget-wise, but if you were close to a metropolitan area there were plenty of players you could chase without spending a lot of money.

Today, when coaches go into a school or home, they're selling their programs. "Hey, look at us. We're Arkansas. We won the national title in 1994; we went to the final game in '95. Look at what we've got to sell. We have the Bud Walton Arena, one of the most magnificent places to play in America. We play in a great conference, the SEC. We're on television all the time."

And if you're a kid and you like Nolan Richardson's fast-paced style of play, you're going to get excited about going to Arkansas. Mike Krzyzewski goes in. He sells Duke. Rick Pitino goes in. He sells Kentucky. Then it's up to the kid to find out where he fits in. A coach from a lesser known school hardly has a chance, and that's too bad. It's sad that the rules restrict those who want to work diligently to bring success to their program.

The big-time programs almost draft players. Rick Pitino has told me he has so many players, he's thinking of having a JV team! If you're coaching at another school and you lose a kid to a program like North Carolina or Kentucky, you can't cry about it, because you're up against so much. You walk into the Dean Smith Center and look up at the ceiling and see all those jerseys hanging — like Michael Jordan's — you know a lot of great players made that same decision. That speaks for itself, and it's hard to recruit against that.

It's also hard for high school kids to say no to the marquee programs, although some of them should. Every kid coming out of high school thinks he's going to be able to play wherever he goes. Most of them think they're just passing through college on their way to the NBA. But kids need to do their homework when it comes to selecting a school. Kids need to take an active role and choose a school, rather than be chosen by one.

Recruits should analyze prospective schools, just as schools analyze them. They should make up charts and rate where they fit in best. With which team can they fit in best? What are the practice sessions like? What other players are already there at their position? Do the players already there seem happy? Do a lot of kids transfer from the program? What is the graduation rate? How will they fit in academically?

A recruit should ask himself a lot of questions before getting excited about wearing a school's jersey or playing on TV. Today, just about everybody plays on TV. And if a player is good enough, the pro scouts are going to find him. Just ask John Stockton, from Gonzaga. Or Scottie Pippen, from Central Arkansas. Or Dennis Rodman, from Southeastern Oklahoma State. The NBA scouting system is so sophisticated today that it's rare for a good college player to be overlooked.

But a lot of kids let their egos get caught up in their decision. They might really want to go to School X, but that school isn't as well known as another one offering a scholarship. So they go to the big-time school to impress their friends and wind up sitting on the bench. Pine City, baby. So they moan and groan and their self-esteem suffers, when they could have gone to a slightly smaller program and been an important part of the team. It's that old question: Do you want to be the big fish in a small pond, or a small fish in the big pond?

Coaches have a responsibility here, too. They have to be realistic regarding their needs and not over-recruit a position. Steve Fisher will go bananas when I say this, but that can create a volatile situation. Don't be surprised if some of the great Michigan recruits from the past couple of years wind up transferring because they became frustrated sitting on the bench. Ndiaye probably won't be the last.

Think about it. At Michigan, you have three frontcourt positions and seven major-league kids trying to fill them. We're not talking about kids who were ranked in the Top 100 out of high school. Most of these kids were ranked in the Top 25.

Traylor will join a group that already includes Willie Mitchell, a Mr. Basketball in Michigan; Jerod Ward, who got rated by Bob Gibbons and some of the other scouting gurus as No. 1 in the nation when he came out of Clinton, Mississippi; Maceo Baston, one of the top high school players in America, from Texas; Maurice Taylor, another Diaper Dandy. Then you throw in Albert White, another freshman All-America from Inkster, Michigan. Something has to give.

But Michigan is one of the hottest schools in America. Kids want to go there. How can Steve Fisher turn his back on a Mr. Basketball from Michigan?

But I have a few questions myself: When does it reach a point where a coach gets too many great players? How can you keep everybody happy in a 40-minute game? Is it fair to the kids to keep bringing in great talent? Do you create more problems than you solve?

Sometimes you need to have a balance. You need players willing to sit on the bench, too. You can get away with stockpiling talent if you win big. Then you shut down all the crying and screaming. But lose a big game at the buzzer — you hear me, Stevie, baby? — and you walk into the locker room and the kids are staring at you and they're thinking, 'Hey, I was Mr. Basketball. When you recruited me, you said I was the best. I should be playing.'

Then you have a nightmare on your hands.

The good news for recruiters is that there are good players everywhere. That's how an Ohio University winds up with a Gary Trent, who was the 11th player taken in the 1995 NBA draft and wound up with Portland. Or Illinois-Chicago gets Sherell Ford, another first-round draft pick. With a little luck, you can find them. Basketball is the most popular game in the country among kids, particularly in the inner city. The days of playing stick ball on city streets are over. Kids go to the playground now and play hoops, which has created a thriving marketplace for college recruiters.

I used to base my recruiting on the summer camps. My first recruiting class at the University of Detroit all came from the Five-Star Camp. I got the job late, but still signed

Walter Smith and Dennis Boyd from New York and Wilbur Ross from Newark. They became the foundation of a successful program.

Five-Star had all the best players in the East. Still does. Founder and co-director Howard Garfinkel, a real Damon Runyon character from New York City, has put together the most dominant camp of its kind. He's been in business 30 years, and his camp has turned out more than 1,000 professional players and some 300 college and NBA coaches who worked there as counselors.

Michael Jordan was discovered there long before he was Michael. Patrick Ewing, Moses Malone, Grant Hill, Chris Mullin, Felipe Lopez, Alonzo Mourning, Isiah Thomas ... they all played on the outdoor courts at Robert Morris and Camp Rosemont in Honesdale, Pa. It was, as Garf likes to say, their Radio City Music Hall, a place to perform and become famous. Bob Knight, Hubie Brown, Chuck Daly, Rick Pitino, Mike Fratello, John Calipari ... they all taught there. No wonder Garf calls it the best teaching camp in the country.

Garf even helped yours truly get his start. I'm not on TV today, I'm not living the type of life I live, without Howard Garfinkel. There's no doubt about it. I was not even on the list for an assistant's job at Rutgers University when Garf got on the phone and sold me to the head coach there, Dick Lloyd, convincing him to interview me. I had to sell myself, but Garf got me in the door. If that interview hadn't happened, I'm probably a principal somewhere in New Jersey. That wouldn't be so bad. I know one thing: all the critics would be sad, because they wouldn't have anybody to put the rip on, baby.

Garf made it happen, and I'll never live it down. Every time he sees me, he screams, "You're nowhere in life without me, baby! And don't you forget it!" He used to bring us in to speak — Hubie, George Raveling and myself. He'd pay us $50, give us a baloney sandwich and send us home. He hasn't changed a bit.

Garf's camp is basically regional. In 1985, Sonny Vaccaro, who was then with Nike, started the first super camp, inviting 125 of the best players in the country — regardless of class — to Princeton for a week-long athletic and academic experience. Nike picked up the tab for everything from flights to tuition.

Three years ago, Sonny left Nike for adidas. He took his ABCD camp with him. But Nike, which didn't want to lose its hold on the best young players in the country, hired Bob Gibbons, who runs the All-Star Sports scouting service, to keep it going.

The NCAA no longer allows free transportation and merchandise, with the exception of a camp T-shirt, if the camp operates within the three-week live observation period in July when coaches are permitted to watch the players in person.

You'd better believe, baby, there's loads of competition between adidas and Nike for the best players. It's sad at times because a lot of personal vendettas surface. The camps get an even split in talent, but hard feelings always arise when both camps are trying to lure the best players. It's like recruiting; someone wins and someone loses.

I look at it this way: Competition brings out the best in everybody. That's the American way, and it makes for better products. I just worry that we have a situation where street agents are wheeling and dealing kids, obviously for their own gain.

I had the honor of speaking at the Magic Johnson Roundball Classic banquet, where many of the high school superstars were gathered. I tried to point out to each youngster that life is more than jump shots and slam dunks. They need to be able to look in the mirror before they go to bed at night and say to themselves, "I'm not a prostitute. Nobody owns me."

All of us have a responsibility to point out to these kids that anybody who gives them cash that early in their careers is only doing it for one purpose, and that's to leech on to them and try to take advantage of them after they start making the big money in the NBA.

Recruiting gurus, meanwhile, scour the summer camp scene in search of the next superstar. The scouting services, such as HSBI, All-Star Sports and Hoop Scoop, record it all and base their ratings largely on what they see during the summer.

These guys get a lot of criticism from all over. The coaches who land the top players complain that their recruits get too much exposure and praise that goes to their heads before they even set foot on campus, and wish the recruiting analysts would back off. The coaches who don't get the highest-rated players complain that the analysts don't know what they're talking about.

But they sell a product that's in high demand, information on high school recruits, and it makes a lot of people — coaches, fans, even me — smarter. Obviously, they're going to make some mistakes. They're human beings trying to rate human beings, and it's impossible to predict how some players will turn out. When a guy makes the big jump from high school to college, you just don't know how he'll respond to his new environment.

You can look at any list of high school All-Americas and second-guess it. Hey, what about Keith Van Horn? He wasn't on any of those lists. Check him out at Utah, playing for Rick Majerus. What about Wake Forest's sensational center, Tim Duncan? Who had him on their list? Hey, David Robinson was a 6-foot-7 kid hardly anybody had heard of when he came out of high school. He wound up going to the Naval Academy and becoming the Naismith Player of the Year.

But don't forget all the guys they do have on their lists who go on to become great players. A guy says to me, "Hey, they missed Tim Duncan." I say, "Oh yeah, but what about a Rasheed Wallace? They miss him? They missAlan Iverson? They miss Raef LaFrentz? Check their lists and see where they had those guys charted."

They hit more often than they miss. So, you see, Bob Gibbons, Clark Francis and Tom Konchalski, I'm defending you. When the recruiting experts rate players, it creates excitement. The fans eat it up. That's all they want to talk about. Whenever I do a talk radio show, it's always recruiting, recruiting, recruiting. But it does put a burden on the coaches. When a Michigan gets a Robert Traylor, a Louis Bullock, an Albert White, the fans know how good they're supposed to be, and they expect poor ol' Steve Fisher to take them to the Final Four. The best thing for coaches to do is just go on, put the team together, and play. The fans are able to tell if a kid's a bust, and they're just as likely to blame the recruiting gurus as the coaches.

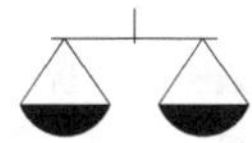

Today, unfortunately, recruiting is a netherworld filled with middle-men and AAU coaches. That's ugly and *Hoop Dreams* showed that. These street agents are sleazy characters who lurk on the playgrounds and latch on to these kids when they're in the eighth, ninth or tenth grade and fill their heads with wild thoughts. Then they try to fill their own pockets with cash by taking money from college recruiters who want to get involved with the kid. They get the kid nice clothes and other stuff before he even sets foot on a college campus. The kid thinks this is the way it's supposed to be, and has a warped outlook from the very beginning.

Then these leeches try to wheel and deal the kid to a high school. Some kids become nomads, going to four or five schools. Or they spend three years in one school and transfer to a prep school for their senior year. That type of recruiting on a high school level troubles me. But I don't know how you eliminate it. You can't prevent a kid from switching schools, or going to a prep school.

Then there are all the AAU tournaments. Most of the good high school kids play 40 to 50 games with AAU teams in the summer. A lot of times they're coached by someone with a strong connection to a major college program who is an unofficial recruiter. Some clubs even have enough money to travel to Europe and Hawaii. You have to wonder what's going on there. There's so much competition between AAU teams for top players that it opens the door for kids to get paid for playing.

All the attention high school kids get from recruiters, recruiting services, all-star teams and AAU teams makes it difficult for them and their college coaches because they expect to be pampered. A lot of times the high school coach gets squeezed out of the picture entirely, which is bad.

When I was coaching at Rutgers, a lot of kids didn't sign until after their senior season. Most didn't decide where to go until after the season ended. But now college recruiters usually have to lock up a player by November of his senior year, during the NCAA's early signing period.

The early signing period takes the pressure off a lot of people. It allows the college coaches to concentrate on scouting underclassmen. It allows the player and his family to enjoy his final season of high school ball in peace, without the phone ringing off the hook all the time. It allows the high school coach to do his job without a lot of distractions.

But the early signing period can force college coaches to make a snap decision that comes back to haunt them. They get caught up in the numbers game. They become worried that they won't be able to sign *anybody,* and decide that they have to sign *somebody*. So they take a kid and hope they can develop him, whereas if they had a chance to watch him play for one more season they would pass on him. Many times a player in this situation winds up transferring or sitting on the bench. And then the coach has to recruit "over his head" by bringing in better players at the same position.

This brings up another issue. A national letter of intent is binding. After a player signs with a college, he can't change his mind without losing a year of eligibility. This is done to protect the coaches, to prevent kids from being lured to another school that has an opening at his position, or has a better chance to win.

But what about when a coach leaves?

I sat and talked with Villanova's All-America guard Kerry Kittles recently. He had signed with Rollie Massimino at Villanova out of St. Augustine in New Orleans. Then Rollie left Villanova for UNLV. Kittles was shocked. He's thinking, 'Wait a minute! I signed to go to Villanova because of Rollie. I wanted to be part of his program. I'm not going to Villanova. I'm going to Tulane with my high school buddy, Pointer Williams.'

But Kittles couldn't do that without losing a year of eligibility right off the bat. He had already signed with Villanova, and was in effect married to that school. It didn't matter that Massimino had left for what looked like a better opportunity at UNLV. The bottom line is, Kittles could have gotten hurt because his choices were restricted. He was locked into staying at Villanova or transferring and losing a year of eligibility. It's totally unfair, and I can't understand why coaches haven't pushed to have this changed.

I don't think there's anything wrong with coaches moving on to another school to improve their situation. As I was saying before, it's difficult these days for a coach to stay at one place for a long time because the pressures mount. Sometimes a change is needed.

But recruits should have the same freedom. Here's an innocent 17-year-old kid who's just had the rug pulled out from under him before he even enrolls in class. That young guy, in my mind, should be given a two-week period to change his mind if he wants to, as long as he doesn't go with the coach who originally signed him in a package deal. If Kittles had gone with Rollie to UNLV, for example, he should have had to sit out a year, because you can't have coaches sign great kids early and then use those recruits as leverage to get better jobs.

Fortunately for Kittles, everything worked out beautifully. He made several All-America teams and led Villanova to the Big East Tournament championship. He was one of the lucky ones. Some kids aren't so fortunate.

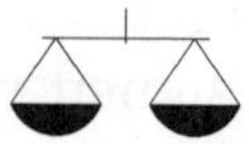

Schools are placing more and more emphasis on academics. And more and more conferences — like the ACC and the SEC — refuse to let coaches take players who haven't met the NCAA standards.

Many coaches have responded to this by building a foundation or plugging holes with junior college players. Cincinnati's Bob Huggins has built a national power with them. Neil McCarthy of New Mexico State has not signed a four-year player since 1989, but that hasn't kept him from winning Big West championships.

Coaches differ on the merit of taking junior college players. Gene Keady of Purdue, who attended a junior college before going to Kansas State and then coached at Hutchinson Junior College, doesn't hesitate to do it if the circumstances are right. Many times a junior college kid is someone who simply matured later than other kids and catches up. A coach who has one hole to fill in his starting lineup can take advantage of the junior colleges because the kid can play right away.

Keady, for example, lost Glenn Robinson to the NBA, but had his other four starters back. He recruited another forward, Roy Hairston, who had been the junior college national player of the year and the MVP of the national tournament.

It seemed like a perfect fit, but Hairston struggled at Purdue. He was playing with and against other great players. He was in a system that placed more emphasis on shot selection and defense. The adjustment for junior college players isn't as great as it is for high school kids, but the juco player usually faces much greater expectations. Many of them are Dow Jonesers at first; their performances go up and down like the stock market. Hairston was an example. He had some good performances early and started the first 15 games in the 1994-95 season, then lost his starting spot. But he came on strong in the NCAA Tournament and appears to be set to have a great senior season.

In most cases, a junior college kid with only two years of eligibility remaining has got to be able to play immediately. I don't think you can bring in a juco to sit on the bench, because you're likely to run into problems. He's impatient because he knows the clock is ticking on his career, and he probably doesn't make a good backup. Why bring in a junior college kid who can play only two years when you can get a high school kid with four years of eligibility left?

But the possibility of a "quick fix" is always going to attract a lot of coaches. Bob Knight used to say he would never take one. He finally signed one, Courtney Witte, to plug a hole in his lineup in 1984. Then he signed two more, Keith Smart and Dean Garrett, when he was shorthanded after the 1985-86 season, and came back and won the national championship the following year with them in the starting lineup. He backed off for awhile, but he has three coming in for the 1995-96 season. He told me he was searching for athleticism, guys who can provide some quickness and athletic ability.

You can't blame coaches for dipping into the junior college pool now and then. Great players like Larry Johnson, Bob McAdoo and Spencer Haywood all went to two-year colleges before going to UNLV, North Carolina and Detroit, respectively, and the NBA is full of former juco players. There's nothing like a Band-Aid for a hurtin' team.

Junior college recruits used to be considered controversial in some circles. But they're nothing compared to the chances some coaches take.

John Thompson certainly did when he took Alan Iverson, the great guard out of Virginia who missed his senior season in high school because he spent four months in jail for his part in a bowling alley brawl.

Here's a teenager who made some mistakes, as his track record shows. But everybody deserves a second chance, and he's getting that. Now it's up to him to take advantage of it. At Georgetown, he'll have an opportunity to get a degree. The graduation rate of Georgetown players is phenomenal. John Thompson has been coaching for 23 years and has always enforced a strong disciplinary code. A lot of kids are looking for that, and I think it's a perfect situation for Iverson. He made it through his freshman season just fine, and believe me, he's going to be a special PTP'er!

Some people ask why Georgetown doesn't give an opportunity to someone else — somebody who's not a basketball star. Hey, John Thompson is there as a basketball coach. His responsibility is to put the best team possible on the floor. If the school's admissions department decides to admit the prospect, why should John Thompson allow the young man to go elsewhere when he has an opportunity to motivate and direct him? There's a saying: "Fool me once, shame on you. Fool me twice, shame on me."

Some critics have been all over John Thompson for taking Iverson, but after Iverson qualified academically over the summer, he could have picked up the phone and been offered a scholarship at 100 other schools in America.

My buddy Jimmy V went through the same thing when he took in Chris Washburn, who was heralded as the No. 1 prospect in America but had a questionable academic background. But Chris could have done the same thing. One call from him to any coach in America, and there would have been 100 guys ready to send a limousine to pick him up at the airport and drive him to the campus.

*John Thompson took a big risk in bringing Alan Iverson to Georgetown, but it looks as though the risk is going to pay off.*

Thompson and Valvano were guilty of one thing — out-recruiting their peers to get a great player. Iverson was destined to become a star from the moment he took the court. In his debut, an exhibition game, he scored 28 points in the first half against Fort Hood. The headline in *The Washington Post* declared "The Age of Iverson." Believe me, every coach in America would like to experience that age.

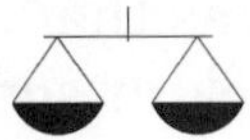

People amaze me. In all my travels, so many people come up to me and accuse one program after another of cheating. It's like some fans believe every school except the one they root for cheats.

Let's face reality. People are not laying cash on kids, providing cars and doing all the things people believe they are. Sure, there's some cheating, obviously. Someone is always looking for the quick fix. But in many cases it involves alumni who get a little too excited during the recruiting process. They want to be Charlie Tuna, the big fish on campus, and they do it by getting to know the student-athlete and doing "favors" for him.

But I think people would be surprised to learn how little of it goes on. I just don't think cheating is nearly as rampant as it was years ago, say in the 1960s or '70s. Every profession, whether it be medicine, law, accounting — pick any line of work you want — has its share of people who break the rules. But I really believe cheating is less common than it was years ago because the rules are much more stringent and specific. For example, years ago an alumnus could entertain a prospect when he visited campus. That can't happen today, and I salute that rule, because a lot of these guys planted the wrong idea in the kid's head. A lot of recruits left campus after a visit with more money than when they arrived. What a way to start a relationship with an athlete. But let's not indict all alumni because many of them love their university and sing its praises in a positive way. I feel for them because it's the sleazy guy who has ruined it for their schools.

Think about it. Why would a coach want to jeopardize a great lifestyle and openly violate rules with all the scrutiny that takes place? Coaches at most schools make a great deal of money with all the extras that are included. Why risk it all on one recruit? You look at some of the guys who have been caught over the years, and they're either out of coaching, working as an assistant somewhere or had to step down to a lower level. It isn't worth the risk.

The NCAA is doing as good a job as possible with its limited staff and resources. The NCAA has come down hard on people, and it's shown it's not afraid to go after the big guys as well as the little guys.

The NCAA's message is very simple: Maryland or Marist, it doesn't matter who you are, the bottom line is that you'll pay big-time if you're caught breaking the rules.

# 3

# Diaper Dandies and other PTPers

The day Felipe Lopez committed to St. John's University, the New York papers went wild. *The Daily News* even came out with a six-page spread. After all, it's not often you get to witness the birth of a savior.

Lopez was born in the Dominican Republic and came to New York City when he was 13 years old. It wasn't long before he had grown to 6-foot-5 and established himself as one of the best young players in the country. Lopez was a prodigy, just like Kenny Anderson had been. He became a two-time high school All-America and led Brother Rice to the New York State Federation 1994 championship. He dominated the two most prestigious postseason all-star games — the McDonald's All-America and the Magic Johnson Roundball classics.

Lopez had achieved heroic status before he ever set foot on the St. John's campus, particularly with the Hispanic population in New York. Season ticket sales jumped for the team's home games at Madison Square Garden. Felipe made the cover of *Sports Illustrated* and was featured in a story about the renaissance of the Big East. *The Daily News* even named him one of the 10 most influential people in sports in New York City. It seemed as if everyone forgot he was only a freshman.

Lopez had a good year statistically, averaging close to 18 points a game. He was one of my Diaper Dandies, along with Alan Iverson of Georgetown, Adonal Foyle of Colgate, Toby Bailey of UCLA, Lorenzen Wright of Memphis and Samaki Walker of Louisville.

I thought the kid did a great job, especially when you consider the personnel around him. If he had gone to a North Carolina or a Kentucky, he could have blended in. At St. John's he was "the man" from the first day of practice. National media outlets were right there from the beginning, banging on his door and knocking it down.

Lopez not only had to play well and make everyone else on his team better, but he also had to lead them to a great season. Unfortunately, it didn't happen. St. John's finished the regular season 14-13, barely good enough to get into the NIT, then lost to South Florida in the first round. If Felipe had a bad night, St. John's was not going to win. And he was going to take the blame.

One day, early in February 1995, I was in New York City for the St. John's-Villanova game that night at the Garden. Several St. John's fans were in the hotel lobby, all dressed up and ready to go to dinner. These were educated people. They came over to me and started moaning and groaning. St. John's was struggling through a losing streak at the time, and they were saying, "Aw, Dick, he's overrated; he's overrated. He's not what we thought." I couldn't believe it. The kid was averaging about 20 points a game and getting eight or nine rebounds. Unfortunately, the expectations were so high he had almost no chance to satisfy everyone.

Anyone who gets a chance to know Felipe will find he's just a beautiful young man. I had a chance to sit with his mother at the adidas All-America Game in Detroit, and the love he has for his mom and his brother is wonderful.

I spoke to the kids before that game. They were given beautiful warm-up jackets. I heard one of the players say, "What's this garbage?" I jumped on them about being spoiled. I said, "Don't you understand? Learn to say thank you; learn to say I love you to the people who care. You're teenagers. People are treating you like royalty." Later, the kid went out of his way to look me up and say to me, "You know, we all really needed this."

But it's not just the players who are spoiled these days, it's the fans. And Felipe is going to have to learn to deal with the expectations and the attention he's going to get. That's part of the formula. If there's a guy who can handle it, I think Felipe will. He's going to be a super player, but people just have to be patient.

Some other great high school players are about to find out what Felipe went through, like Stephon Marbury at Georgia Tech and Ron Mercer at Kentucky. People expect these guys to be giants from the first day of practice. It isn't fair to put that kind of pressure on a young player, but that's what college basketball has become — a game for young players. Most of the best upperclassmen leave early for the NBA these days, so the burden is greater for the freshmen and sophomores to step in and become impact players immediately.

Physically, many of them can do it. The best recruits have played in about 300 games by the time they get to college, with all the summer AAU competition that's out there. But mentally most of them aren't ready to handle the adjustment to college life and basketball. They have to go through a transition period.

A freshman hasn't had enough time to develop his skills, to get a feel for what college is all about. He has to adapt to living in a dormitory, to the academics, to being away from home, to living with a roommate. There's too much going on to be able to jump into major college basketball and be an instant star as well. Remember, these guys are still teenagers. Hey, most of us didn't do anything much more challenging than watch television when we were teenagers. These kids have to play on it. That's why I'm a big believer in freshman ineligibility. Make a kid sit out his freshman year, while still practicing with the team, and then have four years to play.

If freshmen are ineligible, it eliminates a lot of the pressure — on them and on the coaches. The kids have a chance to adjust, to get acclimated to college life outside the public eye like all the other students on campus. They don't have to play a game on ESPN when they're still feeling a little homesick and worried about their English final at the end of their first semester on campus.

By sitting out a year, they have time to get their heads on straight. We hear a lot about the difference between college players today and a generation or two ago. I think today's players are much more spoiled. But it's not their fault. They get so much attention from coaches, street agents, fans, the press, at such an early age. They travel the country playing basketball — not only during the school year, but during the summer — they play on television, they get written up in the newspapers. And everywhere they go, adults roll out the red carpet for them and fawn over them as if they're royalty. This process begins for some of the kids when they're in junior high school. So how can you blame them for not being humble, innocent, down-to-earth young men when they get to college?

Now all of a sudden they get to college and their coach wants to put the handcuffs on them, keep them from playing out of control, fit them into a team concept, because they're no longer the best player on the team. A lot of freshmen are so blown away by this shocking development, they can't adjust. They blame the coach, blame the system, blame their teammates, but never look in the mirror and blame themselves.

Too many kids today forget the basics. They get away from good work habits and fundamentals — the free-throw shooting, the ball-handling drills, the passing skills — and try to rely on athleticism. They focus on making plays that will get them on the late-night highlights package on television.

I've read comments from Isiah Thomas, who is, in my mind, the greatest little man ever to play the game. I can see why he was super, with his work ethic. He's the vice president of the Toronto Raptors, one of the NBA's expansion franchises, and everywhere I go he's sitting in the stands scouting players.

Isiah was a guy who worked on the details of the game. He'd devote hours and hours to improving himself, and he resented anybody who told him he was just a great athlete. And I don't think many kids are doing that these days.

Georgetown's Alan Iverson is considered the next Isiah Thomas by some pro scouts. He's another example of a kid who can't live up to the expectations that are laid out for the supers when they enter college.

Almost from the first time Iverson touched the ball in his first college game againstArkansas, it was said he doesn't understand how to play the game. But he was just a freshman, and one who had not played in a year because of his arrest in high school.

This is a kid with unbelievable quickness and talent. Bob Gibbons wrote recently — and I have to agree with him — that Iverson "does things you can't teach." He started getting better and better as the year progressed. He began to understand how to get Othella Harrington involved in the offense; how to let him touch the ball in the post; how to keep the big guys happy. Alan, you must let the big fellas eat, baby! If you want the rock back, you'd better keep them happy.

I was in the locker room talking to him after one of their games and I just loved his personality, his smile. He seemed to be warm, genuine. He seemed to understand that he'd made a mistake in his life. My heart goes out to anybody who was injured in that bowling alley incident, but there comes a time when a person should be able to get on with his life. Alan Iverson has turned out to be a great thing for John Thompson and Georgetown, and Georgetown has turned out to be a great thing for Alan Iverson.

Like Lopez, he had to come in and contribute immediately. He wasn't surrounded by a lot of great, great talent, but Georgetown had some good runners and jumpers. And the Hoyas got all the way to the Sweet Sixteen of the NCAA Tournament. During the course of the season, Alan learned how to utilize his speed. John Thompson talked to him about not playing in high gear all the time, and tried to get the point across that playing in a basketball game isn't like driving in the Indianapolis 500. Sometimes you have to play like you're caught in a traffic jam at Times Square; you have to slow down and look for someone to pass to.

Georgetown, like Duke, has never had a player leave school early. It will be interesting to see if John Thompson can keep Iverson around for four years. If he can, the Hoyas could be making some noise come tournament time. Georgetown hasn't won the past few years like they did in the Patrick Ewing era. Iverson's got the kind of rare talent that could take them back to the top.

Most freshmen want to play immediately, the way Lopez and Iverson did. Not just play, but star. Ever since Michigan's Fab Five reached the final game of the NCAA Tournament in 1992, kids have that sort of ambition. Hey, it's great to have dreams, but you have to keep your feet on the ground, too.

Sometimes, though, it happens the way it did for 6-11 center Lorenzen Wright of Memphis. He's always been a Windex man, a great rebounder. I'm sure he gets some of that from his father. Herb Wright was a big star in Finland. He used to work as a gym supervisor at a Memphis rec center during the off-season. Then, one night in 1983, his life changed forever.

Herb Wright was getting ready to close down the gym for the night when he ran into a gang of kids he had thrown out earlier. One of them had a gun. Wright was shot and a bullet lodged in his spine. He was paralyzed from the waist down. Lorenzen has dedicated his career to his father.

Herb Wright is coaching junior college these days. But he is constantly working with his son, and it shows. Wright averaged 14.9 points and 10.4 rebounds for Memphis in the 1994-95 season while playing on the same front line as David Vaughn, a first-round NBA draft pick of the Orlando Magic. Wright scored 20 or more points 10 times and had 14 double-doubles for a team that reached the Sweet Sixteen of the NCAA Tournament. I named Wright my Mr. Diaper Dandy for his consistency.

Joe Smith was able to step in and star immediately at Maryland, too, but there was a position waiting for him. Rasheed Wallace and Jerry Stackhouse had to wait their turns when they arrived at North Carolina because they were surrounded by seniors like Eric Montross and Brian Reese. They were great players, but there were many nights their lines in the box score showed seven or eight points. The case of Wallace, Stackhouse and Jeff McInnis led to some internal problems in the locker room. They were high school All-Americas who couldn't remember anything but stardom, and it was a major adjustment for them.

By the same token, if a high school phenom gets a shot immediately and struggles, he might get benched, lose his confidence and wind up watching the coach recruit over his head. The coaches are under such pressure to win that they often don't feel they can afford to be patient with a kid.

Regardless of how it works out, it's easy for young players to lose their equilibrium. A lot of kids have felt the heat to perform from the time they were in eighth grade. That's scary. A lot of them have problems with self-esteem if they don't make it right away. A kid comes in with a big reputation and is afraid to face his friends if he doesn't get it done. Players are reluctant to go back to their old high schools, where their jerseys are hanging in the school's trophy case. They were heroes when they walked down those halls, and now they feel like failures because they're getting zero P.T. And sometimes they take the easy way out, by becoming a Marco Polo, traveling from one school to the next. When 7-

foot center Rashard Griffith signed with Wisconsin in 1993, he was considered the school's most important recruit in modern history. Griffith helped lead the Badgers to their first NCAA Tournament since 1947, but at the end of his freshman year his mother told the Chicago newspapers that her son was considering transferring or entering the NBA draft because Badgers coach Stu Jackson wasn't running an offense that got her son the ball enough.

Wonder where she got that idea? Players should never be able to hold coaches hostage. Griffith did leave Wisconsin early after his sophomore season, but he didn't go until the second round, where he was taken by the Milwaukee Bucks with the 38th pick.

Many of the younger players are better off if they join teams with established players, where the limelight doesn't shine so brightly on them and they're not looked upon as Option No. 1.

I think that really helped players such as Raef LaFrentz at Kansas and Toby Bailey of UCLA. LaFrentz got to play on the same front line with 7-2 Greg Ostertag and 6-10 Greg Pollard. He got to go at his own pace. So did Bailey, who was a supporting cast member for the national champions.

Bailey, a 6-5 guard, had started every game since he began playing organized basketball in Los Angeles. When he arrived in Westwood, he had to adjust to coming off the bench as a sixth man. Bailey eventually moved into the starting lineup, but he never had to be "the man."

When he scored 26 points against Connecticut in the Western Regional finals, he got rave reviews. When he scored two the next game against Oklahoma State, he wasn't hung out to dry. The only thing most people remember about Bailey was the way he went off in the title game, scoring 26 points and limiting Scotty Thurman to five points in the victory over Arkansas.

Bailey got a championship ring for his efforts. Adonal Foyle will never receive that kind of notoriety until he's ready for the NBA draft. Foyle was a 6-10, 260-pound center and one of the top five recruits in the country in 1994 who shocked the basketball world when he selected Colgate, a tiny liberal arts school in Hamilton, N.Y., over Syracuse and Duke.

Foyle grew up in the West Indies on an island with only 800 residents and no electricity. He erupted on the national scene in 1990 after coming to America to study. He averaged 36.2 points, 20.6 rebounds and 6.9 blocks his senior year at Hamilton High, leading his team to the New York Class D state title.

Foyle is a serious student who prefers listening to Broadway show tunes on his headset rather than to rap music. He is taking an acting class and went to see *The Phantom of the Opera* with his guardians, Jay and Joan Mandle, when he was in New York City for the holidays. He has grown to love the theater ever since he saw *The King and I* at a summer music festival in nearby Syracuse two summers ago. He loves to read Faulkner, Shakespeare and Homer. He enjoys history and writing poetry.

If Foyle's priorities are to get a great education and just be a good college player and enjoy himself, fine. Who am I to sit in judgment and say he made a wrong decision? If that experience is one he loves, and he's doing it because he wants to and not because he was pressured by outsiders, then I salute him. Can he become a great college player, a first-round draft pick? Hey, was Dr. J, Julius Erving, a great player coming out of Massachusetts, back in the days when a lot of people didn't know UMass had a basketball program?

The cry we're hearing now is that Foyle can't reach his potential at Colgate, that he can't become a complete player because he won't be playing against the best competition, not just in games but in practice, that he's hurt his chances of making it to the NBA. But, hey, maybe facing constant double- and triple-teaming defenses will help make him better in the long run. He's got a super body and a good touch. He blocks shots and he runs.

And maybe the challenge of going to Colgate, which plays in the Patriot League against the likes of Army, Navy and Lehigh, will inspire him to work hard and make the school a winner. Colgate finished 17-13 Foyle's freshman season and tied for the conference championship as Foyle averaged 17 points and 12.4 rebounds. That could be the start of something big in Hamilton, N.Y.

The Adonal Foyles of the world can rest easy because if you're talented and you can play, it's almost certain you will be discovered. This is true for high school players hoping to get a scholarship and for college players hoping to be drafted by the NBA. It doesn't matter if you're playing at Colgate or in a rain forest in South America, scouts like the NBA's Marty Blake will find you eventually. Basketball is becoming more and more an international game; in fact, it's becoming the favorite sport of the global village.

Increasing numbers of foreign players are finding their way toAmerica's campuses, especially in the Big East, which has become a melting pot of opportunity. Dikembe Mutombo of the Denver Nuggets played for Georgetown. Rony Seikaly of Golden State came to Syracuse from Greece and helped get the Orangemen to the NCAA finals in 1987. Andrew Gaze ofAustralia did the same for Seton Hall in 1989. Nadav Henefeld and Doron Sheffer of Israel have been two of the biggest stars for UConn in the '90s and 7-3 Costantin Popa of Romania helped turn around Miami's program before the L.A. Clippers drafted him in the second round of the 1995 NBA draft.

A lot of people ask me if the college game is becoming too "foreign." Hey, just because the game was invented in this country — by a Canadian, by the way, — doesn't mean we have a lock on it. This is America, baby, the land of opportunity. If a kid from abroad can handle the classwork and proves he can play, I don't see any problem with that. After all, we send our best students to Oxford in England as Rhodes Scholars. Just ask the Prez, Bill Clinton, or Dollar Bill, Senator Bill Bradley.

Three of the four teams in the 1995 Final Four had foreign players on their rosters, and 7-foot center George Zidek of the Czech Republic played a big role in UCLA's championship run.

International players offer a great opportunity for the coaches at less established programs because they don't seem as influenced by reputations. Mike Jarvis of George Washington, for example, has built his program by recruiting overseas. He signed 6-10 center Yinka Dare out of Nigeria and 6-10 center Alexander Koul of Byelorussia. Dare helped GW reach the NCAA Tournament twice before leaving early for the NBA. Koul is a fundamentally sound post player who has a big upside, too.

We're going to see more and more foreign players on American teams. Because of all the coaches from the U.S. going abroad to do clinics and all the international competition that takes place now, foreign players have improved dramatically. They begin playing at younger ages and receive better coaching as they develop. They're becoming an attractive alternative for a lot of coaches, and they're an equalizer, too. A program can improve by leaps and bounds with the addition of one great foreign player, the way Marist did when it had Rik Smits.

Hey, maybe we should change the inscription on the Statue of Liberty from "Give me your tired, your poor ..." to "Give me somebody who can shoot the rock!"

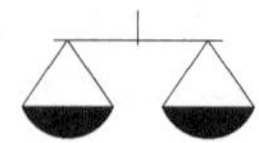

Basketball has had a lot of great success stories in foreign players, but American kids are still writing some great scripts, too. Take Gary Trent, the great forward who did so much to elevate Larry Hunter's program at Ohio University.

Trent had an unbelievable upbringing. He grew up in Columbus, Ohio, and looked like he had no way out. His father, Dexter, was in prison, serving a long-term sentence for drug trafficking. One of his grandmothers was convicted of killing her son. And Gary was headed in the same direction. As a teenager, he admitted selling drugs; and when he was a ninth-grader he missed 80 days of school.

His aunt, Rosalyn Terrell, a stern disciplinarian, and his high school coach, Randy Cotner, who recognized Trent's potential, helped him turn his life around. Trent committed to Ohio U as a junior before Ohio State and the rest of the Big Ten schools discovered him. He skipped the summer camp scene the summer before his senior year to work on his academics and wound up qualifying. He went on to become a three-time MVP in the Mid-American Conference and picked up an appropriate nickname: "The Shaq of the MAC."

Trent stayed at Ohio U for three years before he thought he was ready for the NBA. Michigan State guard Shawn Respert was smart enough to stay four, and look what that did for his stock: he was the eighth pick in the first round. Respert grew up in the same neighborhood in Detroit as Chris Webber and Jalen Rose. He thought about turning pro after his junior year, but called a press conference in May '95 to announce he was coming back. He wound up leading the Big Ten in scoring and became a lottery pick. Now he'll join the millionaire's club. Villanova guard Kerry Kittles made the same smart choice when he decided to stay in school for his senior year. If he has a good season, he could jump to as high as fifth in the draft.

I hate it when great players don't get a chance to reach their potential because of injuries. The three biggest Heartbreak Hotel stories in college hoops in the 1994-95 season were Cory Alexander of Virginia, Keith Kurowski of Notre Dame, and Randy Livingston of LSU.

Cory Alexander really had a tough experience. He suffered a broken foot in the opening game of his junior season and had to sit out the entire year. Then he fractured it again midway through his senior season and had to sit out again. This was a kid who was good enough to turn pro early, but never got a chance to show what he could do. He could have stayed for a fifth season, but he decided to take his game to the NBA. He was the last pick of the first round of the 1995 draft, by San Antonio. Hopefully he'll have better luck there.

But as often happens in sports, one person's misfortune is another's fortune. The break in Alexander's foot turned out to be a great break for Harold Deane. Deane has become a solid point guard, but with Cory Alexander there he would have had to play the off guard. After Alexander's injury, Deane blossomed. He can be one of the best point guards in America, along with Iverson and Jacque Vaughn of Kansas.

It's funny how things work out.

Deane's father was a coach at Virginia Union. He's now a professor. When Deane was in high school, he wanted to go to Virginia, but the coaching staff there thought he wasn't tough enough. So Deane spent a year as a postgraduate student at Fork Union Military Academy, where he averaged 15 points and six assists. Virginia coach Jeff Jones realized he had made a mistake and signed Deane to a scholarship. Good things come to those who wait, and it's certainly true for college athletes. The kids like Respert and Deane have really helped themselves by showing a little patience.

LSU coach Dale Brown thought Randy Livingston would be his next All-America. Livingston was everybody's All-America when he was in high school in New Orleans, but he tore up a knee the summer before his freshman year at LSU. He worked like hell to come back and was leading the nation in assists when he reinjured it against UCLA, and then again three weeks later against Arkansas. Later he had surgery for a fractured knee cap. I called his mom to offer my support and she says to me, "Mr. Vitale, let me tell you something. I'm not worried about Randy. People have to understand Randy has more going for him than just basketball."

"Where is he now?" I asked.

She told me he was back in class, and it was just great to hear.

Kurowski was considered a big-time prospect when he entered Notre Dame in '91. But people never saw what he could do. He came in as a promising recruit from Christian BrothersAcademy in New Jersey. As a freshman, he suffered a fractured foot. Then he had knee surgery and missed six games as a sophomore. Finally, he underwent a 12-hour high frequency radio wave surgery to correct the Wolff-Parkinson-White syndrome that was diagnosed. The condition causes the heart to palpitate, almost like a short circuit.

Kurowski has no history of heart trouble in his family. So, when his heart started fluttering midway through a January 19 practice session at Missouri, he wasn't sure what he was experiencing. The doctors in Columbia gave Kurowski an EKG and he tested out fine, leading South Bend doctors assigned to his case to recommend that Kurowski be put on medication and undergo surgery following the season. After another episode, however, they felt it was in his best interest to move up the timetable.

Kurowski's legs felt like rubber. He lost 11 pounds and tried to come back, but he played only a few games before the doctors told him he had to quit for the season. "I think I need to change my name to get some of that luck of the Irish," he said.

Players like these guys should qualify for battlefield citations. But they also serve as a reminder that athletes, no matter how great they are and how hard they have worked, are not guaranteed a basketball career. That's why they have to hit the books as well as they hit their jumpers, so they have something to fall back on.

Speaking of awards, I'll be giving out more than my share of them on my PTPers show. It's just like the ESPYs, baby, and every year I'll be passing out the envelope.

Take the Albert Einstein Award, for example. It will go to a guy who is brilliant on the court and in the classroom, someone who makes good decisions in life. In 1995 it went to Jacque Vaughn of Kansas. This kid goes to class and is nearly a straight-A student. Then he goes to the gym and passes out eight assists a game. He's a rare student-athlete.

My Thomas Edison Award goes to the most creative playmaker, a 3-D man. That's somebody who can drive, draw and dish the ball with the best of them. I gave it to Tony Miller of Marquette, who ranks fifth all-time in NCAA career assists.

What do Mother Teresa and college hoops have in common? I want to present an award to someone who gives of himself, a player who is very unselfish. He cares about winning, takes the charge, goes after the loose rebound, dives on the floor, plays with intensity. I found Corey Beck. He was the heart and soul of Arkansas' great teams.

We'll present the Arnold Schwarzenegger Award to someone who has a big body, someone who's intimidating, who works out in the weight room. The first recipient was Louis Roe of Massachusetts. The man is a warrior. He was the first player drafted in the second round of the '95 NBA draft, by Detroit. I think he'll be a great player for Doug Collins.

The Human Eraser Award goes to a shot blocker, and the first winner was Roe's teammate, sophomore center Marcus Camby. What does it take to be a great shot blocker? It takes jumping ability and timing, baby, and a player who wants the rock. Camby averaged a block every 6½ minutes.

The Velcro Award goes to the best defensive player in the land. My first one went to Cuonzo Martin of Purdue. He held Shawn Respert to a season-low 12 points, then held Wisconsin's Michael Finley to just nine points three weeks later. Martin wasn't a tremendous athlete, but he was a warrior for the Boilermakers.

The Roadrunner Award goes to the fastest player. There's no doubt who deserved the first one: Iverson. No coyote could catch him.

The Randy Newman Award is named after the guy who wrote that famous song, *Short People.* It honors the best player under 5-10, and in 1995 that was Otis Jones, a scoring whiz from the Air Force Academy who led the WAC in scoring with 24 points a game. This guy can really fly. Literally. He's a pilot, too.

The Ma Bell Award goes to the player who can really dial it up from long distance. Chris Kingsbury of Iowa was the first recipient. He has unbelievable range. He's open as soon as he crosses half-court. He drained almost four three-pointers a game and shot 40 percent from three-point land, and a lot of them were from well behind the line.

The Clark Kent Award goes to a great player who is disguised as an unknown. Texas Christian forward Kurt Thomas deserved the first one. Talk about a great player with no publicity. He's able to grab the rock with a single bound. He's able to leap tall defenders. He was the first guy to lead the nation in scoring and rebounding since Hank Gathers did it in 1989. He didn't escape the attention of the NBA scouts, though. The Miami Heat made him the 10th player selected in the 1995 draft.

The It Takes a Thief Award goes to the player who can pick pockets of ball handlers, and we stayed in the Southwest Conference for the first one. Roderick Anderson of Texas led the SWC in steals with 3.5 a game.

What makes college basketball so special are the supreme efforts these young amateur athletes put out. I'll never forget doing Indiana's game against Michigan for ESPN in January of 1995 and watching freshman guard Neil Reed play with a separated shoulder. He had tears in his eyes as he kept picking himself up off the floor. His performance against Michigan reminded me so much of Willis Reed's performance in Game 7 of the NBA finals against the Lakers in 1970.

I'd like to see a Most Courageous Award named for Jimmy Valvano, so his name could carry on. It would go to a college basketball player who demonstrates great courage, who battles the odds. I think the trophy should be handed out at the same time they hand out the Naismith and the Wooden awards.

Every season would produce a lot of great candidates. Guys like Ed O'Bannon, who some people thought would never play again after he tore up his anterior cruciate ligament. Not only did he play again, but he became America's best player at the end of the year. Or Alan Henderson of Indiana, Shawn Respert of Michigan State, and Randolph Childress of Wake Forest. These guys all had to undergo major surgery and spend hours and hours of rehab to be able to play again.

The Jimmy V Award would be something special. And Jimmy, who was such a battler, would be proud to know a student athlete would be carrying a gold trophy with his name shining on it.

*Jim Valvano was Mr. Courage for the way he battled cancer. I really loved working with the V-man because he had a special passion for college hoops.*

# 4 Hit-and-Runs

In the end, University of Maryland sophomore center Joe Smith got tired of answering the same question over and over.

Smith needed a police escort just to get to Maryland's basketball banquet. There were 900 people there, and most of them were in his ear, pounding away, wanting to know whether he'd be a Terp or a pro next season. Two days later, Smith decided to end the suspense. He said he was going to make himself available for the NBA draft.

Joe said he wasn't doing it for the money. He wanted to do something for his mother, Letha, who had raised seven kids. Then he leaned over into her lap and started to cry.

Personally, I would have been crying if I were Smith's coach at Maryland, Gary Williams. Lots of tears.

Smith was primarily responsible for making the Terps a contender in the Atlantic Coast Conference for the first time since Lenny Bias had played there. He was voted MVP in the conference, finishing ahead of sophomore center Rasheed Wallace and sophomore forward Jerry Stackhouse, both All-American out of North Carolina. He also won several national player of the year awards.

It's a little scary to think what might have happened if Smith had been able to follow through on his childhood dream. He grew up in Norfolk, Va., wanting to play for North Carolina. He even convinced his mother to spend $70 for a Tar Heel jacket when he was in junior high school. But he never heard from Dean Smith and eventually signed with Maryland. Can you imagine how good Carolina could have been with a front line of Joe Smith, Rasheed Wallace and Jerry Stackhouse? Are you kidding me? There might have been another banner hanging in the Dean Dome by now.

But maybe Maryland was the perfect place for Smith to develop, without having to share the ball or the limelight. He led Maryland to the Sweet Sixteen for the second consecutive year in March 1995. But after his team lost to UConn in the Western Regional semifinals, he started to investigate his options. When he learned that he would go anywhere from 1 through 3 in the NBA draft, he followed his heart and did what he thought was best for his family. He wound up going numero uno, to the Golden State Warriors.

You can't blame Smith. You have to think about the kind of dollars he's going to make. We're not talking about a million dollars. We're talking $40, $50, $60 million dollars from his first contract alone. We're talking about stacks and stacks and stacks of cash. How can a kid turn that down when his mother is struggling to get by?

The Joe Smiths of college basketball have all seen the megadollars that players like Glenn Robinson of Purdue and Chris Webber of Michigan are making in the NBA, and they want to be part of the gold rush. In 1994, Robinson, the first pick in the draft, signed with the Milwaukee Bucks for $60 million. In 1993, Webber got $74 million from Golden State. With all the talk about the NBA imposing a salary cap, they want to get in before the golden goose lays its final egg. And who can blame them?

I didn't like salary caps for assistant coaches in college, but I think caps for NBA rookies will bring some reality to the game. The marketplace is out of whack in professional sports because rookies are being paid more than established veterans. The kid coming out of college who has never stroked the J on the big-time level doesn't deserve as much money as the star.

And remember, the rookies won't be living in poverty. They'll make plenty of money and have a chance to become free agents after a few years. Then they can break the bank if they have produced. The kids coming out of college who are entering the corporate world don't make more money than the vice presidents who have been there for several years. It should work the same way in professional athletics.

But even if the NBA does decide to institute a rookie cap, I expect it to be challenged in the courts. I might have a problem with untried rookies making more money than veterans who have proven themselves, but I don't know if the courts will agree.

Smith was just one of several underclassmen who took part in the NBA's gold rush. Within a week of the 1995 Final Four, Arkansas' 6-foot-8 forward Corliss Williamson and Arizona State's 6-9 forward Mario Bennett, a pair of juniors, both declared for the draft. They were joined shortly by Smith, 6-8 Ohio U junior forward Gary Trent, Arkansas junior guard Scotty Thurman, Kentucky's junior forward Rodrick Rhodes, Southern Illinois' junior forward Chris Carr, both Wallace and Stackhouse, Antonio McDyess of Alabama, and Rashard Griffith of Wisconsin.

Kevin Garnett went them all one better by jumping in straight out of high school. Garnett, a 6-11, 215-pound forward from Farragut High in Chicago, averaged 25.2 points, 17.9 rebounds and 6.5 blocks and was voted Mr. Basketball in Illinois.

He was thinking about Michigan, North Carolina and South Carolina, but he decided to enter the NBA after he fell one point short of the ACT score of 17 required for NCAA Division I eligibility. He took the test again to become eligible, but it didn't matter. He had made up his mind. And it paid off for him, too. The Minnesota Timberwolves made him the fifth overall selection.

Anyone who questioned the judgment of these kids in coming out early only had to watch the draft. The first four players selected — Smith, McDyess, Stackhouse and Wallace — had two more years of college eligibility remaining. Smith was 19, McDyess, Stackhouse and Wallace were 20. Garnett also was 19.

When I turned 19, in June of 1958 — wow, I'm giving my age away! — I was like a lot of kids today. I had just graduated from East Rutherford High School in New Jersey, and I was begging for a college to give me a chance. I wasn't even thinking about a scholarship because I didn't have that kind of ability. I just wanted an admission slip. I finally got one from Roanoke College in Salem, Va., and I was ecstatic. It was like heaven had opened up.

So compare Garnett at 19 to Dickie V. A little different, huh? But you know what? I wouldn't change a thing. I later transferred to Seton Hall-Paterson — that's right, an extension campus — and got my degree. That school doesn't even exist any more. They closed the doors on it after I left, something the people at Seton Hall have never let me forget. But I wouldn't trade my degree for anything.

---

*Guess who? This is me at East Rutherford High School, before nature took its course. I can't believe it. I really did have hair!*

Garnett is just the fourth player to turn professional shortly after returning his tuxedo from the high school prom. Moses Malone has been the most successful, but he started out in the American Basketball Association, which wasn't as competitive as the NBA. Darryl Dawkins had a decent NBA career, too. Some people bring up Shawn Kemp, but he went to Kentucky and a junior college for one year after high school.

Garnett has the talent to succeed in the NBA, but there's more to it than hitting a jump shot. It's the lifestyle — endless travel, fitting in with players more than 10 years older, dealing with all the hangers-on in the hotel lobbies, dealing with all the people who are trying to get into your pocket.

One of the challenges Garnett, and all young NBA players, must contend with is boredom. He'll have a lot of free time on his hands at all those hotels he'll be living in, and he'll have a lot of money, too. That will make for a real challenge for him. And he could find himself in a situation where he doesn't get a whole lot of playing time right out of the gate. It's going to be tough for him to handle all the new challenges.

I would love to have seen Garnett develop, both as a player and as a person, in college first. To me, that should have been his whole focus. Even if he couldn't have gotten into an NCAA school, he could have gone to the NAIA. He would have benefitted a great deal just from being a part of the college scene, with the structure and discipline and challenges. He's going to have to grow up awfully fast, and the Timberwolves will have to bring him along slowly.

Of all the underclassmen in the draft, Stackhouse and Williamson are the two who appear physically prepared to take the pounding over an 82-game NBA season. Most underclassmen simply aren't ready for it. But that doesn't mean they can't contribute immediately and become great players in time. And they'll all be Mill-ion-aires, with a capital M, baby. And you can take that to the bank.

My daughter has an MBA from Notre Dame. She's putting her resume together, going all over the country, trying to find a job for $25-30,000 a year. If somebody would have come to her when she was a junior and said, "Tell you what, Terri. We'll put you into the corporate world and give you $1 million," something tells me she would have said, "You know, Dad, I can go to school at night and get my degree later." And something tells me I wouldn't have tried to stop her.

Some players, like Juwan Howard of Michigan who left after his junior year and was selected by the Washington Bullets with the fifth pick in the 1994 draft, have done just that — finishing their degree requirements while they play.

Howard is one of my new heroes. He never forgot his No. 1 goal — to walk down the aisle and get his diploma. To see the smile on Juwan's face in all the newspapers was a thing of beauty. So let's give a big cheer for Juwan. Hey, I'm going to be a Michigan cheerleader! I'm going to cheer on Juwan.

I hope more guys follow his path. Wallace and Stackhouse said they were going to do the same. But a lot of players say they're going to do it and don't. After the checks start rolling in, it's tough to get motivated to enroll in an English literature class or whatever and prepare for tests again.

But another North Carolina star named Michael Jordan did it. Michael wrote down his goals, and one of them was getting a degree. He vowed to come back during the off-season and work on it, and he did just that. Money can buy a lot of things, but it can't buy a degree, and Michael said he felt like a million dollars when he walked down the aisle and received that piece of paper. That, my friends, is a winner.

Unfortunately, we don't have enough Michael Jordans. College basketball is becoming a three-year sport for the great ones, or two years in special cases. The first four-year player chosen in the 1995 draft was Bryant Reeves, from Oklahoma, who went to Vancouver with the sixth pick. That bothers me. You look at the players who should have made the 1995 All-America team and they were playing in the NBA: Glenn Robinson, Juwan Howard, Chris Webber, Jason Kidd, Donyell Marshall. Not a bad team. Hey, even I could coach that team and win a few games.

Everything is getting moved ahead. Every season now, it seems the best players are underclassmen. They come in for a couple or three seasons to get their feet wet and then they dive into the NBA. One big splash and they're gone.

That's why we don't have the dominant teams in college basketball, the heavyweight knockout teams. When a player like Smith declares, it leaves a huge gap that's hard to fill. I wish they would stay because it would be great for college basketball and great for the kids. But how can you argue their decisions?

But you know what? There's always a new group of stars on the horizon. Off the top of my head, my preseason first team All-Americas would be Jacque Vaughn of Kansas at point guard — I give him a slight edge over Harold Deane of Virginia, Alan Iverson of Georgetown and Brevin Knight of Stanford — and Kerry Kittles of Villanova at shooting guard. He can flat-out run the floor, shoot the rock, score in transition. At small forward, I'm staying in the Big East and going with Ray Allen of Connecticut. He scored 32 against UCLA in the NCAA Regional finals in 1995 and should have a big year.

My center is Tim Duncan of Wake Forest. He'll be blocking shots, dunking, dominating. He's just getting better and better. Marcus Camby of UMass is my power forward. Can you imagine Camby and Duncan in the lineup at the same time? It would be Rejection City. I want Ryan Minor of Oklahoma as my super sixth man, drilling the jumper, tickling the twine with the Nothing-But-Nylon jumpers, letting it fly from trifecta land.

I was as surprised as anyone that Duncan decided to return for his junior season. I've talked to a lot of pro scouts about him, and he's a hot item. Already, no less an authority than Lakers GM Jerry West has called Duncan the best player in the country and a potential No. 1 pick in the draft if he leaves school in 1996. Jim Simpson, who gave me my biggest break in TV when he was at ESPN — and who now lives in St. Croix — had told me about Duncan several years ago.

Duncan reminds me so much of the Admiral, David Robinson. Like Robinson, who went to the Naval Academy and was never heavily courted, Duncan was never spoiled by the recruiting system. He didn't even know what sport he liked best as he was growing up in St. Croix. He had Olympic aspirations as a freestyle swimmer and he was being groomed to follow in his sister Tricia's footsteps and represent his country in the 1992 Summer Games at Barcelona. But his athletic career took a different direction in 1989 after Hurricane Hugo destroyed his club's pool.

*I'm lucky. I have a job that enables me to meet a lot of classy people, such as the Hills, Calvin (left) and Grant. Calvin was a star running back in the NFL, and Grant is making it big in the NBA.*

Duncan got tired of training in the ocean and took up basketball. He averaged 25 points, 12 rebounds and five blocked shots for St. Dunstan's Episcopal School, but he received no attention from major programs until Chris King, a former Wake Forest player, saw him play. King was in St. Croix with a group of NBA rookies to play a series of exhibition games to promote an anti-violence, anti-drug campaign and saw Duncan go head-to-head with Alonzo Mourning.

When Wake Forest coach Dave Odom asked King if he had seen any prospects during the trip, King told Odom about Duncan. Only he couldn't remember his name or the island he came from. Odom followed up the lead. Once he got the details and a phone number, he arranged to fly to St. Croix to watch Duncan play in a Sunday afternoon pickup game on an outdoor court. Hey, nobody said recruiting was easy.

Odom quickly realized that Duncan had star potential. But he had no idea Duncan would emerge as a giant who would grab 20 rebounds when Wake defeated Carolina to win its first ACC Tournament in 33 years toward the end of the 1994-95 season.

I hope Duncan stays four years, like Duke's Grant Hill did. But Hill was the only one of the first seven players in the 1994 NBA draft to do so.

Grant told me he loved college life, but unlike a lot of players in college, he came from a prosperous home. His father went to Yale and played in the NFL; his mother went to Wellesley, where she roomed with Hillary Rodham Clinton. So money wasn't a factor for Grant. But the Grant Hills of the world are becoming dinosaurs. And this isn't *Jurassic Park*, baby.

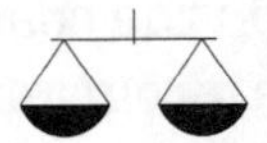

Underclassmen now have an option if they decide to turn pro. They can enter the draft, be selected by a team and even practice with that team but still return to college within 30 days if they still meet eligibility requirements and haven't signed with an agent.

Minnesota guard Voshon Lenard was drafted by the Milwaukee Bucks with the 46th pick in 1994. Center Charles Claxton of Georgia was taken by Phoenix at 52. Both guys decided to return to school for their senior season after they were offered the NBA minimum salary of $150,000 per season.

I've talked with some coaches who don't mind the rule because they figure the kids have nothing to lose. But I hate the rule because it benefits the NBA and not the player. If an underclassman gets drafted and returns to college, he's locked into the spot where he was drafted. He can't improve his situation. It made no difference what Voshon Leonard did his senior year, he couldn't play his way into the first round and make more money.

I think it can be a big distraction for the player and his college team, too. Can a player really be focused on his college season when he's already had a taste of the NBA? In Lenard's case, you have to wonder. He averaged 18.9 points a game as a junior, with a high game of 38. He shot 47 percent from the field and hit 41 percent of his three-pointers. But his numbers dropped his senior season. He averaged 17.3 points, hit 41 percent of his field goals and 33 percent of his three-pointers. Even his free-throw percentage dropped from 84 to 76 percent. You have to wonder if he didn't have one eye focused on the Minnesota Golden Gophers and one on the Milwaukee Bucks.

I'm selfish. I'm hoping a rookie salary cap will at least slow down the mass exodus. I want to watch them play for more than two years. So do the coaches who recruit them. A coach wants to develop a program over stretches of three and four years, not sit on pins and needles wondering if his star player is going to turn pro.

But the life span of an average NBA player is less than five years, and a growing number of the great college players are afraid of what might happen to their futures if they suffer a serious injury. Most of the blue chippers in college have the option of signing a $1 million NCAA-sanctioned insurance policy with Lloyd's of London. But that pales in comparison to the money they could make in the NBA. So it's hard to tell a kid to return to good ol' State U and risk a serious injury.

Most of the players know what happened to all-star forward Danny Manning. Manning gave up a $35 million offer from Atlanta to sign a one-year, $1 million deal with the Phoenix Suns because he wanted to play for a team that had a chance to win the championship. But he tore up his anterior cruciate ligament in January and missed the rest of the season. Think about what that is going to cost him financially. I guarantee, when he goes back to talk contract again, even though he may be healthy, there'll be all kinds of stipulations because of the knee.

Agents are going to point that out to all of the great young players in college: "Hey, are you going to roll the dice?" I think that's what spurred on some kids to leave early.

UCLA All-America forward Ed O'Bannon bucked the trend, but he had no choice. He thought he would get a chance to roll the dice, too. When I first met him before he signed with UCLA in 1990, he was considered the best prospect in the country. He thought he would stay in school for two years, then go on to the pros. He thought he would hit the lottery. But a month after he entered UCLA in 1990, O'Bannon wrecked his anterior cruciate ligament during a pickup game on campus. A lot of people thought he would never recover, but he was determined to come back and he finally made it to the top last season.

Eddie O was my Rolls Royce PTPer of the Year for the way he carried UCLA to the 1995 championship. He scored 30 points and grabbed 17 rebounds as UCLA defeated Arkansas, 89-78, at the Kingdome.

O'Bannon only wound up postponing his destiny. Not only was he a first-round pick in the draft, he also found time to graduate with a degree in history. His maturity was the thing that got UCLA over the top.

College basketball would be a lot better off if there were more Ed O'Bannons.

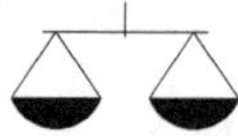

The NCAA could do something that would help slow the mass exodus into the NBA: pay the players. I'm not talking about thousands of dollars, but why not some spending money? Something more than room, board, tuition and books. Back in the 1960s, athletes were allowed $15 a month for laundry, but they don't even get that anymore. Why not?

Money is becoming a major issue for college athletes in the 1990s. The vast majority of them won't get a whiff of NBA dollars, but they're still helping produce millions of dollars in revenue. They see packed arenas all over the country. They see their coaches making hundreds of thousands of dollars a year. They see coaches and schools striking deals with shoe companies. They see kids on the street wearing their school's jersey, sometimes with their name on it. They see CBS paying the NCAA an average of $214 million per year for TV rights so millions of people can watch them play.

And they wonder why they never see any of it.

I do, too. I believe some of that money ought to filter down to the athletes before someone files an antitrust suit. The NCAA is operating on thin ice. It has always benefitted from being a non-profit organization. Revenues are not taxed, and it is exempt from federal labor laws because the players are not considered employees. You have to wonder how long this can last.

I read in the *Seattle Times* where Dick DiVenzio, the former Duke player who is an advocate of paying players, said he would love to get the 52 scholarship players in the Final Four in a room for an hour and encourage them to attach conditions to their participation. That might get a response.

The athletes have been slow to organize because they're afraid of being labeled troublemakers and the logistics make it almost impossible. Somebody is going to have to do it for them. They do have a voice on an NCAA advisory committee, but that's about all, and it doesn't carry much weight.

I know, I know. Paying only the players on revenue-producing teams would open up a can of worms because of Title IX legislation. But let's eliminate the nonsense. Give the kids a $200-per-month stipend while they're in school. Those kids deserve some spending money. They deal with a lot of pressure and put in a lot of hours. It's a 12-month cycle now. They're expected to be on campus during the summer, working out and playing. And while we're at it, let's give the parents or guardians of any player who makes it to the Final Four two free airline tickets plus tickets to the Big Dance so they can share in one of the greatest experiences of their lives.

When you think of the megacontracts signed between television and the NCAA — CBS bid $1.7 billion in its new deal for the rights to televise the NCAA Tournament — plus all the revenue gained through the sales and advertising of merchandise, why not give some of it back to the student athletes who bust their guts on a regular basis for their university?

I would love to see all scholarship athletes paid, regardless of sport. But at the very least those athletes on revenue-producing teams should receive some form of compensation. Not enough to make them rich, just enough so they can enjoy some of the simple pleasures most college students get to experience.

My girls have been on tennis scholarships at Notre Dame. I'm fortunate to be in a position where I can afford to write out a check for them to come home for Christmas. I can afford to send them a few dollars for clothes. But what about all the moms and dads who can't afford to do that? Some college athletes can't afford to buy themselves a shirt or tie, or go on a date.

That's what leads to a lot of Mickey Mouse cheating. Here comes the alum who wants to be Charlie Tuna, the big fish on campus. He says to the athlete, "I'll slip you a few bucks. Just don't tell coach." Or, "I'll get you a job. Turn off the lights, baby, and it'll be worth $500 a week."

The NCAA is well-intentioned, but it has some wacky rules; and there are times when those rules hurt kids rather than help them. The NCAA believes if the rules are in the book in black and white, so be it. But sometimes you have to make adjustments.

The first commandment of college athletics always should be, "Thou Shalt Help Young People."

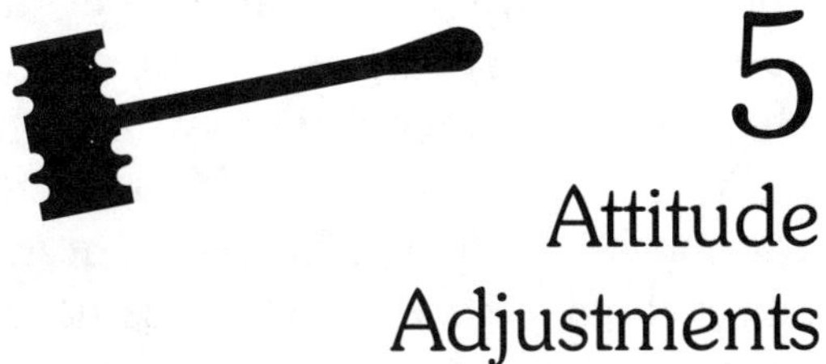

# 5 Attitude Adjustments

Hey, baby, love him or hate him, you better believe he is a giant in the world of college basketball. That's right, I'm speaking of the big fella, Robert Montgomery Knight.

The General is bigger than anyone in the state of Indiana, including the governor. The guy is a giant, and he's divided the fans there into opposite camps. Some love him and some loathe him. You don't find many people who are ambivalent about him.

I always think it's one of the special moments in college hoops when Knight comes strutting onto the floor at Assembly Hall in Bloomington before a game with his red sweater on. You know hoops hysteria is about to take place in Hoosierland.

Knight has coached Indiana to three national championships, in 1976, 1981 and 1987. He won the NIT in 1979. He coached the U.S. Olympic team to a gold medal in 1984, with Michael Jordan, Patrick Ewing, Sam Perkins, Wayman Tisdale and others. He's won 11 Big Ten titles, including four in a row in the 1970s. He's won more games than any coach in the history of the Big Ten. He coached the last unbeaten Division I team, in 1976. He's in the Hall of Fame.

If I had to win one game, I'd want Knight on my side. All things being equal, give him a week in the gym to prepare, and he'll usually win because of his understanding of the game and his ability to get the maximum out of his players. He has the track record to prove that.

You talk about powerful. I traveled with Knight to see Damon Bailey when he was a high school star in Bedford, Ind., which is about 30 miles south of Bloomington. We went down there, and I couldn't believe it. The place was packed with people who all came out to watch Damon.

When we walked in, I said, "Bob, I can't believe all these people came out for me."

He burst out laughing.

As soon as Knight entered the gym, they gave him a standing ovation. I thought I was walking in there with a king. Basketball is so big in that state and Knight commands that type of loyalty.

I just hope people remember him as one of the legends of the college game, a guy who has drawn from the likes of Pete Newell and the late Hank Iba, instead of a guy who has been involved in a lot of incidents, such as throwing a chair onto the floor or pulling his team off the floor against the Russians in a preseason exhibition game.

Obviously, I don't agree with everything he's done over the years, just as I'm sure he doesn't agree with everything I've done. We've had our disagreements.

For example, The General and yours truly had a skirmish during the shooting of the movie *Blue Chips*. I haven't said much about it, but let me tell you what happened. I walked into a room and saw Knight, who was sitting down. I snuck up behind him and threw a bear hug around him and screamed, "Do you want to fight, baby?!" I really caught him off-guard. Little did I know he wasn't having the best of afternoons. He instinctively swung back his left arm and I went to the deck. He didn't hit me with a punch, it was a jab with his arm to get me off his back. And believe me, I got off his back.

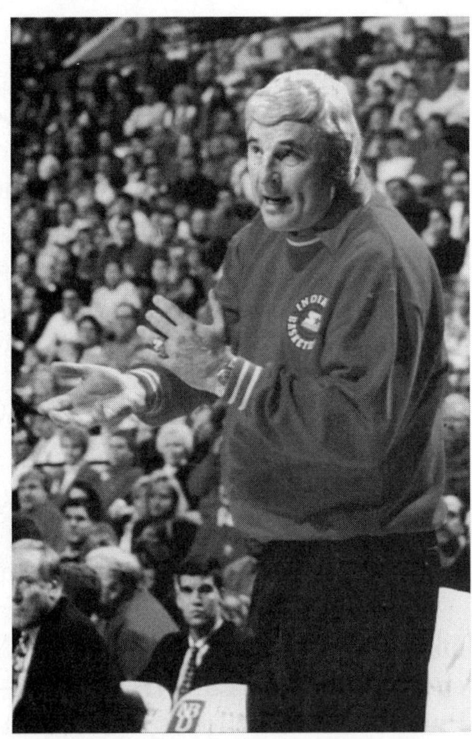

*If you want to win a big game, you've got to put in a call to The General, Bob Knight.*

---

We've laughed about it on a number of occasions. In fact, he later told me he wanted to give me a lesson on how to protect my left side. He told me, "When you're blind in your left eye, you don't sneak up on somebody like that and expose your left side."

That's what the guy is all about. He has an outburst, and then it's simply forgotten. It's history, baby. Tuck it away. The bottom line is, this guy has tremendous loyalty to those who are loyal to him. He'll go to the mountaintop for his friends.

He's been involved in a lot of controversies over the years, but if you look at the total picture, he's got a lot more positives than negatives. We have a tendency to look at Knight as a mean-spirited, tough, my-way-or-the-highway guy, but if you get to know him you discover he does a lot of beautiful things behind the scenes — like reaching out to youngsters in a hospital who may need a helping hand, or helping his ex-players. When Landon Turner, one of his stars, was paralyzed in a 1981 car accident, no one did more to raise funds for his rehabilitation and treatment.

I've seen letters in his office from guys he coached at West Point who went over to Desert Storm as officers in the Army. They were heartwarming. "Coach, all the things you've taught me about discipline, about life, I'm applying them in the real world. Please, coach, watch out for my family if something happens to me." I wanted to put them on the air. They were so moving. But the General said, "No way."

"Dick," he said, "I really don't need any publicity. These are just beautiful people who I love dearly."

Knight has established a reading program in the state for elementary school kids and a drug awareness program. He contacted all the NBA stars — Michael Jordan, Charles Barkley and all those guys — to come do two minutes apiece for a video on the importance of staying away from drugs and alcohol. He made it available to all the schools in Indiana.

Unfortunately, some people don't get a chance to see that side of his personality.

Any time he blows up, tongues start wagging. The media jumped all over him in the 1992 NCAA Tournament when he playfully whipped some of his players in response to accusations he was too tough on them. His players took it in stride, but when the wires moved a picture of him whipping Calbert Cheaney, one of his black players, some people took offense.

Knight's latest outburst occurred after Indiana lost to Missouri, 65-60, in the first round of the 1995 NCAA Tournament in Boise. Knight had been on his best behavior throughout his brief stay, but he ripped into Rance Pugmire, the moderator of the postgame interviews, after Pugmire had been incorrectly informed that Knight wouldn't be coming to the news conference and announced it to the media.

Knight's actions obviously were inexcusable, but it was set up by some miscommunication among the NCAA representatives running the postgame news conference.

The NCAA later came down big on him, fining him $30,000. He responded in vintage fashion, with a statement that jabbed the members of the NCAA's committee that imposed the fine by pointing out that most of them had worked at schools that had been guilty of NCAA rules violations.

Knight's just an explosive, competitive person. He lets it blow in one outburst, then sits down and says, "Why, why did I do it?"

I've had the pleasure of sitting down with Knight on several occasions for a one-on-one for ESPN. Let me tell you something, he's an absolutely intriguing personality. He's so bright on so many issues that he amazes me. When he sits down to converse, he has you listening to every word. I told him point blank, you have to be disappointed with some of the things you've done in the past. He simply said, "Obviously there are some things I wish I didn't do, but that's true for everybody."

One of the great ironies of college athletics is that coaches want their players to react in a disciplined manner during games and practices, but all too often they have difficulty controlling themselves.

Hey, I was as guilty as anyone. I was absolutely wacky on the sidelines. I was up from the moment the game started to the moment the game ended, screaming, cajoling, trying to get the maximum out of my players — and yes, the zebras, too. I was fortunate because college basketball wasn't covered then like it is today, otherwise I probably would have come in for some criticism.

The NCAA addressed the issue of crazy coaches over the summer of 1995. Because of incidents like Knight's press conference fiasco and Memphis' Larry Finch complaining about the officials in his team's tournament loss to Arkansas, it is going to come down harder and harder on coaches who have eruptions in the tourney.

In the past, many of the outbursts and eruptions might have been overlooked. The local media would report what happened and that would be the end of it. Coaches would settle their problems in private. But today, everybody's watching. Because of the increased visibility of college sports and the growth of cable television, anything that happens gets broadcast and reported all over the country.

How many times did we watch the rerun of that videotape showing John Chaney of Temple going after John Calipari of UMass a few years back?

Chaney is one of the top coaches in the country; but he totally lost it after a particularly heartbreaking one-point loss to UMass at Amherst. When word got back to him that Calipari was trashing the officials after a win, Chaney charged into the press room and had to be restrained from going after him.

He screamed, "I'll kill you! I'll kill you!" The cameras caught it all, and it was shown over and over.

Several days later, when he accepted a one-game suspension from the school, he offered an apology, suggesting he had let his team, his family and his players down by his actions. But the buildup for the rematch a week later in Philadelphia looked like the promos for a heavyweight championship fight. Fortunately, the players on both teams had enough common sense to concentrate on the game and not the hype.

Television also captured the confrontation between Dean Smith of North Carolina and Rick Barnes of Clemson in the ACC Tournament. Dean had been complaining all year about Clemson's physical, Big East-style tactics. After a Clemson player gave Jerry Stackhouse a particularly hard foul on a breakaway, Smith went off, pointing his finger at the player and yelling at Rick. The two went toe-to-toe at midcourt before officials broke it up. And that's in the ACC, the best league in the country, where they work at camaraderie.

Gene Corrigan, the ACC commissioner, acted immediately in reprimanding the coaches and letting everyone know this sort of incident cannot be tolerated.

The NCAA has difficulty regulating outrageous behavior by coaches. If a player gets ejected for fighting, he faces a one-game suspension. If ejected a second time, he's gone for the season. The rules attempt to control trash talking, but the sanctions aren't as severe.

I have no problem with a kid who wants to express himself with a theatrical dunk and show some jubilation over it. I do have a problem with a player who tries to embarrass an opponent, who gets in an opponent's face, points at him or laughs at him. A couple of times in his career at Michigan, Jalen Rose showed that kind of immaturity. I don't want to single out Jalen. I've seen a number of players get into a guy's face. They see a guy on the floor after he's been dunked on and they point their finger right in his face. That kind of gesture is totally uncalled for.

The referees are the ones best equipped to control this sort of thing. Dick Paparo, Eddie Hightower, Lenny Wirtz — all you big zebras of the world — slap a T and you'll end that nonsense quickly.

Officials can T up a coach, even eject him, but it's up to the conference office to discipline him. They have penalties they can inflict if coaches get out of line. A commissioner can suspend a coach or fine him.

It's a funny thing, though. Nobody can touch the officials. If coaches question a call publicly, they can be fined or suspended — even if that call dictated the outcome of a game. This is wrong. Coaches and players have to be accountable after games, why not the referees? If the coaches and players have to stand up to the media and answer questions about their performances, officials should have to face the music as well. I don't mean officials should have to explain every call they make, but when a call helps determine the outcome of a game, I see no reason why they can't explain it.

A lot of times a coach's job is on the line. Some of these guys are headed for Ziggy-land if a call here or there goes against them. There's a lot of money at stake, and the coach is right in the middle of it.

Coaches are no longer instructors in the physical education department who coach on the side. They're celebrities, institutions, almost like rock stars in some cases. You walk into the baseball dugout during spring training and what do guys like Jimmy Leyland of the Pirates want to talk about? "What about Bobby Knight? What about Rick Pitino? What about Mike Krzyzewski?" These guys are like CEO's of large corporations with the kind of dollars they're generating — the TV revenue, the tournament dollars, the marketing, the T-shirts, the alumni donations.

When you hear what all the corporate giants are paid, why shouldn't a coach reap some of the same rewards? What is Bob Knight worth to Indiana? What's a Denny Crum worth to Louisville? A Rick Pitino at Kentucky? Not just financially, but in other less tangible ways? If a coach works for a Top 50 program, he has the potential to make megabucks. It's not just the base salary, but all the extras: the summer camps, the shoe deals, the TV shows, the speaking engagements. Hey, the big stars in coaching deserve their big salaries, just like the big decision-makers in the business world.

Let me share a story with you. The story gets better and better every time I tell it, but it happened something like this: When I interviewed for the head coaching job at Detroit in the mid-1970s, they asked how much it would take for me to accept the job. I was making about 11-thou a year as an assistant coach at Rutgers at the time. I said, "Give me $15,000 and I'll take the job."

It sounded like a nice raise to me, but they looked at me like I was some kind of wacko. They're thinking to themselves, "We're a nice little Jesuit school. We have $21,000 budgeted. We'll hire this sucker, save $6,000 and we won't have to pass the basket."

They got me really, really cheap. But, you know what? I was so excited to be a collegiate head coach I never thought about the money.

A lot of young coaches are out there today thinking the same thing. They just want a shot. But the established coaches have opportunities to make a great deal of money. They can negotiate their own shoe contracts. Many of them owe a thank-you to Sonny Vacarro for increasing their bank accounts. When he was working for Nike, he started the trend of paying coaches at the major programs big bucks for putting their teams in his shoes. Until then, companies only paid the NBA stars for wearing their shoes. Some coaches get six-figure deals off of shoe contracts alone.

Mike Krzyzewski signed a 15-year deal with Nike, at $375,000 a year plus stock options and a $1 million signing bonus. Dean Smith signed a $300,000 deal with Nike, with a $500,000 signing bonus. In Smith's case, he donated his entire bonus to charity and will split his annual payment between his assistant coaches and the school library. But CBS' *Sixty Minutes* blasted the coaches for those deals, suggesting, among other things, that players should receive some of the revenue.

My shoe deal when I coached at the University of Detroit suffered by comparison. Back in the early 1970s — are you ready for this? — the Converse rep, Donnis Butcher, came in and said, "Hey, you wear our shoes and I'm going to give you some free sneakers." So my players wore Converse, and I got a pair of free Cons.

Then I made the big jump. When I became coach of the Pistons, Pro Keds laid 5,000 big ones on me. I was thrilled. Hey, Michael K, how does my deal compare to yours? Are we in the same ballpark? The same zip code?

Several schools have even come up with $1 million annuities in an attempt to hold on to their coaches. We've seen it at Louisville with Denny Crum, at Kentucky with Pitino, at Texas with Tom Penders. I have no problem with that. But I do have a problem with the sort of thing that happened with Nebraska's football program, telling coach Tom Osborne before he went to the Orange Bowl they would give him a $50,000 bonus if he won the national championship. When you start giving out bonuses for winning national championships, when you start giving incentives for success, you create a problem.

Just recently, the University of Minnesota gave Linda McDonald-Hill, the women's coach there, a five-year extension, but stated that in order for the deal to be valid she had to take her team to the NCAA Tournament in three of the next five years. What kind of message is that?

You're opening the door for potential problems. Suppose you're a coach recruiting a heck of a player who happens to be a borderline kid. Normally you wouldn't take a chance on a kid like that, but now you're thinking, "Maybe that kid can help get us into the tournament. And, if we qualify, I get an extra $50,000." So now you start taking short cuts, start sacrificing standards. It would be much better if schools rewarded coaches for graduation rates and for how they run their programs. A coach who graduates all of his or her players, who teaches positive messages about life — now that's a winning coach.

All the money being tossed around these days is a double-edged sword for the coaches. You can argue that they deserve a lot of cash because of the revenue their teams generate and the pressure they have to endure. But the money also increases the pressure. Fans argue that if a coach is making hundreds of thousands of dollars, he should be producing champions. Everything becomes escalated — most of all the scrutiny.

When Rollie Massimino left Villanova to replace Jerry Tarkanian at Nevada-Las Vegas in 1992, he found himself in the middle of a full-fledged civil war in the desert. That marriage was doomed from day one. And not only because of Rollie Massimino. Whoever succeeded Jerry Tarkanian was going to have problems. It was a three-ring circus. Former president Robert Maxson, who brought Rollie in, had divided the town with his attempts to get rid of Tark.

Maxson never understood how big Tark was. Tark was bigger than all the stars on the marquees on the Vegas strip. Yes, put them all up there. Tom Jones, Wayne Newton, David Copperfield. Tark was the biggest of bigs. In fact, they even had a big disco in town called "Sharks." He was a major star at Vegas, and why not? His teams had gone 509-105 in his 19 years there, had made nine straight NCAA appearances from 1983 to '91 and won the school's first-ever national title in 1990. The only team Vegas was afraid to play during that period was the one with the four-letter acronym. Not UCLA, baby, NCAA. Tark resigned in the wake of a never-ending NCAA investigation that eventually put the program on a one-year probation.

In the two years Rollie spent at Vegas, UNLV never made it to the NCAA Tournament, and attendance at Thomas and Mack Arena dropped below 10,000. And then there was another scandal.

Maxson was so desperate to hire Massimino, he gave him a contract worth $510,000. Then reports started to come out about Rollie receiving an additional $375,000 from a private slush fund with the booster club that was never reported to the Board of Regents. That's $885,000.

Nothing was done illegally. It might have been shady, and it wasn't out front. I only wish it had been. Rollie wanted it out front. It's my understanding that the school president, the general counsel and the AD were there at a special meeting, and they were the ones who wanted to keep it quiet. They were a little worried that if it got out they were paying that kind of cash for a new coach, all heck would break loose.

Everyone involved wound up losing. The most unfortunate thing is that a man who dedicated his life to basketball, who graduated his players and abided by NCAA rules at Villanova, now finds his career in jeopardy. Sure, he got a $1.8 million settlement. But it's not the same. I know Rollie. He's a fighter and you'd better believe he wants to be on the sidelines.

As with anyone else in the limelight, one mistake can cost a coach his career. Within the span of a week in the spring of 1995, Seattle Seahawks coach Dennis Erickson was arrested for driving while intoxicated and ordered to enter an alcohol treatment program. Atlanta Braves manager Bobby Cox was arrested after his wife, Pamela, called police to report a domestic dispute. According to reports in the media, when police arrived, they found his wife with the left side of her face swollen. They arrested Cox and charged with him with simple assault. And Michigan football coach Gary Moeller was arrested following a drunken outburst at a Southfield, Mich., restaurant. According to the police, Moeller was intoxicated and punched an officer. Earlier, he had harassed a waitress, bothered other patrons and challenged the manager to a fight.

Moeller was fired by the university. He didn't fight it because there was no way he could have won that battle. Now he's coaching the tight ends for the NFL's Cincinnati Bengals — quite a step down from being the head coach at the University of Michigan.

Moeller will be the first to admit he was wrong. He made a major, major mistake. That kind of stuff is not going to be tolerated on the college scene. And it's all too easy to blame his problem on job-related stress. My idea of stress is a single parent making $800 a month and trying to support three kids. The guy who has a six-figure contract only has to learn how to manage it.

Moeller just gave ammunition to those who were unhappy with his productivity. I find that mind-boggling because I know the guy's record during his years at Michigan: 44-13. Are you serious? Those numbers usually get you into the Hall of Fame. But at Michigan, with 105,000 fans at every home game, they expect nothing less than the Rose Bowl.

That just goes to show the hypocrisy in college athletics. I ask a very simple question: If Gary Moeller's team had gone 11-0 the previous season and gone on to win the Rose Bowl, I wonder if Michigan officials would have called a press conference and said something like, "Hey, sure, Gary made a mistake, but let's take a deeper look at this. Here's a guy who has represented us with class for more than two decades in the business. He admits he made a mistake. He will grow from this error. Let's not allow one hour to destroy his entire life."

Let's face reality, if a coach — or athlete — is on top, he gets second and third chances. Not being involved, it's tough to comment about somebody else's life. But I do know this: Anyone who is a leader has a responsibility to himself, his players, his fans and the school he represents.

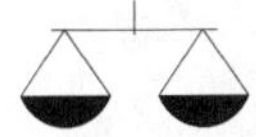

But the spotlight never burns out. In the fall of 1994, the glare fell on Massachusetts.

I've seen a lot of Frank Lloyd Wright jobs in my day, where a coach comes in and builds a program from scratch. I saw it at Georgetown with John Thompson, at Arizona with Lute Olson, at Georgia Tech with Bobby Cremins. But the best rebuilding job I've seen in my 16 years at ESPN and ABC is the one coach John Calipari has done for the University of Massachusetts up in Amherst. He took a program that had no visibility, no recognition — other than the fact that Dr. J once played there, 20 years ago — and turned it into a national power.

John Calipari was a 29-year-old unknown assistant from Pitt when he applied for the head coaching job at UMass in 1988. He got some help from Rick Pitino of Kentucky, who knew him from the Five-Star Camp, was impressed by Calipari's enthusiasm and spirit, and sold the selection committee on giving him a chance. That's right, another Garfinkel protege. I can just hear Garf calling Calipari. "I got you your job. Right baby? I did it. Don't you forget that!"

And what a golden move it's been.

Calipari inherited a program that had gone through 10 straight losing seasons before he arrived inAmherst in 1988. But he has been a master architect who has built UMass into a Top 20 program and won four straight Atlantic 10 Conference titles. They've even reached the Final Eight.

Calipari's done it the hard way, selling a dream that has finally come true. Kids want to play in bigger programs, the programs that are always on top. So Calipari had to build

*John Calipari is one of the real architects of coaching, a Frank Lloyd Wright who built the UMass program from scratch.*

his program around lesser-known recruits like Jim McCoy, Will Herndon, Tony Barbee and Harper Williams. He was able to sell the school to a lot of kids who were bypassed by a lot of other schools. UMass reached the Sweet 16 with that group in 1992.

Lou Roe, a two-time All-America forward, was a freshman on that team. Roe was Calipari's first real breakthrough recruit. He was a star at Atlantic City High in Jersey, and Calipari was able to establish a relationship with him because he had once recruited his cousin, Bobby Martin, to Pitt. Then he convinced Donta Bright, one of the nation's top players at Baltimore Dunbar, and 6-10 center Marcus Camby, a shot blocker deluxe, to come along, too. Remember me saying I didn't think an upstart program could get the big-time recruits, the way we got Phil Sellers to go to Rutgers? Maybe Calipari has been an exception.

John has always been a workaholic as a recruiter. Can you imagine him if there were no restrictions on recruiting? He'd be relentless. He'd be a machine. He'd be out every minute, be in your face all the time, because he's such a tenacious competitor.

He wants his kids to be that way, too. That's why he stole a page from John Chaney's book at Temple in his approach to scheduling. He said, "OK, I'm going to take some hits, but I'm going to go out and play the best." So he went out and played the best. And he sold that to recruits. In the 1994-95 season, Massachusetts played non-league games against Arkansas, Kansas, Maryland, Saint Louis and Louisville. People thought he had gone bananas. But John knew what he was doing. All of those games were on television. I remember back when UMass used to have to beg for games on TV. They played midnight games with Siena, Manhattan and Southwestern Louisiana, just so they could get on ESPN.

Calipari also benefitted from the fact that the Atlantic 10 has jumped out of the shadow of the Big East. The A-10 is going gangbusters these days. UMass was ranked No. 1 on two different occasions in 1995. The fans have responded. The new Mullins Center on campus is filled for each game, 9,000 strong.

But now, because of all his success and his flamboyant nature, Calipari is coming under a lot of scrutiny.

When you look at the Top 10, you expect to see certain schools like Duke, North Carolina, UCLA, Indiana, Arizona, Kentucky there every year. Nobody moans and groans about them. But Massachusetts didn't fit the profile. So now, if you have any problems, people who are a little envious are ready to jump on you. Jealousy, man. The green monster rears its ugly head in athletics just like in all walks of life. And that is what John Calipari has faced at Massachusetts.

In the fall of 1994, the *Boston Globe* blasted the program because four of his players had finished the previous semester with grade point averages below 2.0. They were screaming about Calipari taking short cuts. So were some rival coaches. You hear it all the time: "We couldn't touch this kid academically. We couldn't have taken him." That's an old excuse. I hate to hear a coach, when he doesn't get a kid, go around trying to knock the kid, bring him down because of academics.

Sean McDonough and I did a halftime piece for ESPN during the Tipoff Classic between UMass and Arkansas. Sean, who is from Boston and did baseball for CBS, was livid. Sean's always had the courage to speak his mind and he thought it was highly unprofessional to print the transcripts of players in the newspaper because of the student privacy laws. Non-athletes don't have to undergo this kind of scrutiny, why should athletes?

As it turned out, Calipari had graduated six of the eight players he had recruited. Of the two who didn't get degrees, one, Harper Williams, was playing pro basketball in Europe. The other, Jim McCoy, was playing in the CBA. UMass is not going to play kids if they're academically ineligible. Six of the kids mentioned in the *Globe* story had a horrendous semester. One semester. But they were eligible under school standards.

Sure, Calipari has taken some marginal prospects. Let's be honest, when you're building a program from scratch you can't be like the Dean Smiths and Mike Krzyzewskis and skim off the cream of the crop every year. And whenever you give people an opportunity, you're going to have some who let you down, who go to the wrong side of the tracks. But I've always preferred to talk about the ones who made it rather than the ones who didn't.

Talk to Calipari's players and they'll tell you he loves to get into the winner's circle, but he's not afraid to draw the line.

Calipari's handling of the Michael Williams situation is a perfect example. Williams was a four-year starting guard for UMass. He was their best shooter. If he had played against Oklahoma State in the 1995 Eastern Regional finals, UMass might have been headed to Seattle for the Final Four.

But Calipari had suspended him in February for the rest of the season after he missed curfew and came in at 5 a.m. after a game at Southwestern Louisiana. With Williams, it wasn't just one transgression, it was a culmination of things that had happened. Some coaches might have said, "I'm going to punish you. You're going to come in early and run sprints, run the steps. You're going to be disciplined." Some coaches keep stretching the rules, keep trying to save a kid, maybe use basketball to try to instill discipline in a kid.

Calipari didn't bend too far. He said, "Michael, the party's over." Calipari didn't forget about him, though. He brought in scouts from the NBA teams in Toronto and Vancouver and let Michael work out for them. He helped get Michael an invitation to the NBA-sponsored Portsmouth Invitational, a postseason tournament for college seniors. He kept preaching to Michael, "Go to class. Get your degree. We're not going to take your scholarship away from you."

So don't tell me Calipari doesn't care about his kids.

In many ways he epitomizes what coaching in the 1990s is all about. Stress, stress and more stress, with a capital S. It's tough even when you're winning because of all the pressures. The job is with you 24 hours a day, and it's always on your mind. One of your players always has a problem to deal with. There's always a group that wants you to come speak to them. There's always a talk radio show dissecting your program. And, most of all, there's always a recruit to chase.

I remember when I was coaching at Detroit, we would go on vacation in Wildwood, N.J., during the summer. I'd be there maybe 10 minutes, sitting on the beach, and I'd say to my wife: "Wait a minute, I got to go. I got to get to the phone. I got to call some recruits. I'll bet Michigan's on the phone. I'll bet Johnny Orr and Bill Frieder are talking to players we want right now. I got to catch a plane. I got to get out of here. They're going to try to steal Terry Tyler."

That kind of pace, those kind of worries, can cause physical problems. I had bleeding ulcers and had to be hospitalized when I coached at Detroit. I'm surprised we haven't seen more coaches suffer from physical problems. The hours and the eating habits can get to you. You're always on the go and you're eating like crazy. You're a nervous wreck after a game you just lost. You're already thinking about the next day of practice. The game ends at 11. You have the press conference. By 12:30, you're at a restaurant eating hamburgers and fries — or maybe steak, if you're one of the Rolls-Roycers. The next day, you get up at 6 in the morning. You're eating bacon, eggs, pancakes. Before long, that stomach is churning and churning. It's Maalox Time even when you're winning — and it's no wonder coaches boil over occasionally.

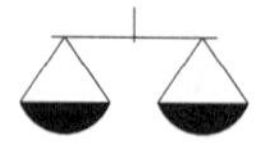

One of the biggest challenges coaches face, and one of the many things that can drive them crazy, is the student half of being a student-athlete. Getting a prospect into school has become much tougher with the increasingly difficult academic standards that have cut into the heart of the recruiting pool.

After a prospect enrolls, coaches often find themselves in the role of social workers. Many of the kids they recruit come from single-parent homes where it's a struggle to get three meals on the table. So the coach has to take on the responsibility of being a father figure. He can't just worry about X's and O's anymore. He has to help those players adjust to being away from home, help them deal with growing up.

Sometimes, players bring their problems with them from their old neighborhoods. When a kid plays poorly and shoots 4-for-18, there could be a lot of reasons why. Maybe his best friend back home just got shot. Maybe his father just got laid off. Maybe his mother is ill.

And if a player has a problem with drugs or alcohol, it seems to fall on the coach. It fell like a ton of bricks on Maryland's Lefty Driesell following the death ofAll-America forward Lenny Bias on June 19, 1986.

Driesell had built Maryland into a national power and Bias, who was twice selected ACC Player of the Year, was his star. Former Virginia coach Terry Holland compared Bias favorably to Michael Jordan in terms of his effect on the league, and Bias was chosen by the Boston Celtics with the second pick in the NBA draft.

But he never reached the pros. Two days after he was drafted, he was dead. He had ingested a lethal dose of cocaine at a private party in a campus dormitory. His passing sent shock waves through the university community. When the school conducted an investigation, it was discovered Bias was attending summer school at the time and was woefully deficient in his academic standing. That led to further investigation into the athletic department.

Maryland president John Slaughter called for drug testing of all athletes and closer monitoring for academic progress. The Terps' season was cut back and the season opener was pushed back until January.

Before the end of the summer, AD Dick Dull resigned and Driesell was forced out, reluctantly resigned to another position in the department. The tragedy proved to be a major setback for Maryland basketball.

If it happens to an English major, the English teacher doesn't get blamed. Nobody even bothers to find out who the English teacher is. But the basketball coach gets blasted in the headlines for a players' problems. He used the kid to further his own career. He didn't make sure the kid kept up with his classwork. He never gave him the proper direction.

Coaches take too much heat for their players' problems. Following the 1994-95 season, I read that Cincinnati forward Daniel Fortson and center Arthur Long were arrested after getting into an altercation with a mounted policeman. I've spoken at several Bearcat functions, and I can tell you Bobby Huggins is constantly reminding his players about the importance of carrying themselves in a proper fashion. But a coach can do only so much. A player has to look in the mirror and say to himself, "Hey, I've got to make some good decisions in life. I'm not a little kid anymore." Being responsible comes with the territory. A coach can't hold a player by the hand 24 hours a day.

I haven't met a coach yet who doesn't constantly speak to his players about the importance of academics, about the importance of going to class, about being good citizens. He's giving constant lectures about academic support services.

Even a guy like Denny Crum of Louisville, who has won two national titles and was voted into the Hall of Fame, has been criticized for the graduation rates of his players. Back in 1990, the *Louisville Courier-Journal* investigated the program and discovered that just eight of 39 players from 1981 through 1990 had earned their degrees, although part of the reason was players who had left early for the pros.

That remark set off a wave of criticism from some leaders in the black community, who accused Crum of exploitation. *Sixty Minutes* even took up the cause.

Crum's defense was that the purpose of a university is to provide students with educational opportunities and that the athletes he recruited in the 1980s were no different than the ones he recruited in the '70s. Some of them simply were better students who had different career goals.

In the 1990s the focus is on dealing with players. Even a successful coach such as Lou Campanelli of Cal can be fired if it's perceived he stepped over the line. Campanelli built a solid program at Cal. He had signed Jason Kidd, maybe the best high school prospect in the country, and the Golden Bears appeared to be headed for the Top 20.

They made it, but without Campanelli. Midway through the 1993 season, when the Bears were floundering with a 10-7 record, AD Bob Bockrath pulled the plug, citing player abuse and unhappiness with the direction the program was headed. He gave the job to a 29-year old assistant, Todd Bozeman.

If you talk to Jason Kidd's family, they'll tell you Campanelli was good for Jason, that he was a tough disciplinarian, that he really stressed academics. Yeah, he yelled. Yeah, he screamed. Yeah, he cursed. But, are you serious? If you're going to fire a guy who built the program from no-man's land into prosperity, that's your prerogative. But why not call him into the office first and tell him the things you're unhappy about and issue a warning? When I hear about the AD firing the guy because he hears some profanity outside the locker room, I wonder if there wasn't a personal vendetta. A man's career was seriously affected. Fortunately, P.J. Carlesimo later gave Campanelli a shot to remain in the sport as part of the scouting staff with the Portland Trail Blazers.

Coaches work in an era with intense media scrutiny and a sensitive public. They have to be careful about what they say, even in the privacy of a locker room, and that makes their jobs much more difficult. They're in a business where emotions run high, particularly in the moments immediately following a game. We shouldn't go overboard in passing judgment on everything they say and do.

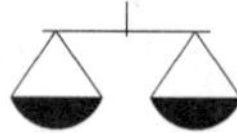

In 1994 there was a raging debate in New York City all winter about Seton Hall's decision to sign Richie Parker, a 6-3 forward from Manhattan Center who was one of the top prospects in the country. Parker was accused of sexual assault on a 15-year-old girl and eventually pleaded guilty to sexual abuse and was sentenced to five years probation. Seton Hall backed off, refusing to accept the kid.

Utah jumped into the picture in the spring, but the president of Utah vetoed that after Donny Daniels, one of the assistant coaches there, was quoted as saying that Parker may have suffered more than the girl. Wow. I'm sure he wishes he had that statement back. Women's groups in Salt Lake jumped all over Daniels, and head coach Rick Majerus had no choice but to suspend him.

George Washington's Mike Jarvis jumped into the picture too, attempting to give Parker a second chance — a chance to learn from his mistake and get on with his life. But the pressure got so intense, with people in the Washington, D.C., area sending letters galore to the president of the university, that an announcement was made by the president that Richie Parker would not be recruited by George Washington.

Let me say this. Having two daughters of my own, I'm disgusted by Parker's actions. I know he was sentenced to five years probation, and I know he's been humiliated and embarrassed by the entire scene. Above all else, let's not forget the victim and what she's gone through.

However, the young lady has announced she is willing to forgive Parker. She has an agreement that if he becomes an NBA player she'll receive some sort of financial compensation. Shouldn't Richie Parker have a chance to get on with his life? If he met all the penalties and requirements that have been placed on him, and a university believes it wants to give him an opportunity to get on with his life in a positive way, I have no problem with it.

Sure, the dad in me cannot accept what he did. But I think fairness must prevail; and if Parker is a changed person, can you hold this against him for the rest of his life? If basketball can help him grow into a positive citizen, then why not use it as a means toward that end?

# 6
# The Bottom Line

My favorite to win the 1996 NCAA Tournament is Kentucky. I can just hear Pitino. "What's Vitale screaming about now? He can't believe we're that good!"

Forget about it.

How good are the Wildcats? Their first team will be my preseason No. 1 for the 1995-96 season. And their second team will be 1-A. That's right. The best two teams inAmerica on one roster.

Hey, Rick even said to me on the phone, "Do you know what we're going to do this year? We're going to have a JV team."

I said, "A what?"

He said, "A JV team, so my subs get a lot of P.T. I may redshirt three or four guys."

Of course, that was the same day he got a commitment from Ron Mercer. I was at the Kentucky Derby. I wanted to talk about horses like Serena's Song and Talkin' Man — can you guess why that was my favorite horse? I wanted to talk about Thunder Gulch, who was trained by Wayne Lukas, the former basketball coach who is a real hoops junkie. (Hey, here's a little trivia for you: Johnny Orr wanted to hire Lukas as an assistant coach before he hired Bill Frieder. That's right, Lukas could have been going head-to-head with The General, who's now one of his best friends.) But the Kentucky fans, all they wanted to talk about were the Cats: "Wait 'til you see us next year. We're going to be awesome, baby, with a capital A!" They were stealing my lines.

How deep is this Kentucky team? Kentucky's deeper than any team in the country. They return a lot of size up front with Mark Pope, Walter McCarty, Antoine Walker, Jared Prickett, plus guards like Tony Delk, Jeff Sheppard and Anthony Epps.

For years, we've heard rumors about Pitino leaving to go back to the pros. The rumors start and every year we hear he's out of town. It's amazing with guys like Pitino and Larry Brown. Once you get a reputation for moving around, it sticks. But Rick loves the Bluegrass and loves coaching on the college level, and if you're going to coach in college, not many places are better than UK. If he does leave, it will be for the NBA. But with his recruiting rolling the way it is, believe me, it will be awhile before he goes anywhere.

Pitino signed another Top 5 class, headed by Mercer and Wayne Turner, a point guard from Beaver Country Day in Chestnut Hill, Mass., who also is ranked among the top 10 prospects in the country. He also picked up forward Derek Anderson, a transfer from Ohio State who averaged double figures in the Big Ten and becomes eligible this season. They have so much talent.

Hey, I wonder if Rick will get on the phone with Dean — that's right, Dean Smith. Oh, I know Kentucky lost to the Tar Heels in the 1995 tournament. But he can get some advice about being overloaded with talent. Dean's had some teams in Chapel Hill that were absolutely loaded. Maybe he can give Rick some advice on how to handle such a situation.

But if I was an AD and I had to choose one guy to put some excitement into my program and win right out of the gate, I'd make the call to Lexington and I'd say, "Hey, C.M.

Newton, I want to talk to your guy. I know he makes a lot of cash down there, but I'm going to double it. I'm going to triple it, because I want this guy."

One thing I like about Rick, he's honest about his players. When I was coaching I would cry if I had a guy who had a sprained ankle, even if he was my 10th man. But not Pitino. I was in Louisville to do the big Kentucky-Indiana game in December 1994 and he told me, "We're not really there yet, but we're going to be really good at the end of the year. This may be the best team I've had."

A lot of guys would try to come up with alibis. "Oh, I lost my point guard. I lost Travis Ford. We're going to struggle." But he puts it right on the line. He's already taken Kentucky to one Final Four and two final eights in the last four years, and I marvel at the way he's handled the popularity of the sport in Kentucky. It's a way of life there. The spotlight shines brighter there than anywhere in America, and it's more than some coaches can handle.

*Nobody can inject excitement into a college basketball program like Kentucky coach Rick Pitino.*

Kentucky fans are starving for another national championship. They haven't celebrated one since 1978, when Joe B. Hall had Rick Robey and Mike Phillips up front, and Kyle Macy and Goose Givens in the backcourt. Givens poured in 42 points as the Cats beat Duke in the championship game. Everybody expected Kentucky to win that year, and the pressure was enormous. Hall admitted they didn't have much fun along the way.

Pitino is going to face the same kind of heat now. Kentucky fans expect this team to be super and they'll be screaming if their Cats don't win it all. But are you telling me if they go 28-2 but lose in the tournament they've failed? Give me a break!

College basketball, unfortunately, has become just like the NBA. Everybody judges coaches by what they do in the tournament. The regular season becomes almost an exhibition schedule. It's crazy, when you think about it. Coaches should be judged more by what they do over the course of a long season, when they have more control over their players' performances and their motivation. Luck plays too much of a factor in a single-elimination tournament. One bad call by a referee, one missed shot by a sophomore, one poor shooting night by a star player, and it's over. Too many factors are out of a coach's control during the tournament. The breaks even out over the course of the regular season, but not in the tournament. One bad one and you're done. But that's what so many fans judge coaches by today.

I'm sure a lot of Big Blue fans felt empty after the 1995 tournament when North Carolina eliminated Kentucky. After all, how many programs had started the season with slogans like "The Battle for Seattle" or "Sleepless 'til Seattle"?

Some Kentucky fans had already purchased tickets for the Final Four in Seattle by the time the Cats played Carolina. They had their bags packed. It must have been a long ride back to Lexington after the Cats went down, hitting just 21 of 75 shots and only eight of 36 three-pointers.

Teams have a major dilemma when most of their production comes from the perimeter. The key to success is to have balance, because if you rely on the three, baby, there will be nights when it's Brick City, USA. And that means it's time to pack the bags.

People have to realize that Kentucky's defensive style of play creates a lot of points through turnovers. Pitino is a genius at working that sideline when it comes to changing defenses and getting the most out of his people. And with his depth he'll be able to utilize all 94 feet. It will be pressure, pressure, pressure, with fresh bodies coming at you all night long.

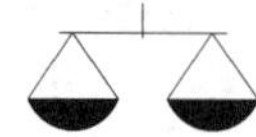

For the fans of many programs, the Final Four is the primary goal — except the schools that have already been to the Final Four, in which case the goal is nothing less than winning a national championship. The coach is right in the middle of it, caught up in the expectations.

Coaches become victims of their own success, because the more success a coach has, the greater the expectations. Connecticut won 30 games in 1994. But a missed free throw against Florida in the Eastern Regional semifinals and people say UConn had a bad year. A couple years back, Kansas had a sensational year but got beat by Texas-El Paso in the second round, and Roy Williams had to walk around hearing people say "What happened?" instead of, "Hey, man, you had a great year."

Arkansas was ranked No. 1 in both preseason polls for the 1994-95 season. Nolan Richardson said he welcomed that challenge. In fact, during the team's Midnight Madness to kick off preseason practice, he said, "Let me introduce you to the 1995 national champs." That is confidence, my friends. They came close to making that a reality, too, reaching the tournament finals. But all season long Richardson had to hear criticism that his players were underachievers. And ultimately a lot of fans felt let down because the Razorbacks didn't repeat.

North Carolina went through a similar experience the previous season. The Tar Heels won the 1993 national championship and they were the favorites to do it again. They had all five starters back, and they had recruited the two best prospects in the country, Stackhouse and Wallace.

North Carolina won the ACC Tournament and was the team to beat heading into the tournament, but it was knocked out in the second round by Boston College. Some fans even called for Smith's retirement after that game, saying he was washed up. That's unbelievable. Just like it's unbelievable that some fans jump on the fact Smith has won "only" two national championships.

We're not talking about just any coach here. Smith has had the kind of career at North Carolina that will get him into the Hall of Fame. It used to be 20 victories a year was a magical thing. Well, Dean's got 830 wins in 34 years — an average of nearly 25 a season. His numbers just blow my mind. Before long he'll become the coach with the most wins in the history of college basketball, surpassingAdolph Rupp of Kentucky, who won 876 games.

But fans can be fickle.

Remember, they once hung Smith in effigy. He became the head coach at Carolina back in 1961, after Frank McGuire had resigned to go to the NBA. Smith took over a program saddled by NCAA probation, and his first three teams were good, but not great. On January 7, 1965, Carolina lost to Wake Forest, 107-85. When the bus returned to campus, a dummy made to look like Smith was hanging in effigy. Billy Cunningham, the team's star player, bolted from the bus and tore it down. That was the only time Smith ever questioned whether he had chosen the right profession.

Smith went on to build North Carolina into a perennial national contender. But it took him an entire year after the loss to Boston College to feel vindicated. The team that beat Kentucky was not nearly as talented, not nearly as deep as the 1994 team. No way they could match that team.

Everybody, including yours truly, thought Carolina didn't have enough depth to play with the heavyweights in the tournament. The Tar Heels were so thin Smith was forced to use Pearce Landy — a walk-on — as his sixth man and play all of his starters more than 30 minutes apiece.

But El Deano proved us all wrong. Carolina had much better chemistry. Hey, I'm not talking about chemistry in the classroom. I'm not talking about scientific formulas. I'm talking about winning formulas on the hardwood, players with clearly

*It's always a pleasure to sit and chat with Michaelangelo. North Carolina's Dean Smith has built one of the nation's premier programs over the last 30 years. It's hard to believe some of the school's fans once hung him in effigy.*

*I look up to a lot of players I interview. Here I am talking with North Carolina's Rasheed Wallace, while Donald WIlliams looks on.*

---

defined roles who know how to play to one another's strengths. Smith got the most out of his 1995 team. He allowed Wallace and Stackhouse to play starring roles before waiting to become upperclassmen. But it didn't affect the team's unity or chemistry. In fact, before the tournament began, some of the players — Stackhouse, Williams and Jeff McInnis — got their heads shaved as a sign of unity. I understand they tried to get forward Dante Calabria to do the same, but Dante refused, saying it might upset the coeds on campus. I'm jealous, Dante. Just give me what they cut off.

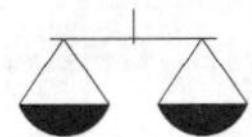

Most schools only dream about doing what North Carolina and some of the other heavyweights have done. Every year brings another game of musical chairs as larger schools attempt to muscle their way into the Top 20 and mid-majors attempt to move up the ladder by hiring new coaches or moving into different conferences.

Fresno State did it by hiring Jerry Tarkanian to rejuvenate its program. Tarkanian built UNLV into one of the nation's most powerful teams by using transfers — both from junior colleges and other four-year schools — and the type of kids other programs were reluctant to touch. He was at his best when dealing with players who had a reputation for being hard to motivate. That's why I labeled him the Father Flanagan of coaching. I have yet to find a kid who moans and groans about his playing days at UNLV.

Tarkanian has always had a super relationship with his players. They love his intensity, they love his work ethic and they love the fact the competition on an everyday basis in practice is very keen. Kids really want to work, and they want to work in a winning environment. Tarkanian knows how to get the most out of his people. Go to a practice session and watch sometime and it's amazing. The guy just loves to coach.

Jerry and the NCAA have been battling for years. I mean, it's been like Frazier and Ali. This is a heavyweight battle that has been raging for years. He was forced out of his job at UNLV after the 1992 season by all the pressure — not just from the NCAA, but from his ongoing battle with UNLV's president at the time, Robert Maxson. (Hey, here's a trivia question: Prior to P.J. Carlesimo, who were the two most recent coaches to make the jump from college to an NBA head coaching job without prior NBA experience as an assistant coach or player? That's right, baby, yours truly and Jerry Tarkanian.)

Tark spent part of a year as head coach of the San Antonio Spurs, but he never liked the NBA. And he found out life in the big leagues was a little different than in college. Jerry got into a battle with his owner over personnel. When that happens, the ziggy is sure to come. Jerry returned to Las Vegas where he spent the next two years working as a consultant with Nike and doing a variety of TV and radio shows, including a sports talk show. I'm sure Rollie Massimino was discussed many times.

When Gary Colson resigned from Fresno State after a disappointing 13-15 season, the school put out a call to Tark to come back to his alma mater, and he jumped at the chance. I think he missed coaching. He missed what most of the great coaches love — being in the gym and putting the pieces together.

When Tarkanian coached all those great teams at Vegas, he had the whole town behind him. He dominated the Big West, but it wasn't a dominant conference. The Western Athletic Conference is going to be a lot tougher, especially now that Tulsa, Vegas and TCU have joined. You still have to go to BYU, Utah, UTEP, New Mexico and Hawaii. Those are not easy road trips. It's going to be interesting to see if he can get the same kind of personnel he had at Vegas and how he handles the transition.

I talked with Tark at the Final Four. I said, "Tark, I know you better than you know yourself. How can you possibly handle a 15-12 season? There is no way in the world you can handle this at 64 years of age."

"Now, let me ask you this," he said. "Do you think I'm going there to be 15-12? If I didn't think the pieces were there, I wouldn't have taken this. We already have two very good players. I plan on being involved with certain kids who I think are going to take us to the next level. I think we're going to win, and win big."

Tark is convinced he can recruit enough players to win 20-some games. I've never been to Fresno State, but they say the fan support is enormous. The Red Wave follows the club religiously. Tark feels at home there. He loves the school. His wife went to Fresno. The Armenian population there loves him.

Only time will tell how Tark does at Fresno State. He's hired his son, Danny, as an assistant coach, and who knows, if Tark produces big time, Danny — who's a lawyer by trade but was a heck of a point guard for his dad — might eventually take over. Tark is already so big at Fresno State that they claim they've already raised hundreds of thousands of dollars since his arrival.

As far as the NCAA goes, Fresno State president John Welty said there will be a compliance officer assigned to the athletic department to watch everything he does. All the I's have to be dotted, the T's have to be crossed. I think Tark is smart enough to know every little thing he does is going to be examined.

Since the NCAA had given him clearance to coach, I'm not really surprised someone gave the guy another shot. Tark's record is unbelievable. He's 625-122 overall. That's a winning percentage of .837. He's rested now. He's in great shape physically.

This guy loves to win, but I don't know in my heart if he can win there like he believes he can. I think 15 to 18 wins is going to be a good season. But he'll create a lot of excitement, just by his presence. Already, Fresno State has been invited to compete in the preseason NIT for the 1995-96 season. Believe me, that wouldn't have happened if Tark wasn't part of the program.

It didn't take Tark long to start making some recruiting waves. He signed two blue chip forwards, Terence Roberson out of Saginaw, Mich., and James Gray from L.A. City College. Then he picked up a high profile transfer, Chris Herren from Boston College, who will have to sit out a year but could be a great one. Herren was expected to be a star in the Big East but suffered a season-ending wrist injury in the first game of his career and didn't get the job done academically.

Tark's back, and it's going to be fun to see what happens.

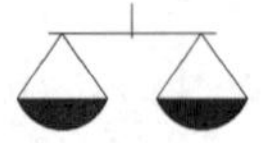

There have been more careers made in March during the NCAA Tournament than any other time of the year. Getting to the Big Dance can do wonders for a coach's profile. Winning a marquis game in the tournament can do even more.

Just ask Tubby Smith, Fran Fraschilla, Herb Sendek or Scott Edgar. They were the hot coaches to come out of the 1995 tournament. Tubby Smith coached Tulsa to the Sweet 16 two years in a row and got the Georgia job. He was an easy sell to alums because he had appeared on CBS for two straight weeks. Sendek, who trained under Rick Pitino at Kentucky, coached Miami of Ohio to an upset victory over Arizona and became a serious candidate at Vegas. Edgar coached Murray State in a competitive first-round game with North Carolina and got the Duquesne job in the Atlantic 10.

When Manhattan got a shot, Fran Fraschilla got a chance to be a star. And when the Jaspers defeated Oklahoma in the first round, Fraschilla became the toast of New York. That city desperately wanted to fall in love with St. John's at the beginning of the season, but when the Redmen struggled, long-suffering college hoops fans jumped on the Manhattan bandwagon after they received an at-large bid out of the MAAC.

Even Mayor Rudy Giuliani, a Manhattan alum, was among the 3,000 fans jammed into Draddy Gymnasium for a couple of home games. Fraschilla was contacted by six schools after the season. He was offered the Tulsa job, but he decided to stay put for another year. He's a guy people are aware of now. He's probably the next Tubby Smith, a guy who will go on to bigger and better things. Manhattan is going to have a difficult time hanging on to Franny Fraschilla.

But just as the Big Dance can make a coach's career, it can break it. Some coaches lose their jobs when they don't get their teams into the tournament, and others have to save them by getting in. Jim O'Brien of Boston College had to beat North Carolina and Indiana in the NCAA tournament a couple years ago to get his five-year extension. I couldn't believe it. O'Brien represented everything they talk about in the NCAA guide. His players did everything the right way. They went to class. They graduated. He had coached at his alma mater for nine years, but the AD kept him dangling until after the Eagles reached the regional finals. Then, they had no choice but to extend his deal.

I get a big kick whenever I hear administrators talking about the ideals of the student-athlete. Because these same guys, come March and April, are calling coaches into their office and saying, "Hey, take a look at the numbers. They aren't what we were hoping for." And it's bye-bye, baby.

In Division I, the reality is you're going to be packing your bags if you don't get enough W's. With that in mind, is it any wonder we have some coaches who are willing to take a gamble on a kid whose character or academic performance is a little questionable but can help him win a few more games?

Some coaches want to relieve some of the pressure by forming a union and establishing tenure for coaches after a certain number of years. That might be something for the NCAA's president's commission to look into. They're always seeking reform, but those same administrators are also quick to fire a coach if he doesn't perform.

Years ago, Al McGuire said coaches should have tenure, just like teachers. I don't think it's a bad idea. If a guy puts in, say, 10 years, he should at least be taken care of by the university if it wants to move him away from the sideline. I mean, a guy gives his blood and guts to the school and proves he can coach, but then all of a sudden a key player gets hurt or flunks out and the record drops and the coach pays the price. That's totally ridiculous. Coaches should be protected like other faculty members.

The negative side to this is a coach can get a little complacent once he or she gets some security. But coaches by nature are so competitive, and their results are posted every day. I don't think you would see many guys coast. I just can't see sending a guy into Ziggy land. It's awfully tough to get another job in coaching after you receive the ax.

Then again, look who's talking. I know what it feels like to get fired as a coach, so I can sympathize with the coaches. Hey, I've always said I should be the president of the coaches association because I've always been a coach at heart. Anything good for the coaches excites me.

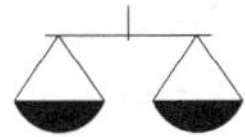

We all get carried away with evaluating coaches. Let me tell you this: coaching is made up of three elements. No. 1 is recruiting. No. 2 is the ability to motivate and communicate. No. 3 is the ability to manage practice sessions and games and handle the X's and O's.

You learn the X's and O's by attending clinics and reading books. There's no shortage of them, and everybody has equal access to them. The game really isn't that complicated, and nobody has any great secrets nobody else knows about. If you want to know what another coach is doing, watch a video tape of one of his games.

The other two elements are more difficult to achieve, and are what separate the truly successful coaches from the others. It's one thing to know about ball-you-man defensive positioning and all that, but it's another to get your players to execute properly and play hard consistently.

And you can't win without players, no matter how much you know and how hard you work. Do you think John Wooden would be in the Hall of Fame and UCLA would have won all those championships without players like Bill Walton or Kareem Abdul-Jabbar? You have to have thoroughbreds to be able to cross the finish line first.

Some coaches are better in one area than another. I felt very confident in the recruiting area. Other coaches love to study the game, break it down to its minute details, but aren't salesmen and can't get the blue chippers. The great ones combine all three aspects of the job.

Because of the media's impact on today's game, some coaches have enhanced their status with their "performance" before the microphones. They're like politicians in that regard. It's not always the best man who gets ahead, it's the one who can win over the pubic with his charisma.

It's not a matter of simply looking at the bottom line. Coaches do not work on a level playing field. Some have bigger budgets, better facilities, more tradition behind them. Just look at what Dean Smith has to work with at North Carolina — a premier conference, a phenomenal campus, a beautiful 21,000-seat building named after him, incredible tradition. You walk into the Dean Smith Center and it's an awesome sight, looking up at the rafters and seeing all those retired jerseys: Jordan, Worthy, Cunningham, Perkins. It's like a special branch of the Hall of Fame. Put Dean Smith at a school with less going for it in the way of tradition and facilities, and he wouldn't win as many games. But it wouldn't be his fault; he'd be the same coach. And keep in mind Smith helped build the tradition at North Carolina.

But not everybody gets the opportunity to coach at a place like Carolina or Duke. It was a lot harder for me to build the program at Detroit, for example, than it was for Johnny Orr who was coaching at Michigan at the time. The Wolverines' telephone budget was probably bigger than our total basketball budget at Detroit. But there's no use complaining. You just have to do the best with what you've got, and hope you get your break.

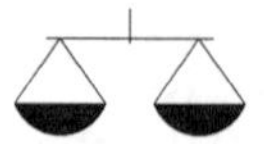

Eddie Sutton has certainly made the most of his opportunity at Oklahoma State. Sutton left Kentucky in near-disgrace, but he's rebounded at his alma mater in Stillwater, Okla. He did one of the great coaching jobs in recent history, turning his 7-foot, 292-pound center Bryant "Big Country" Reeves into a star.

Reeves looked like he might be overwhelmed when he first arrived in Stillwater before his freshman year in 1991. He was a flabby 265 pounds then and couldn't complete a 2-mile run. When you looked at him then, you didn't think there was any way he could be a major star on the collegiate level. People laughed at him. The late Henry Iba, Oklahoma State's former coach, showed up at the arena to watch Reeves on his first day of practice. He sat with Sutton and shook his head. "Ed," he said, "that boy's got a long way to go."

But Reeves was brought along patiently under Sutton, who is one of the game's best teachers. He climbed the mountain and became one of America's best players — the sixth player taken in the 1995 draft.

Reeves scored more than 2,000 points and grabbed more than 1,000 rebounds during his career, and was an All-America his final two seasons. He led the Big Eight in scoring, rebounding and field-goal percentage as a junior. The last guy to do that was a big guy from Philadelphia's Overbrook High by the name of Wilt Chamberlain. Big Country brings back fond memories of another former small town Oklahoma State star, 6-10 Hall of Famer Bob Kurland, who led the Cowboys to NCAA championships in 1945 and 1946 when the school was still known as Oklahoma A&M.

I love coaches who make their players better and make their teams better over the course of the season. Gene Keady of Purdue falls into that category. Indiana's program is so big in the state that the Boilermakers are almost treated like a second-class citizen, and that's a shame. Keady, year in and year out, does as good a job as anyone in the Big Ten. He's won five league titles in his 15 years at Purdue, including the 1994 and '95 championships. He's done it with great players such as Glenn Robinson and with unknown talent. Only one of his championship teams was predicted to finish among the leaders, but he keeps doing it.

Keady's always screaming. "Dick Vitale doesn't even know we exist. His lips can't say, 'Pur-due, Pur-due, Pur-due.'" He cries and screams about lack of respect. I've sung their praises so often, but Gene always feels like he's the forgotten guy.

Keady has played Knight almost even, and my guy in the ESPN studio, Digger Phelps, wouldn't even play Purdue when he coached at Notre Dame. I used to tease Digger about that, and he'd laugh and say the roads didn't run from South Bend to West Lafayette.

But the best way to build exposure is to win, baby, win at tournament time. That's what has hurt Keady — Purdue got to the final eight in 1994, but has never reached the Final Four — and that's why I admire what Dean Smith, Bobby Knight and Mike Krzyzewski have done, advancing deep into the tournament on a regular basis. It's not about winning a national title. There's only one guy who can do that each year. It's all about sustaining excellence in an increasingly competitive atmosphere.

In my mind, the great coaches have passed the test of time. Think about it. Guys like Dean Smith, John Chaney, John Thompson, Gene Keady, Bob Knight, Mike Krzyzewski, Rick Pitino, Denny Crum and Nolan Richardson all fall into the same category. They've been there for 10 years or more and gotten the job done year after year. Their teams are consistently in the Top 25.

Jud Heathcote passed the test of time, too. He coached at Michigan State for 23 years before retiring in the spring of '95. He's an amazing story when you consider he had a heart attack late in his career and still maintained his emotion.

Heathcote wasn't able to out-recruit Michigan very often for talent. He usually finished No. 2 in the battles for the Chris Webbers in the state. A lot of his stars, such as Shawn Respert and Steve Smith, weren't all that highly recruited coming out of high school.

Heathcote did have that great team that won the national title in 1979 when Magic Johnson was a sophomore. After Jud won the championship, his 2-3 matchup zone was the talk of the clinics. Jud would get up and talk and then I'd remind everyone, "Come on now, guys. You could have played man-to-man or zone; you could have put Magic in anything you wanted to play and it would have been what America wanted." I told the coaches, "Well, that's great. Everybody's writing down the 2-3, but you got a little problem. You don't have Magic or Greg Kelser or Jay Vincent in the backline."

All too often, guys on the high school level get too carried away with trying to emulate the guys on top. A guy wins a title and all of a sudden his wrinkle is the only way to play. Some coaches forget that the most important ingredient in coaching is to evaluate your personnel and adjust your style to the players on your roster. In college, you can recruit players to fit your style. In high school, you've got to play with what you have.

I was so happy to see Jud go out on a high, battling Purdue for the Big Ten title before finishing second and earning a No. 3 seed in the NCAA Tournament. Guys like him have earned a lot of credibility, especially from within the profession, and have made more contributions to the game than fans realize.

One coach who hasn't earned the respect he deserves is Jimmy Boeheim at Syracuse. Boeheim coached the Orangemen to the NCAA Finals in 1987. He came so close to winning it all against Indiana, but Derrick Coleman missed the front end of a one-on-one with 28 seconds remaining and Keith Smart won it for the Hoosiers with a baseline jumper in the final two seconds.

If Coleman hits his free throws, or if Smart's shot rims out, Syracuse wins the national championship and Boeheim's a hero. But the fans have never let him forget finishing second. Now he's branded. You walk down the streets in Syracuse and you always hear people moaning and groaning about him.

I'll flat-out guarantee there's no way Boeheim could survive a 14-14 season at Syracuse. That's a crying shame because the guy has averaged close to 24 wins over 19 years. He played there, was an assistant there. If Tommy Lasorda bleeds Dodger Blue, this guy bleeds Syracuse Orange. And he has never been given the respect he deserves for winning and surviving in a tough league like the Big East.

People just don't understand how difficult it is to get to the Final Four. Jimmy did a great job in the 1994-95 season. He had Arkansas beat in the second round before Lawrence Moten made a mistake and called a time-out his team didn't have in the final six seconds of regulation. Arkansas went on to win in overtime.

Lute Olson of Arizona is another coach who doesn't always get the credit he deserves. Arizona was 1-17 in the Pac-10 the year before he arrived. He comes in, creates fan interest, turns McKale Center into one of the great environments in college basketball, wins 24, 25 games a year. Arizona carried the banner for the Pac-10 a long time and got to the Final Four in 1988 and 1994.

The program's been super. Unfortunately, it has run into a few buzz saws in the NCAA Tournament, losing to East Tennessee, Santa Clara and Miami of Ohio during a four-year stretch. Fans tend to remember the upsets more than the accomplishments, and the burden can become unbelievable for the coach. It's a shame this deters from what Lute has done, because he's done plenty. He's done it all, in fact, except win a national title — and he can still get that.

Sometimes, the pressure can even catch up to the great ones. Bob Knight is the Big Ten's all-time winningest coach. But he didn't have one of his better teams in the 1994-95 season. He had a legitimate star in 6-9 forward Alan Henderson, who was a first-round draft pick of the Atlanta Hawks, but the Hoosiers were young. They started three freshmen at times. The state of Indiana is known for producing shooters like Steve Alford and Larry Bird and Rick Mount, but Knight didn't have one, and that led to a lot of erratic moments.

Indiana won 19 games, but Knight became so disillusioned at one point that he actually talked about leaving the game after a crazy victory at Northwestern in which the Hoosiers lost an early 19-point lead but regrouped and won by 21.

Knight wondered afterward if the game had passed him by. He reiterated the same sentiments to me later in the year. "What am I doing?" he said. "The '90s have become baggy shorts, black sneakers, black socks, chains and earrings. It's become three-point shooting, the 35-second clock. Everything I don't believe in is part of the game. Maybe I'm getting too old, and I should get out."

Knight later admitted he wasn't going anywhere. He'll just try to beat the system. When it comes to the end, I really believe The General will head for the fishing pond and never look back. Until then, he'll keep doing it the Robert Montgomery Knight way — playing solid defense, getting a high-percentage shot and playing with intensity.

By the time Knight retires, he might join Dean Smith with more than 800 career victories. He finished the 1994-95 season with 659.

By the time Don Haskins of UTEP leaves the game, he should have more than 750. Haskins has coached at UTEP for 34 years, and he was on the sidelines for one of the most historic NCAA championship games. He did his part to help the cause of the black athlete back in 1966 when he coached a Texas Western team, with five black starters, to a stunning victory over an all-white Kentucky team, the 'Rupp's Runts' squad that included former Knicks coach Pat Riley and my ESPN broadcasting partner Larry Conley.

That was the first time a team with an all-black starting lineup won the title. Haskins received a lot of hate mail after that tournament, including some death threats. He had the courage to integrate a team in the deep South at a time when segregation was still the norm. For that and his other accomplishments, he certainly deserves a spot in the Hall of Fame, and I think it's a sin he hasn't been inducted.

Haskins doesn't have the advantage of coaching in a power conference or in a major media market. Haskins coaches in El Paso, in the WAC. Rick Majerus of Utah is another guy who works in a blackout zone for national TV in Salt Lake City. Majerus may have the best program in the West outside the Pac-10. Utah is traditionally the second choice of instate kids. Most of the Mormon stars go to BYU.

But Majerus has been a consistent winner, and he's an excellent teacher. He's bound to have a breakthrough eventually. I've never done a game in Salt Lake City. Do you hear me, Rick? Send me an invitation?

For some coaches, the NBA is an option. The Portland Trail Blazers went after Mike Krzyzewski in 1993. When they couldn't get him, they went after P.J. Carlesimo of Seton Hall and lured him with a five-year contract worth $7.5 million. For P.J., that was a no-brainer. The dollars were unbelievable. How could you turn that down?

John Calipari spoke with Detroit, Golden State, Boston and Miami before deciding to stay at UMass. Other pro teams like the Lakers, the L.A. Clippers, the Indiana Pacers, the Atlanta Hawks and the New Jersey Nets have also made a run at the big names in college coaching, speaking to the likes of Rick Pitino, Nolan Richardson and Roy Williams.

But I don't think they can get the megastars away. They can't get the Mike Krzyzewskis, the Bobby Knights, the John Thompsons, the Dean Smiths. They can get the guy who has been successful, but not the guy who's become an institution in his own right. There's that automatic relationship. That type of guy isn't going to subject himself to a league where people on the bench are making more than he is and where he can't control the situation. In the college game, he has total command.

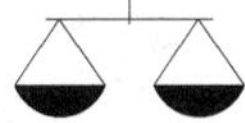

Lately, some ex-pro players have wanted to get into college coaching. Kareem Abdul-Jabbar showed interest in replacing George Raveling at USC, for example. Kareem was the greatest all-around center ever to play the game, but I don't believe guys like that can jump onto the sidelines from out of nowhere and be successful. It's not simply X's and O's. There's the academic side, the NCAA rule book, fund-raising, dealing with alums. Let me tell you, I think it would be easier for a guy like Kareem to make the transition to coaching in the NBA, where it's just basketball, basketball, basketball.

In the NBA, you can get it done if you've got the right players and you put them together in a system and you get them motivated. Coaching experience isn't as great a factor. Pat Riley had no coaching experience when he stepped out of the broadcast booth and began coaching the Lakers. He certainly benefitted from having Magic Johnson on the perimeter, James Worthy on the wing and Kareem in the middle, but to Pat's credit, he did a good job blending their egos together. The Lakers won five titles in the 1980s.

Don't get me wrong, they do a superb job coaching on the NBA level. Guys like Riley are among the best in the business, but they don't have to deal with the various strategies that exist in college, such as the multitude of defenses — the triangle-and-two, diamond-and-one, all the zones. Yeah, they play helpside defense in the NBA and zone the weak side, but there aren't as many strategic adjustments as in college, where each game is so unique.

Just because a coach's name is Kareem Abdul-Jabbar, kids aren't automatically going to go to his school. Besides, hiring someone simply because he was a great player is a slap in the face to all the guys who have busted their guts as assistants, or guys who have worked their way up the ladder as head coaches at smaller schools; guys who have worked 25 to 30 years, learning the game, waiting for an opportunity.

It's getting tougher and tougher to get into college coaching because the number of assistant's positions has been reduced. The NCAA eliminated one assistant's job to save money, but it has denied a lot of young guys an opportunity. The guys who work in the trenches in high school today don't get the same opportunity I had.

In 1971, I'm teaching sixth grade and coaching high school basketball in New Jersey. I finally got a chance to be an assistant at Rutgers. I brought in some quality players for Dick Lloyd, and that was my ticket to getting a head coaching job at the University of Detroit. I don't know if I could get the same break out of high school today with the limited staffs.

There are a lot of outstanding young college assistants out there who coach until they're 30, then want to make the break. They've learned when to call time-outs, how to manage a team, how to blend a team together. They learn the intricacies of the recruiting wars. They've learned from their head coach. I learned so much from Dick Lloyd, my boss at Rutgers. And he learned a lot from the guy who preceded him, Bill Foster. Foster was way ahead of his time. He coached Rutgers, Utah, Duke and South Carolina into the NCAA Tournament. He had it down to a science.

So I got the benefit of all that knowledge. I learned how to write recruiting letters, how to raise money, how to promote the team. All of those things came because I got a chance.

If a head coach does leave and the program has been successful, it's the result of a combination of people — the head coach and the assistants — who made it happen. So why not give the assistant a shot? Michigan State did the right thing and elevated assistant Tom Izzo after Heathcote retired. This created a sense of continuity. But a lot of athletic directors lack the courage to go with an unproven assistant. It's hard for assistants to get jobs unless they're at a program that's winning big or the head coach is such a monster in terms of recognition — like Rick Pitino, Bob Knight, Dean Smith or Mike Krzyzewski — he can pick up the phone and call on their behalf.

It seems to be happening more often, though. It's good that UNLV will give Billy Bayno, one of John Calipari's assistants at UMass, a shot. It's a chance to bring in some new blood. Duke assistant Michael Brae got the job at Delaware. UCLA assistant Mark Gottfried was hired at Murray State. Kansas assistant Mark Robinson got the Tulsa job. Bring in some new guys, some new ideas, new concepts, new excitement. Schools should reach out to these guys. They do a great job in the trenches. Sometimes they just don't get the chance.

It appears that going the Division II or III route is a dead end these days. Of the 46 Division I schools with coaching vacancies after the 1995 season, only two — Southwest Missouri State and Texas-SanAntonio — went for Division II or III coaches. Southwest Missouri hired Steve Alford, the former Indiana star who coached Manchester (Ind.) College to the Division III championship game in 1995. But Alford had name recognition, having been an All-America in college who played in the NBA. But, many times, Division I athletic directors will not give a shot to a Division II or III coach because they want names they can sell to alums.

Hey, virtually all the great head coaches working today were eager assistants at one time, and somebody took a chance on them. Hopefully enough athletic directors today will have the courage to keep providing those opportunities.

# 7
# Changing Times

NBC dropped a giant bombshell a few years back when it plunked down $35 million for the rights to broadcast Notre Dame's home football games. Dick Rosenthal, ND's former athletic director, negotiated the deal. He angered many people in the collegiate community, but let's face reality. He did a superb job in serving the university he represented from a business standpoint. No AD would turn down a deal of that magnitude.

But the network felt it was worth the gamble. Notre Dame has the most powerful athletic program in the country. Lou Holtz usually has the Irish in the hunt for the national championship. Oh, they slipped in 1994, but they'll be back.

Notre Dame's football program has always been strong enough to operate as an independent. But you simply can't survive any longer as an independent in college basketball. Al McGuire said that independents are going the way of the dinosaur, and I agree with him.

McGuire — street-wise, down-to-earth — was one of my favorite coaches when I was at Detroit, and he should know about independents. His 1977 Marquette team is the most recent one to win the national title. Since Al retired after that season, Marquette has joined three different conferences — the MCC, the Great Midwest, and, most recently, Conference USA — in an effort to regain national prominence.

If any basketball program had a chance to survive outside of a conference, it was Notre Dame. It's like Digger Phelps used to cry before he left the head coaching job there to join us in the studio at ESPN: "We are national. We are not just provincial. We are the Golden Dome." He used to drive me crazy. At first I thought he was wacky. But after I became familiar with Notre Dame, I discovered Digger was 100 percent correct. No question, the Irish are national.

But perhaps not as national as they used to be. A lot has changed since the Irish had enough talent to end UCLA's 88-game winning streak on Dwight Clay's jumper at the buzzer back in the 1970s, when they had players such as Adrian Dantley, Gary Brokaw, John Shumate and Kelly Tripucka.

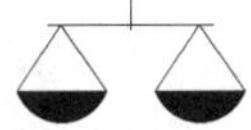

Notre Dame hasn't qualified for the NCAA Tournament since 1990, and hasn't reached the NIT since 1992. The Irish slipped as low as 9-18 in the 1992-93 season, went 12-17 the following year and still missed out on postseason play in 1994-95 despite finishing 15-12. They had impressive victories over Indiana and Xavier on their home court, but lost to San Diego, Dayton and Fordham (in a game played at Madison Square Garden). They lost to Butler for the fifth consecutive season. And they suffered truly ugly defeats to UCLA at Pauley Pavilion and to Kentucky in South Bend.

No one is afraid to play Notre Dame anymore. And the major reason the program has faltered is that it doesn't play in a conference. It was finding it impossible to keep up with recruiting in the Midwest and East — its traditional bases — because of the dominance of the Big Ten and Big East. Kids want to play on television, and an independent program — even Notre Dame's — isn't going to get on television as often. A conference also offers "name brand" recognition. When John MacLeod inherited the job in 1991, he quickly discovered the name "Notre Dame" wasn't going to be enough to impress a kid.

That all changed in the summer of 1994 when Notre Dame accepted an offer from the Big East to join the conference starting with the 1995-96 season. Up in Providence, R.I., the Big East headquarters, they were calling it the marriage of the year.

Notre Dame's players were excited. Ryan Hoover, one of their starting guards, was quoted in the student paper saying he couldn't wait to get into the Big East because he wanted to play against high-class competition on a regular basis. Potential recruits said they would look at Notre Dame more seriously now, and the Irish had their best recruiting class in some time. Athletes want to play in big-time games that are meaningful. Think about it. Duke plays North Carolina and then makes the trip up to South Bend to play Notre Dame. The game is little more than a scrimmage to the Blue Devils, because it doesn't have the same impact as an ACC battle.

Get ready for some beautiful nights now. Here comes Georgetown, with Alan Iverson and big John Thompson on the sidelines. Do you think the Athletic Convocation Center will be rocking and rolling? Do you think the TV cameras will be rolling?

I think so highly of Notre Dame, because both of my girls received scholarships there based on their academic and tennis ability. I have attended as many home football games as possible, and always walk the campus before the games. I really soak it up. After having met many of the professors and coaches, I cannot be convinced the Irish can't find two or three quality players a year who would like to wear a Notre Dame uniform.

I hear all this cry about academics, how Notre Dame's high standards exclude most of the blue-chip recruits. Sure, but there are plenty of recruits who can qualify and can do the work, such as the Grant Hills and Eric Montrosses and Chris Webbers of the world. The Irish have to draw from a smaller recruiting base, but they have something special to offer — a degree from Notre Dame. And along with that degree comes the national networking among all the university's alums.

It's one great university. It's time Notre Dame started getting results and forgot about all the excuses and alibis. I'm not saying it should win a national title, but you can't convince me Notre Dame can't be a member of the Top 20 on a regular basis.

The Big East brings exposure and political clout to Notre Dame. Finish in the top half of a 13-team league and you've got a shot at the tournament.

Notre Dame brings a lot to the Big East, too. It offers advertisers exposure in Chicago, the nation's No. 2 TV market, and offers automatic drawing power. It's one of those elite programs capable of attracting enormous corporate sponsorship.

That's probably the wave of the future in college athletes. We got a vision of the what is to come when Nike supplied 24 of 26 programs at North Carolina with shoes, apparel, uniforms and luggage. AD John Swofford figures the deal will be worth $1.9 million over the length of the four-year contract.

That was just the beginning. With most states putting a limit on funding for a university, colleges are always looking to generate new sources of revenue for their athletic programs. More and more are turning to corporate sponsorship. A major sporting goods supplier or shoe company provides the university's athletic teams free uniforms and equipment and pays a substantial amount of cash in return for the university's endorsement.

This is the wave of the future, and I have no problem with it. Colleges need more and more money because of increased costs, particularly with the growth of women's programs, and this is simply another method of generating revenue. You can't blame colleges for taking advantage of every opportunity they get. Establishing a program is tougher than ever these days. When I was coaching at Detroit, we never played on television. And we were an independent, a tiny Catholic school. But Detroit had some tradition with Dave DeBusschere and Spencer Haywood, and I always thought it could be a sleeping giant because of all the talent in the city. We were able to get some of the best prospects in the city — guys like Terry Tyler and John Long — and turn the program into an NCAA Tournament team. And we did it on a shoestring budget.

My first year we had a 24-hour paint-a-thon in which we painted all the seats in our gymnasium. I was on my knees, painting seats. Can you see Dean Smith or Bob Knight doing that? People thought I was wacky, which I am, but the school had told me there wasn't enough money in the budget to hire painters. So I said, "I'll tell you what I'll do. You pay for the paint. I'll get the student body to paint the seats."

They said, "You've got to be kidding."

Sure enough, we got some students together and we painted the seats. It made a big difference.

Then we had a 24-hour basketball marathon. We opened the gym and had 10 games, starting every two hours. The Police Department vs. the Fire Department. Joe Strawder's Cafe (Joe was a former Bradley standout and Pistons player) vs. Willie Horton's cafe (Willie had been a Tigers slugging star). We culminated the day with our red-white intrasquad scrimmage.

We were just trying to create some excitement in the city. Detroit had a winning tradition, but people didn't think fans would come back from the suburbs at night to watch a game. I believed that if you had a first-class product, all these beautiful people — black, white, it didn't matter — would come out. And they did.

Even my players thought I was wacky. At my first meeting with them I said, "My biggest thrill will be when you arrive at 5:30 for an 8 o'clock game and there'll be a sign that says S.R.O. — Standing Room Only. You will absolutely feel like a million dollars as a player." When that finally happened, it was such a thrill.

We made our home games a special event. We turned off the lights, turned on a spotlight and had the players run through a big hoop as they were introduced. It got to the point where the visiting coach wouldn't bring his team out on the floor until after we were done. I wasn't afraid to give away tickets, either. I was like Santa Claus. I wanted to make sure those seats were filled.

That's the sort of thing smaller programs have to do to become successful, but it's even tougher today because of the dominance of the power conferences. Year in and year out, the ACC, the Big Ten, the Big East, the Big Eight and the SEC are going to be in the top echelon. The Pac-10 is coming on strong, too. It's obvious every year when the NCAA bids come out. In 1995, the Big Ten received six bids, the SEC and Big Eight received five and the Pac-10, Big East and ACC received four apiece.

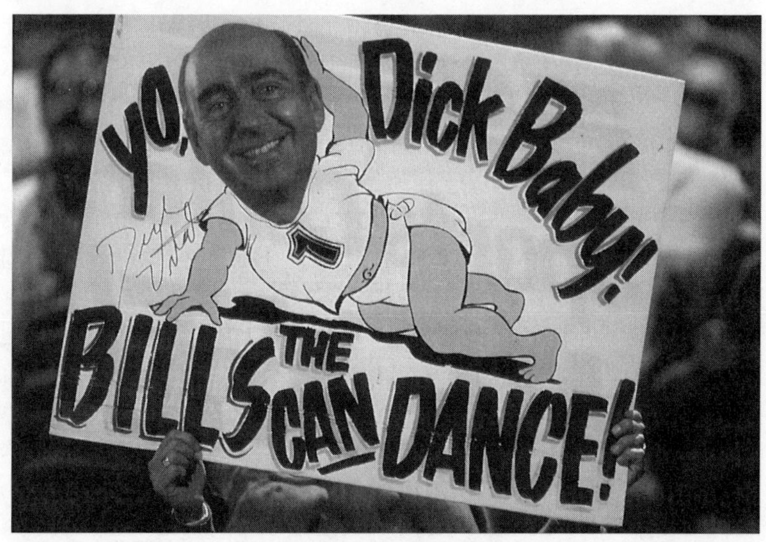


*Fans of the Saint Louis University Billikens were hoping to reach the Big Dance in 1995.*

Notre Dame's program is going to be rejuvenated within a three-year period now that it has joined the Big East. It won't happen overnight, but if it can bring in just two or three worthy recruits each year it will make some noise. Just two or three kids who want to play on national television against Syracuse, Georgetown and the rest.

Notre Dame also should rejuvenate the Big East, help it become the force it was in the 1980s when six conference schools — Georgetown, St. John's, Syracuse, Villanova, Providence and Seton Hall — made it to the Final Four and both Georgetown and Villanova won national titles.

The Big East is a made-for-TV league. It does not have the beautiful, bucolic campuses like Duke, Virginia and North Carolina in theACC. It does not even have on-campus arenas. What is does have is an enormous population base and a gigantic television market. The Big East has been so successful in basketball that it has been able to promote its own football league as well.

But the conference has not sent a team to the Final Four since 1989. By contrast, the ACC has sent six. I thought Connecticut had a shot to get there on two different occasions, but Christian Laettner hit a big shot to knock them out in the 1990 regional finals and then they drew eventual champ UCLA in the Western Regional finals in 1995.

The Big East is still powerful, with plenty of great players. Its biggest problem is that it has to deal with the comparisons to 1985, when Villanova, St. John's and Georgetown all made it to the Final Four, and Rollie Massimino's team played that perfect game in the finals to beat Patrick Ewing and company. The league had Ewing, Ed Pinckney and Chris Mullin then. That was royalty.

That set a standard that has been impossible to duplicate. But programs become the victims of their own success, just like coaches. People always want more. And when a league takes a small step backward, as it is bound to do on occasion, people say, "Wow. What happened?" Then comes some talk show host: "Hey, they're slipping in recruiting." And it becomes so difficult to get back.

The biggest problem the Big East faces in my mind is that so many schools lack campus facilities. That's why I've always put the Big East a step below the ACC and the Big Ten. They play so many games in public arenas like the Hartford Civic Center, the USAir Arena in Landover, the Spectrum in Philadelphia and the Meadowlands. The only exception I would make is Madison Square Garden, because it's special. It's the mecca of college hoops.

I like the idea of playing a big game like Syracuse vs. UConn at Gampel Pavilion in Storrs, on the UConn campus. I know Jimmy Boeheim might not agree, and I don't blame him. But that is what college hoops is all about. That is hoops heaven. The priorities are in order. The students are part of it. The whole school feels the electricity.

I got a chance to spend some time on the Georgetown campus for a Dickie V sound-a-like contest, and I told the students they ought to build a John Thompson Arena right on the campus of Georgetown. Right in the middle of Hoyaland. Forget about Landover. Carolina's got the Dean Dome; we're going to build the John Thompson Dome.

If Georgetown put up its own facility, it would be paid off in no time. The fan interest would be unreal. Students would line up forever to get a ticket. But the size of the facility is important. Don't make it too big. That's the problem Kevin O'Neill faces in Tennessee. The facility is such a big place that no matter what the guy does, it's going to be tough to get 25,000 people in there. With all those available seats, people are less inclined to buy season tickets. They know they can always get a ticket.

Rutgers is going to give Seton Hall a real run in Jersey. I think Seton Hall has a major problem now. Rutgers will steal a lot of its spotlight because it has a great facility on campus. The Hall, meanwhile, plays all its home games at the Meadowlands. For me, the pro arenas are just too sterile. Unless you have a dominant club, it's just not an exciting collegiate atmosphere.

P.J. Carlesimo, with that big contract you have in Portland, can you hear me? Hey, I'll throw in a few dollars. You donate $2,990,000, and I'll swing for $10,000 for my alma mater, and we've got $3 million to break ground for a new arena on campus. We'll even let them call it the P.J. Carlesimo Dome.

With the Collegiate Football Association contract about to expire, several teams have opted to leave their current conferences to join newly formed super conferences that span entire regions of the country. It is geographic chaos. I can't even keep up. I have no idea who belongs to what conference, who's going where. Take the new Conference USA. It's going to be exciting now that they've combined teams from the Great Midwest with teams from the Metro. But if you asked me who's in it, I'd have to stop and think about it. Oh yeah, the University of South Florida's in there. So are Tulane, Louisville, Memphis, Cincinnati. They're going to have Houston in 1997. But how do you keep up? And if I don't know, the average fan who doesn't make his living broadcasting college basketball games isn't going to know either.

We get back to that one magical word that a lot of us don't want to talk about in intercollegiate athletics: money. Why are these conferences put together? For green, green and more green, piles of George Washingtons. It's BIG business.

But we've got some schools playing in leagues that absolutely make no sense for them. Penn State became the 11th member of the Big Ten. Texas is one of four Southwest Conference schools that joined the Big Eight to form the Big Twelve. Miami is in the Big East. The travel alone makes it a bad idea, especially for the non-revenue sports that don't get to fly on their road trips. Schools talk about not wanting kids to miss class, and yeah, maybe the football player doesn't have to miss class because the team's got a charter jet. But how about the tennis player, the golfer? If you're a Penn State athlete riding in a car or bus to Ann Arbor for a match with Michigan, how do you do that in one day? How do you not miss one or two days of class in situations like that? We've got some crazy alignments that make no sense whatsoever.

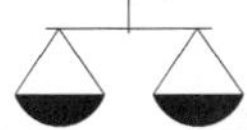

One thing I know for sure: The strongest conference for basketball in the country on a regular basis is the Atlantic Coast Conference. When I think about a conference, I don't think just about the quality of teams, because, obviously, the ACC is always going to have one or two teams in the hunt for a national title. What makes the ACC so special is the facilities, the crowds, the excitement, the media coverage, the glossy images of the programs.

I would put an all-star team from the ACC against the rest of the country. I'll take five guys from the ACC, you take the rest of the country. I'm not going to say it's a lock, but I know I've got a great chance to win. Just think, in 1995 I could have had Joe Smith, Rasheed Wallace, Jerry Stackhouse, Cherokee Parks and Tim Duncan up front, with a backcourt of Randolph Childress, Travis Best and Bob Sura. That's the start of a pretty good club. Nobody could have screwed up those guys.

You can count on the ACC to be strong every year. The same goes for the Big Ten, although it's been in a slump lately. The Big Ten has been hurt more than any other league by kids leaving early for the pros. If the Michigan kids had stayed in school, do you think the Fab Five would have been highly ranked the past couple of years? Do you think maybe if the Big Dog, Glenn Robinson, had stayed at Purdue, they wouldn't have been ranked among the top five teams in America? They still won the Big Ten without him, but they would have been a true national power with him in the 1994-95 season.

Ohio State's fall from glory also was a blow to the Big Ten. The Buckeyes won back-to-back league championships in 1991 and '92, and they seemed destined to become a national power. But they finished a bleak 6-22 overall and 2-16 in conference play in the 1994-95 season. The Buckeyes were devastated by the loss of five scholarship players from the junior class and an NCAA investigation that found the school guilty of 17 violations in the recruitment of Damon Flint from Cincinnati, who now attends the University of Cincinnati. It's been an absolute enigma, and I don't understand it. If there was a guy who was really charted as a hot coach in America, it was Randy Ayers.

A lot of people don't realize this, but I got a call from somebody really influential asking for advice on the job opening at Notre Dame after Digger Phelps resigned. This person asked me, "If you had to name a guy from the college ranks who is young and has a great future, who would it be?"

At the time I didn't know that John MacLeod was going to leave the NBA for the college ranks. The first person that came to mind was Randy Ayers. I tried to recruit Randy as a player when I coached at Detroit; he could really shoot the ball. But he went to Ohio U and was a terrific player in the MAC. He had just come off two seasons in which the Buckeyes won the conference title and he had been named the league's Coach of the Year. He nearly got his team into the 1992 Final Four, but it lost an overtime heartbreaker to Michigan in the Southeast Regionals in Lexington after beating the Wolverines twice during the regular season.

Randy was at the pinnacle then, but it seems from that moment on things began to change. It was just a steady slide downhill. Derek Anderson and center Nate Wilbourne both transferred at the end of their sophomore year. Then before the season began, junior forward Charles Macon — a former Mr. Basketball in Indiana — ran into trouble with the law and flunked out of school. Ohio State's athletic director, Andy Geiger, removed junior center Gerald Eaker from the team after Eaker allegedly fired a gun at the tire of teammate Antonio Watson's car. Finally, junior guard Greg Simpson was kicked off the team after he was charged with assault on a former girlfriend. Simpson, who was later acquitted, has since transferred to West Virginia.

It all goes back to recruiting. Ohio State's coaching staff made some mistakes in evaluating the players they brought in. In a sense, you can fault the current recruiting system, which limits the number of times coaches can talk and meet with recruits. Coaches just can't get to know recruits personally like they once did. Many of the players Ohio State brought in had problems off the court. And the problems just kept mounting and mounting. It's an example of what can happen if a coach doesn't pay enough attention to character and takes too many chances. Sometimes kids mature and turn out fine; sometimes they don't.

Now Randy Ayers has to start over. He's lucky to have Geiger in his corner. He's the kind of AD who will be patient. Just the way he was at Maryland. When Geiger arrived there from Stanford, he found Gary Williams going through some tough times after he had inherited a team that was going on probation. And look at the Terps today.

Bill Bayno, one of John Calipari's assistants at Massachusetts, faces a rebuilding situation of his own at Nevada-Las Vegas. Bayno has a difficult job ahead of him. I was in Vegas in 1994 for a heavyweight championship fight, and fans there were excited about a new guy coming in — one who doesn't have a track record in terms of wins and losses, but who's coming in to rebuild from the start, rather than taking over during the season and trying to apply bandages. I think that a lot of people out there are going to give him a chance and understand that he's just not going to get it done — get Vegas to where Vegas was under Jerry Tarkanian — in a year or two.

I really believe Tim Grgurich could have turned it around after he replaced Rollie Massimino in November. Grgurich was Tark's top assistant and had done such a good job as an assistant with the Seattle SuperSonics in the NBA. I watched him work with kids at the ABCD Camp in New Jersey once. The guy is a pure gym rat who loves nothing better than to help a player get better. He'll coach anybody. At ABCD, he would take a bunch of the kids aside and work on post moves. He'd be sweating as if he was playing. Sonny Vaccaro would say, "C'mon let's go get lunch." And Tim would say, "Forget it. I've got to work with these kids."

That's just the way he is. He can't help himself. Everybody who knows him says he would work 30 hours in a 24-hour day if he could. But he couldn't deal with all the outside distractions of the Vegas situation after he took over. It didn't take long for it all to catch up with him. The stress and the exhaustion put him in the hospital. Doctors advised him to spend six weeks away from the game, but he never returned. He's probably a guy who's better off being an assistant, where all he has to do is teach. He can make more contributions to the game in that position, instead of dealing with all the outside distractions.

UNLV went through two more coaches, assistants Howie Landa and Cleve Edwards, but neither had a real chance to resurrect the program. Vegas finished 12-16 in 1994-95, their worst record ever.

It's hard to bring a program back, as Gary Williams discovered at Maryland. Maryland had been an elite program under Lefty Driesell, with 15 winning seasons from 1972-86. Lefty came in and proclaimed, "We're going to be the UCLA of the East." He did that to bring attention to his program and it worked. He went out and recruited great players such as Lenny Elmore, Tom McMillen, Buck Williams, John Lucas, Albert King and Len Bias.

But it all fell apart after Bias died from a cocaine overdose. It took the Terps nine years to get back to the national spotlight. Gary arrived on the scene in 1989. He had been on a roll at American, Boston College and Ohio State, but he always wanted to coach at his alma mater.

I don't think he would have made the move, though, if he knew the NCAA was going to give Maryland a three-year probation in 1990 for violations committed by Driesell's successor, Bob Wade. In addition to probation, the school was prohibited from competing in the NCAA Tournament for two years, from appearing on TV for a year, and was forced to return $407,000 in revenue accumulated from two previous NCAA Tournament appearances. The sanctions killed recruiting at first. Maryland almost landed Donyell Marshall, but he signed with UConn because he said he wanted to play in the NCAA Tournament right away.

Gary really had to battle. But he just kept fighting and fighting. That's all he knows. I was coaching high school ball in East Rutherford, N.J., the same time he was coaching at Woodrow Wilson in Camden. The thing you could see even then was the spark, the intensity he brought to the table. He was that way as a player at Maryland, too. He got the maximum out of his ability. He was such a heady competitor. But please, Gary, I hope you are not the shooting coach for Maryland. You were Brick City, USA when you played there, baby. Hey, only kidding, Gary. Please, no phone calls.

Eventually, he was able to recruit enough super quality kids to make a dent in the ACC. He signed blue chippers from the D.C. area like Duane Simpkins and Johnny Rhodes. He broke down some of the barriers in Baltimore and got Keith Booth from Dunbar, where Wade used to coach. He signed Joe Smith from Norfolk and turned him into a star. Gary is a great teacher.

It was just a matter of time before Maryland started to win. The Terps beat UMass to reach the Sweet 16 in the 1994 tournament. That gave them a great buildup for the following season, when they finished in a four-way tie for the ACC title with North Carolina, Wake Forest and Virginia.

Gary paid the price, though. Just before the start of the ACC Tournament, he came down with pneumonia and had to be hospitalized. Maryland got to the Sweet 16 again, but Gary was never the same in the tournament. He had just worn himself out.

Some programs fall and have trouble getting up. Look at DePaul. It was No. 1 in the country back in 1980 when Ray Meyer was still coaching, and had Mark Aguirre and Terry Cummings. But the Blue Demons haven't been to the NCAA Tournament lately, and the fans are getting restless.

DePaul fell, too, and is still trying to get back on its feet. Sure, Ray's son, Joey was able to recruit Tom Kleinschmidt, but if DePaul's going to make noise it has to get more great kids from the city. If there are three great ones in Chicago, they've got to get at least one of them. Their argument will always be that many kids can't meet their academic standards, but they've got to find a way to make sure those who can, find their way into a Blue Demon uniform.

It doesn't help when you hear behind-the-scenes comments that there's a battle going on between AD Bill Bradshaw and Joey. That just fans the fire. It's tough enough to get a job done when everybody in the boat is rowing in the same direction; it's impossible when the leaders aren't working together. I happen to like both guys and it's about time they quiet the critics who say they don't get along. They need to get behind closed doors, resolve their differences and come up with a plan to get DePaul back into the upper echelon.

The people at DePaul want more than 16 to 18 W's a season. Joey's been around DePaul forever, as a player, assistant coach and head coach. After awhile you're kind of taken for granted, and that's sad. It's the same with Jim

Boeheim at Syracuse and Larry Finch of Memphis, both of whom played at their respective schools. I think they would have been a lot more appreciated if somehow, some way, they would have moved on. But they're in a comfort zone.

If a program gets stuck in a rut too long, the coach eventually finds himself out of a job. Hugh Durham coached at Georgia for 17 years and took the Bulldogs to the Final Four in 1983. He came very close to getting to the NCAA Tournament in 1995, winning 17 games, but after Georgia lost in the first round of the NIT it was over. You look at his numbers over the long haul and the university had no right to fire him. If you win more than 60 percent of your games and you're shown the exit, something's wrong with the formula.

But sometimes change is good for everybody involved. Sometimes coaches need a change of scenery and schools need new blood. When Billy Tubbs left Oklahoma for TCU after the 1993-94 season, I think it was a good move. And I think Oklahoma made a great choice, going after Kelvin Sampson of Washington State. Sampson built his entire offense around Ryan Minor and Oklahoma won all its games on its living room floor. Sampson won several national Coach of the Year awards. He should get even more publicity once the Big Eight expands to the Big Twelve.

I've never been to Starkville, Miss., but I may have to make the trip soon to watch Mississippi State. Coach Richard Williams never played college basketball when he went to school there. He was a student worker in the physical education center and used to attend practices when Babe McCarthy was the coach. He worked his way up the coaching ladder after he graduated, from junior high to high school to junior college, and finally was offered a chance to join Bob Boyd's staff in 1982. After Boyd retired, Williams got his chance and he's made the most of it. His team reached the final 16 of the NCAA Tournament in 1995, and it has great talent coming back. Starkville is going to be a difficult place for the teams that dare go there.

Mike Montgomery at Stanford is in a similar situation. You don't hear Montgomery's name mentioned often, but he's an outstanding bench tactician. He's finally starting to get some talent. I love Tim Young, Stanford's young 7-footer. And I love the lead guard, Brevin Knight. His dad, Mel, was a Thomas Edison special when he played at Seton Hall. He was a 3-D man. He had the ability to drive, draw and dish the rock when he played. He later served as an assistant to Bill Raftery, and was an assistant athletic director there. Brevin's mom still works at Seton Hall, but the school showed no interest in him. He went out to Stanford and has become a diaper dandy in a league that has produced point guards galore — guys like Jason Kidd, Gary Payton, Damon Stoudamire and Tyus Edney.

Winning 10 games might not seem like a big deal, but it represented a great accomplishment for Pitt coach Ralph Willard when you studied his personnel. He made the most of what he had. Now wait until his recruiting efforts start to pay off. Ralph has instilled an unbelievable spirit in his players with his enthusiasm and positive attitude.

I'm a big fan of Pete Gillen at Providence, too. I loved him when he coached at Five-Star. I loved him when he coached at Xavier, and I was shocked he didn't take the Notre Dame job after Digger Phelps left; he had been an assistant there and it seemed a natural for him. When Rick Barnes left Providence for Clemson, Pete finally decided to move on. I think one of the big reasons was the fact Xavier joined the Atlantic 10. When Pete saw all the traveling involved, he thought, "Well, I might as well do it in a league that has a built-in national profile." I think Gillen has Providence headed for the Top 20 now that Shamgod Wells, a sensational lead guard from LaSalle High in the New York City Catholic League, has made his test score. Howard Garfinkel of Five-Star rates Wells only slightly behind New York's finest, Stephon Marbury. Enough said. This kid must have a world of potential.

One last thing. It's a shame that hardly anyone talks about the Ivy League. Penn was a legitimate team the past two years. Fran Dunphy's players went through two undefeated Ivy League seasons, then held their heads high in the NCAA

Tournament, beating Nebraska one year in the first round and then playing Alabama to overtime in the first round of the 1995 tournament.

That's a rarity. Of course, how many times is an Ivy League team going to get a backcourt of Jerome Allen and Matt Maloney? Remember, this is a league where there are no scholarships, and tuition and board run close to $26,000 a year. Allen was a big time player who was recruited hard by both Temple and UMass and certainly could have gone to a lot of the power schools. Maloney played in the SEC at Vanderbilt before transferring after his freshman year. Maloney comes from great stock. His dad, Jim, is an assistant at Temple and should be a head coach somewhere. Jim has done an amazing job with his son in terms of understanding the game. They're a typical father-son combination, a lot like Bob Hurley and his dad, Bob, Sr., at St. Anthony's of Jersey City.

Occasionally, an Ivy League coach gets lucky and lands a great player who wants the academic challenge — a player like Sen. Bill Bradley, who went to Princeton in the 1960s. The Tigers have been lucky a few times. They've also had players such as Geoff Petrie, John Hummer, Brian Taylor and Teddy Manakas play for them. Columbia had some great teams, too, with player such as Jim McMillian, who went on to have a solid NBA career.

It's always a great story when a PTPer goes to an Ivy League school. These schools are so good academically that a player has an unlimited future when he gets his degree. It's a shame it doesn't happen more often.

What does continue to happen is Pete Carril pulling off an occasional upset against a higher-ranked team. It's not going to happen on a regular basis, but it can happen anytime Princeton plays a highly ranked team. The Tigers run that patient motion offense, with all those backdoor cuts, and sneak up on a team that's not playing at its peak. He does an amazing job when you consider he's dealing with athletes who, obviously, are not the same level of recruits as the kids who go to the big Division I schools. The fan on the street might not know much about Carril, but if you talk to his peers they will tell you he can flat-out get a team to perform to its maximum. He beat Bob Knight's first Indiana team in the 1972 NIT at Madison Square Garden, and he lost to Georgetown by just one point in the first round of the 1989 NCAA Tournament.

Pete Carril is a genuine superstar in the coaching fraternity. That's one thing that hasn't changed over the years.

# 8 Lights! Camera! Action!

I'm a dummy, baby. Hey, I didn't go to Harvard. So I'm not into high-level corporate negotiations. I'm into doing games on TV. But you don't have to be a genius to realize the $1.7 billion that CBS paid to maintain control of the NCAA Tournament is a lot of gravy. I know Billy Packer must have jumped with joy when he heard the news. I can just hear him shouting, "If I can get just a little of that!"

Television has made the NCAA Tournament so big that it seems everybody follows it. People who haven't followed basketball all year get excited about the tournament and dive into office pools. The Final Four has become a megaevent that ranks right up there with the Super Bowl and the World Series. And ESPN has been right in the middle of the growth. We reach more than 60 million viewers. When we do Conference Championship Week in March, we draw big ratings numbers. We've given the game tremendous visibility, and I can't believe the way it's taken off.

All the college basketball coverage has given a major assist to the NBA by introducing the stars of the future to the public. By the time a Joe Smith, Jerry Stackhouse or Rasheed Wallace enters the draft, they're household names because of their television exposure in college.

I think the extensive schedule ESPN puts on — starting with the Hall of Fame Tip-Off Classic, the Preseason NIT, the Great Eight and the preseason tournaments in Hawaii and Alaska — whets everyone's appetites. We continue serving up games all season long, and by the time the NCAA Tournament selection show comes around, ESPN, ABC and CBS have set the table for a grand feast.

Basketball's not like football, where teams need large numbers of outstanding players to win. College basketball teams can win with one superstar and some role players, or a couple of late bloomers — like David Robinson at Navy. Nobody wanted him when he came out of high school, a fairly ordinary 6-foot-7 player. So he goes to Navy, has a major growth spurt, and all of a sudden he's on TV whipping Syracuse at the Carrier Dome in the NCAA Tournament and taking his team to the East Regional finals against Duke in 1986. He's putting on a show, carrying the Midshipmen on his back. It was beautiful to see, and ESPN helped it happen. The game just keeps getting bigger and bigger and bigger.

Basketball is the perfect game for television. The players are so agile and mobile, and they're performing on a small stage where you can see their every move. There's so much drama and emotion, and the cameras capture everything. The players and coaches are all right out there; there's no place to hide. You can see the pain on a coach's face when he's slapped with a technical. You can see the jubilation of the players. You don't see all that in football and hockey, where the players wear helmets. You can't see it very well in baseball, either, where everybody's in the dugout. Basketball's large ball is easily picked up by the cameras, and the games last about two hours — perfect for a television show. Baseball and football can last up to four hours, beyond the attention span of many viewers.

Some college coaches would rather not have the celebrity status television brings. Dean Smith once told Sport Magazine that before the birth of ESPN, the National

Association of Basketball Coaches was worried that North Carolina was on TV too much. How often was that? Three or four times a year. Now just about every Carolina game is televised somewhere, and the same is true for many of the major programs.

Smith says he enjoys the coaching, not the attention that comes with it. But coaches have become such a dominant force in college hoops. College basketball is different from the pros in that way. The NBA's sense of stability comes from the players. A Kareem Abdul-Jabbar, Larry Bird or Michael Jordan stays in one city for several years and establishes a relationship with the fans. But in college, the players can play no more than four seasons and often leave before playing that long, so the sense of stability must come from the coaches. That's why they're the stars of the show.

I was lucky to get into the boom in basketball coverage on the ground floor. I got the ziggy from the Pistons in November of 1979, just 12 games into the season. Bill Davidson, their owner, pulled up to my house in a big limo. The chauffeur knocked on the door. My wife knew what was coming down, so she left the house. Davidson comes in the door, taps me on the shoulder and whispers to me, "I've just made a coaching change." Wow. I couldn't believe it. I'm not going to lie. I cried like a baby.

I was in a state of deep depression for awhile. I slept a lot, moped around a lot, and hardly left the house for a month. It got so bad I even considered psychoanalysis. But I wanted to coach. So when Scotty Connal, the head of production at something called ESPN, contacted me about doing a few games for this all-sports cable network, my mind was still on getting back into coaching. I realized I had made a major mistake in taking a coaching job in the NBA, because my personality wasn't well-suited for it. I'm so up-tempo, and 82 regular-season games is too much for my type of personality. I wanted to get back into college coaching or into administration at the NBA level.

But nothing was happening for me. I was writing letters all the time, but I got more rejections than the Dean of Admissions at Harvard hands out in any given year. I wrote to Joe Taub, the owner of the Nets. I said, "Please, bring me back home. Let me work in the front office." He finally did offer me a job — selling tickets. I thought I had a little more to offer than that.

The first game I did for ESPN was one that DePaul played at Wisconsin in Madison during the last week in November. Joe Boyle and I handled the broadcast. Rod Thorn, who's now the NBA assistant commissioner, was scouting for the Chicago Bulls at the time and was up there to see Wes Matthews and Mark Aguirre. We went out afterward and I felt so relieved. It was my first time out of the house in a month. I thought it would be a hoot for a few games, a great short-term run doing a few games on TV before I landed on my feet with another coaching job — in college.

*As a member of the media, I enjoy interviewing other people, but as coach I learned what it's like on the other side of the microphone. Here, I bid farewell to the Detroit Pistons after getting the ziggy in 1979. It turned out to be the beginning of a new career for me.*

It still amazes me that I have a career in television. I still can't believe my name ever was considered by the ESPN executives. Connal had worked for NBC sports, and had helped hire McGuire and Packer. He was producing many of the games in the NCAA Tournament, including the last one I coached in college. It was against Michigan, when the Wolverines were ranked No. 1 in the nation. It was truly a special moment for our program at Detroit. For us, playing a tournament game on regional TV was a big deal. The fact two legends broadcast the game — Curt Gowdy handled the play-by-play and John Wooden the color commentary — made it even more special.

I hear that Connal became aware of me through that game, that he liked my enthusiasm. Looking back, it makes our loss to Michigan that day a lot easier to digest.

Connal was the perfect guy to get me started. I'll never forget him telling me, "You've got several things we can't teach, like your enthusiasm, your knowledge, your candidness and passion. But you have absolutely no clue about the world of TV." That's when Scotty assigned Jim Simpson, a pro's pro, to work with me on a regular basis. I owe a great deal to Scotty C for having the guts to hire me, and then sticking with me through my growing pains in broadcasting. Steve Bornstein, the chief honcho at ESPN and Dennis Swanson atABC also have continued to support me.

I've watched the cable network grow from the grass roots, housed in a little trailer in Bristol, Conn., into a huge, bureaucratic corporation. We have a lot more meetings, more memos now. ESPN is a giant, and it's still growing. We have ESPN 2 and ESPN International. I tell people that when ESPN wanted to hire me I said, "What is that, a disease?" Now, every place we go people roll out the red carpet. They can't do enough for us.

I would broadcast games all night if they'd let me, but a lot of people — coaches, fans, players, even some announcers — are upset about how much control television has over the game. We have games starting at 9:30 p.m., which means they end not long before midnight and nobody gets home and in bed until about 1 a.m. — and that's if they live in town.

But I've learned you have to accept things that are out of your control, that you have to adjust and go along with the system. I'm certainly not going to complain. I'm happy whenever they give me a game, regardless of what time it starts.

I don't buy the argument that the players miss class as a result of the late starting times. Are you kidding me? Go to a dorm sometime. I've been on campuses all over the country for more than 25 years, and kids everywhere stay up late and rap until well past midnight.

Obviously a late start is not the most ideal situation, but if kids really want to study and are willing to organize their day, they have plenty of time to study. If that's the toughest problem those kids have to face, they are heading for an easy life. Besides, players aren't asked to do this seven days a week. I've heard all the complaints, but I don't consider it a major dilemma.

And I guarantee you this: Give any program in America a choice between starting a game late in the evening or not playing on television at all, and I flat-out guarantee they'll choose to be on the late show. Conferences want air time, coaches want exposure to help their recruiting and the players want to play on TV so their families and friends back home can watch them.

I know some people, including Wooden, believe all the games on television give players a tendency to play for the camera. They become hot dogs in search of relish, trying to make the fancy pass or the difficult shot. I guess I agree to a certain extent.

Wooden also believes television can bring out the worst in the coaches, encourages them to make a scene on the sidelines to be noticed. There might be some truth in that, but I can't believe many coaches are thinking about a TV camera while the game is going on. They're so wrapped up in the moment.

If anything, I think guys become sharper mentally because they're aware of all the criticism out there, whether it's right or wrong. They're aware the whole nation might be watching every maneuver, and therefore they want to be at their best. That's just human nature. TV can help guys develop, because they want to stay ahead of their competitors.

With all due respect to Mr. Wooden, who makes some good points, I believe TV has brought about more positives than negatives to the world of college hoops. It's helped to make it one of the most popular games in the world.

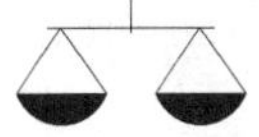

Television has made all of the participants celebrities, including the commentators. Believe me, I love the life I lead and I feel extremely fortunate to have the opportunities I have. But the doors to the profession didn't open for me because I was a great player or a Hall of Fame coach. I was lucky to be in the right place at the right time, and I've had to prove myself every day. I'm paid very well now, but in the beginning I was making $300 a game, doing 30 to 40 games a year. You can do the math and figure that's not a lot of money.

But I do not believe in the word "can't." To all the young people out there: Don't allow the word "can't" to become part of your vocabulary. A lot of people will doubt you, and you'll doubt yourself at times, but if you love what you're doing, if you have a passion for what you're doing, and if you prepare, it all works out. There are always going to be people who are negative toward you as you climb the ladder, but that comes with the territory.

Some people seem to think all I do is shout things like "Awesome, baby!" or "Get a T.O., baby!" but I know I always go the extra mile to get that little bit of information that's going to make a telecast more interesting. I've been criticized a lot over the past 16 years. I get a lot of positive press, too, but I've earned my stripes the hard way.

I've had to make a lot of adjustments, and that's the key to surviving in television. I learned to adapt to different announcers. I had to learn to tell the why of it — why a team is scoring, why a team is playing great defense, and basically leave what is happening to the play-by-play guys. To me, they're the real pros in the business. They're the pilots and the analysts are the copilots. I've been blessed to work with some real superstars.

My biggest adjustment has been learning how to utilize my information. Sometimes I get so wrapped up in trying to use all the tidbits that I try to jam them into one game. I had to learn to pick out my spots and use my enthusiasm and maintain my discipline behind the mike.

The bottom line is, the key guys at ESPN and ABC have told me emphatically that whatever I do, I shouldn't change from being myself. I don't think that's possible, but I think we all can learn to grow and mature along the way. Believe me, at times I've listened to some tapes of games I have broadcast and said to myself, "Why, why did you say that?" Sometimes you just get so caught up in the excitement you let your emotions run wild. I try to be as wild and enthusiastic as I can be, and if I feel I've given every player and coach a fair shot, that's all I can do. I still get highs that you can't believe from broadcasting, but it's certainly not the same as in coaching, where you're either super high or super low after every game. The television world contains a middle ground that certainly helps me live a normal life.

How long do I want to go on? I try to keep myself as young as possible. I'm 56, but I act like I'm 14 according to my daughters, and that's the greatest compliment I can receive. I keep in shape and I maintain my enthusiasm. The day I lose my enthusiasm is the day I'll pack it in. Who knows how long I can go? Harry Caray, the Chicago Cubs announcer, is my new hero. He's in his 70s. And if Bob Dole can run for president when he's in his 70s, why can't I still be working then? I'm having too much fun along the way. I'll let my bosses and the fans decide when it's time for me to move on.

I realize I'm not like most of the commentators. I was kidding one of my bosses after he told me I had won the Cable Ace Award as the top sports analyst. I said, "If I can do it, anybody can." I had been nominated six or seven times and didn't get the call. I was the Bud Grant of cable analysts, always one of the also-rans. The same was true for Chris Berman, and he finally won it. I'd love to do an ESPN special with Chris. Can you imagine the two of us on the air together? I just don't know if he would give me any air time. I'd be in the back-back-back-back-background.

People say I'm a hot dog, and I couldn't agree more. When the cameras go on, it's flat-out Hoops Heaven for a junkie like yours truly. I absolutely love it.

The players love it, too. TV might be the biggest single factor in recruiting today. The teams that are on the most have a huge advantage in signing kids.

Think about it. The players on the best teams are on national television at least once a week. They're like the stars of a weekly television show. They're part of a long-running series — as long as four years for some. How many times do you think Ed O'Bannon played on television, either in games shown around the Los Angeles area or nationwide, during his career at UCLA? Hey, he became better known than a lot of the actors around Hollywood.

Before TV took over, the ACC used to have the best selling points: the beautiful campuses, the weather, the arenas that were rocking and rolling. Kids wanted to be part of that. But TV has helped closed the gap and negated some of the advantages the ACC had.

Over the last 16 years, ESPN has been able to showcase programs that never would have received TV exposure otherwise. In the past, you had all the Rolls Royce programs — the Indianas, the Kentuckys, the UCLAs, the North Carolinas — but you never saw the Virginia Commonwealths or South Floridas or Tulsas. Now fans can see dozens of teams. Now they get to see the Gary Trents of the world. They can see there are a lot of good teams and players.

Television helps the players being recruited, too. They can watch the teams they're interested in and see how their style of play would fit in, get a look at how the coaches operates, get a feel for the atmosphere of the home games. Television has really been a positive force in the entire recruiting process, and has played a big role in helping some programs close the gap on the big-time programs.

TV was responsible for making the Big East one of the power conferences. When former commissioner Dave Gavitt put that conference together in 1979, the original members were Seton Hall, St. John's, Providence, Boston College, Connecticut, Syracuse and Georgetown. Within three years, he added Villanova and Pitt. That gave the Big East large markets like New York, Philadelphia, Boston, Washington and Pittsburgh.

Gavitt was able to sell that to CBS and NBC at the end of the 1982 season for a combined $9.7 million. Two years later, he negotiated a $13.3 million deal with CBS that has since escalated. Gavitt also signed a deal with ESPN in 1979 that eventually became a major part of the Big Monday programming.

All of this exposure did wonders for Big East recruiting and keeping the likes of Patrick Ewing, Chris Mullin, Ed Pinckney, Pearl Washington and Charles Smith from heading off to other regions of the country. It also enabled the conference to recruit both nationally and globally. A campus used to be a major factor in recruiting, but that has been diminished. Look at the success a school such as Seton Hall — with an urban campus in North Jersey — has had because it plays in the Big East, and plays on TV frequently. It was able to recruit enough good players from North Jersey and New York — along with Andrew Gaze from Australia — to advance to the national championship game in 1989.

With that in mind, TV executives have become the power brokers of the 1990s — along with the sneaker companies and the "agents" — because they decide who gets the exposure. When *College Sports Magazine* listed its Top 50 Most Influential People in College Sports, five of the top 10 were from television.

The combo of David Kenin and Len DeLuca of CBS were No. 1 because of the NCAA contract they put together. The others were John Wildhack, the vice president for programming at ESPN; David Downs, the Senior VP at ABC; and Rick Ray, the CEO of Raycom, Inc..

DeLuca gets kidded all the time. People are always saying, "Who are you, Vitale's son?" He's got the little bald dome, like I do. He has to go around carrying that with him, and I feel sorry for him. Obviously, he's done an amazing job in keeping the NCAA Tournament at CBS, and that's certainly a big plus. My boss at ESPN, Steve Bornstein, has made the cable network a big-time player in college hoops. I think Dennis Swanson has made a super commitment to college sports on ABC. He loves college sports. He went to Illinois, and is a big Illinois fan. And I know he loves you, Lou Do. That's right, Lou Henson has a big fan in Dennis Swanson.

Let me tell you a quick story. I was in Champaign for a game and they were honoring me at halftime because I had said I would stand on my head if Austin Peay beat the Illini in an NCAA first-round game. Sure enough, Peay won and I had to live up to my promise. I did it on ESPN and at Peay's postseason banquet, and the people in Champaign wanted me to do it again for them. Well, I did and the place was going wacky.

*In 1987, I opened my big mouth and told ESPN viewers that I would stand on my head if Austin Peay upset Illinois in the first round of the NCAA Tournament—which, of course, is exactly what happened. Here a few Austin Peay players, Mike Hicks, Lawrence Mitchell and Richie Armstrong, help me keep my promise at their postseason banquet.*

---

Then I got on the mike and I said, "I love what I'm doing. I'm the luckiest guy alive to make my living talking about a game I love. In fact, I love it so much I'd do it for zilch, but please don't tell my bosses."

Well, guess who was standing in the background. It was Dennis Swanson. He tapped me on the shoulder as I came off the floor and he said into the mike, "Well, Dick, it's great to know you'd do this for nothing."

Fortunately, they haven't held me to it.

I guess I don't realize how much influence announcers can have. One mention of a coach's name or a player's name can make a big difference in someone's career. It can get a coach a job or land a player on an all-conference team or an All-America team. At least that's what people tell me. It's hard for me to believe we have that kind of power. I still think it's up to the individual to perform. But I guess a good, honest evaluation, and a little publicity, can go a long way.

I've always tried to be a positive guy. I get criticized at times for being too involved with the coaches, never taking a shot at them. I always get a kick out of that because I know there are some coaches who feel analysts like Billy Packer and yours truly are always second-guessing them. But look at the games we're involved in. We're always involved in the megagames involving the big-time programs where the coaches are super success stories. When you're broadcasting a game that involves North Carolina, Duke, Kentucky, UCLA, Indiana, Arkansas — teams like that — you're obviously dealing with great coaches. So it's pretty tough to sit there and rip those guys. For what? They're all future Hall of Famers. I'm a Hall of Shamer, man. I mean, I got fired. What am I going to rip these guys for? If critics want to rip me for that, so be it. I try to look at positives, and I think those guys bring a lot of positives to the table.

I've had my share of magic moments on TV. I've also had some crazy moments. The craziest occurred at Midnight Madness in Shoemaker Arena at the University of Cincinnati in October of 1994. ESPN's Robin Roberts and I were there for the unveiling of an Oscar Robertson statue. We were going to pick somebody from the crowd and ESPN was going to give a kid a full scholarship if he could drain a shot from midcourt. We figured it wouldn't happen, right? You could put Jordan, Magic, Barkley, all of them, at the half-court line and they wouldn't be able to step up and hit a one-and-only shot. It would be Brick City.

So here comes this kid, Corey Clause. When he arrived that night he had no idea he was going to take a shot in front of 12,000 fans. He was selected randomly. The place was really rockin' and rollin', and of course I got caught up in the excitement — and once again my mouth got me into trouble. I said, "If this sucker can knock this down, ESPN's giving him room, board and tuition. And I'll throw in the books!" Well, I no sooner say that than he lets go with a running one-hander that would have made Bob Cousy proud and drills it. NBN, baby. Nothing but nylon. I was so excited

*Everybody went bananas — including me — when Corey Clause drilled a shot from halfcourt during Cincinnati's Midnight Madness, which ESPN broadcast live. This is before it sunk in that I had promised to pay for the kid's books if he made the shot. It cost me $750.*

I jumped into the kid's arms. Then later I found out the kid was an electrical engineering major! His books cost me 750 big ones.

At least I'm lucky the kid didn't go to Princeton, where it would have cost me double. But he was so thrilled, and I got a thrill just seeing him so happy. I also ran into him at the ESPY awards, where the shot won an honor. You should have seen how excited he was when I introduced him to the superstars who were present. You could see the look in his eyes. He felt like a million dollars, and I felt the same for having the chance to share the moment with him.

That's the difference between Billy Packer and me. I don't think he would have approached things the same way that night. Let's face it, if we were both ice cream I'd be rocky road and he'd be pure vanilla. People try to create this big rivalry between us, but I've never been jealous of anybody.

I've never had time for that. Life's been too good to me. Packer has stood the test of time. I've said it once, I'll say it again. He'll be in the Hall of Fame. He deserves to be in the Hall of Fame. He's done 22 Final Fours. I haven't done one.

Obviously, I'd love to broadcast a Final Four, just as all the coaches would like to coach in one. But I can't sit around and worry about the things I can't have. Hey, I'd like to have hair and two good eyes, but I don't. I'd like to be handsome, but I'm not. There's a lot of things in life that I'd like to have, but I'd rather be grateful for what I do have.

Fortunately, I still get to be involved in the Final Four. ESPN does such a heavy volume of work from the site, I probably get more A.T. than anybody there because of the selection show, the one-hour specials, breaking down the teams.

One thing I have to say about Billy: He stands up and speaks his mind whenever people say the network TV ratings for college hoops are down. The ratings aren't down if you total all the people watching college basketball, because there are so many avenues today to watch the sport — not just the networks and ESPN, but other cable outlets such as Prime and Sports Channel. You have so many games on, it's just incredible.

Billy takes a purist's approach to his job. He's an X and O kind of guy. I like to entertain a little more. But I think we have one common denominator: We both have a great passion for the sport. And I think we both would agree the game has been great to us. It's a two-way street. Guys like Billy and Al McGuire made it happen for guys like me. They were the pioneers who showed that you can make a living doing it.

A lot of people talk about my unique type of chatter, my language — you know, PTPers, Brick City, All-Airport and all that. A lot of that came from the players I coached. Guys would say, "Coach, I get no P.T.," or "Coach, he doesn't give up the rock." I've taken those things to the microphone. Billy is going to stick with the technical aspects of the game and tell you about the 2-3 zone and so forth. I give a lot of that, but I try to keep an 80-20 ratio — 80 percent X's and O's and 20 percent pizazz. I know that's true, because I've studied the tapes.

Obviously, if you've coached at every level like I have, you'd like to think you know a little about the X's and O's. But I don't want to put people to sleep. That's one thing I see in television that drives me bananas. All the analysts want to be geniuses, analyzing every play. The fans want to be educated, sure, but more than anything they want to entertained. That TV box, it's supposed to be fun, and I've never forgotten that. That's why my favorite guy on TV is John Madden, who brings so much passion for what he's doing when he does NFL football for Fox and always keeps it fun.

When the players get excited I do, too, especially when someone throws down a hellacious slam dunk. Bob Ryan of *The Boston Globe* got all over my case about that. He said the dunk has taken away from the art of the pass, learning to shoot the jump shot. I don't buy that. Hey, when a guy can get up and fly through the air like Michael Jordan, it's a special moment. What's taken away from passing and shooting is the fact kids don't work on fundamentals, and that's a separate issue. Does eating dessert take away from the main course? I rest my case.

I treat every telecast like it's the most special game in the world that given night. I learned that from working with Jim Simpson and Bob Ley early in my career. Simpson would take me aside and work with me during lunchtime before we'd do a telecast. Ley was the valedictorian at Seton Hall. We all know where I finished. He's really helped me in the studio.

I do as much research as I can to try to prepare for each telecast. Sometimes I do too much, but I'd rather be over-prepared than unprepared. It gets me in trouble occasionally on the air because I have so much I want to share, and I want to get it all out in one telecast rather than save it for another game down the road. I've made some mistakes along the way, but if you try to be as fair as can be, that's all you can do.

Obviously, I'm a little controversial. Anytime you take a stand, you're going to have some people agree and others disagree. Just like Bill Walton. Walton was such a dominant college player when he played for UCLA. His performance against Memphis State in the finals of the 1973 tournament was the greatest ever. Bill scored 44 points, shot 21-for-22. But he expects all the players to live up to his standard, and most people can't do that. They just aren't as good.

Back in 1993, after Michigan lost to North Carolina in the finals when Chris Webber called a time-out he didn't have at the end of the game, Bill said the Five Fab were the biggest underachievers in the history of the sport. Wow. I disagree with that one. If Bill would sit down and analyze what he said, he might not be so harsh. Michigan's achievement — putting five freshmen on the floor and getting to the final game — was amazing. It will never happen again. Ever.

Then, in 1994, he trashed his alma mater, saying UCLA players under Harrick got worse after they entered the program. I know the coaching staff was upset about that one. So was Coach Wooden. But everybody has to be true to himself. You have to be yourself, and Bill is. I'm just happy to hear he's made amends with the Bruins.

If there's anyone who was wired to UCLA in 1995, it was my partner on ABC, Brent Musburger. He told me they were going to win the national title in February. He loved their personnel, the way they ran transition and defended. I should have listened. This guy is a pro's pro. He's so knowledgeable, so thorough. Must be all those shoot-arounds he attends.

During the tournament I spend most of my time in the studio with John Saunders and Digger Phelps. John's our anchorman. He loves handling the microphone. He has no ego about him in any way, shape or form. He's a young guy who I predict will achieve superstardom. We have some other rising stars, too, like Chris Fowler and Mike Tirico, and they take great pride in being involved in the college game. Robin Roberts is also going to be a giant. Wow, if I could be her agent I'd be on Easy Street. By the way, Saunders is a big hockey fan. He earned a scholarship to Michigan as a player and then went to Western Michigan. But he loves hoops as well. And John, I promise that I won't tell them that you're a big Hoya fan. He cheers for the Hoyas like crazy when he's off the air.

I always tease Digger. I say, "Digger, when you were coaching Notre Dame, man, you wouldn't even say hello to me. You wouldn't give me the time of day." I was just this little guy coaching at the University of Detroit then. I also remember the time we walked in with ESPN's cameras to watch a Notre Dame practice and he kicked us out. Now he's one of my best friends. Oh, how times have changed. I have a blast with him. The guy is fun to work with. We have a good relationship, on the air and off the air.

Digger is constantly talking politics. We were 10 seconds from going on the air during the Final Four and he rolls up his sleeves and shows me his cuff links. That's right. They were cuff links from the White House, from President George Bush. I had to tell people about that. Here I was, a Kmart special, and he was Saks Fifth Avenue all the way. He went out of his way to help us get President Clinton on the air during the Final Four. We're sitting around and Digger says, "Hey, let's call the White House right now. We've got to get President Clinton on the air." And he tracked him down in Little Rock, in a restaurant, and got it done.

I think Digger loves TV. But down the road I would not be shocked to see Digger in the political arena. I always tease him about that, too. His son-in-law is Jamie Moyer, who pitches for the Orioles. I was talking with Jamie during spring training. He told me Digger will call him early in the morning on the day of a game he's pitching, talking a little bit about how "you've got to keep it away from this hitter;

you've got to keep the ball low." I'm always kidding him, saying, "Digger, please, you have a tough enough time with hoops. Stay away from Jamie, baby."

As for McGuire, I love all of his French pastry. Al was one of the greatest con men in the history of basketball. He conned people into thinking that he didn't know the game, that he didn't work. I know differently. I coached against him. That team was prepared. His teams came to play. And he knew how to get into the minds of people. McGuire knew how to win.

On TV he's an entertainer deluxe. He has his special way and a special feel. Imitation is the sincerest form of flattery, and I've tried to flatter McGuire and Packer both. When I got started I tried to take a little of Packer and a little of McGuire. Al's got sort of a shtick, some pizazz. Billy's pure X's and O's. I've tried to blend the two.

*ESPN's John Saunders and I meet with movie producer, movie director, movie star and Knicks fan Spike Lee — who obviously is thrilled by the experience.*

Another guy who had a style all his own was the V-Man, Jimmy Valvano. I used to tell him all the time how much I admired his work in the studio. He didn't have a peer who could match him. The V-Man just had that special flair. You never knew what he was going to say. You had to be on your toes all the time. The best stuff was the unstructured stuff.

I believe that Jimmy V would have been phenomenal in a sitcom. I couldn't believe it when my representatives at International Management Group called me about the possibility of being in one. They wanted me to follow in the footsteps of Bob Uecker and Alex Karras and become an actor. My wife and I flew out to L.A. to talk, but it just wasn't me. I really felt Jimmy V could have done it, though. It would have been V at his best. It would have been like *Seinfeld*. I'll never forget the time we went in to do *The Cosby Show*. V had Bill Cosby, the funniest man on earth, on the floor in stitches.

We all owe Howard Cosell, who died in the spring of 1995, a big thank-you. He was a giant in every way. Guys like myself benefitted from Cosell because he was the first to, as he liked to say, "tell it like it is."

Howard fought for rights of people such as Jackie Robinson, Muhammad Ali and Curt Flood. He went to bat big-time for Ali when he refused to enter the Army because he was a conscientious objector to the Vietnam War.

Howard was a legend. The guy had absolute star quality. It was sad seeing him go out bitter, writing the negative book about his partners and the people in the business. I never got a chance to know him that well, except for the fact he once referred to me and I was awed. I said, "Wow. Howard Cosell mentioned me." He was talking about the mentality that now exists in television in hiring all these former jocks and coaches. He called it "jockocracy."

I couldn't agree with him more, because that's all I am. I came out of the locker room, man. I got fired in November of 1979 and they put a microphone shortly after that for the debut of hoops on ESPN. All of a sudden I'm supposed to be a broadcaster. I hadn't gone to broadcasting school, communications school or any kind of school that would prepare me for doing games on national television. I hadn't learned all the ins and outs of the journalism field. So I agree with Howard. But does that mean I was supposed to turn down the work?

One time my wife and I were in New York City and we saw Howard standing near St. Patrick's Cathedral, around 11 in the morning. I approached him. "Hi, Howard, Dick Vitale."

After a 30-second cordial greeting, he left and started walking down Fifth Ave. People in taxis and cars were screaming out his name: "Howard! Mr. C! Cosell!" He stopped traffic in New York City. That's superstardom, baby.

I heard a great story about him from Shelby Whitfield of ABC Radio. After Howard had retired, he came back to the studios and walked into a room where all the technicians were working. He was smoking a cigar. One of the guys yelled out, "Howard, what are you doing here?"

And without missing a beat Cosell said, "Just giving mediocrity a chance to rub shoulders with greatness."

A lot of coaches and ex-players believe television is easy to do. But when they get into the arena they find out it's not as simple as they think. A lot of guys like to get on our cases. Nolan Richardson has said he'd like to announce some games. He's always kidding us. "C'mon, Dick. C'mon, Packer. Where have you guys coached?" He always categorizes announcers as "all those guys that got the ziggy."

But I know one thing. When you're a TV analyst, you're always undefeated. I haven't lost a game in 16 years. Besides, who else in America coaches Indiana on Tuesday, Kentucky on Wednesday and Carolina on Saturday?

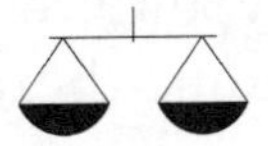

Some teams are just perfect for television. Michigan has that quality. So do Duke, North Carolina, Kentucky and some others. They all have that certain flair for TV because of their reputations and traditions.

There also are certain places I just love to visit. Cameron, where Duke plays, always gets me excited. Just the fact that the kids are that close to the floor. I wish I could sit down there. Come on, Tom Butters, you're the boss down there! I don't want to sit up in the rafters. I don't want a bird's-eye view. I want to be where the action is. Put us down on the floor with all the students!

I also love Allen Fieldhouse in Kansas, the Deaf Dome at LSU, Assembly Hall in Bloomington, Bud Walton Arena at Arkansas, Mackey Arena in West Lafayette. I even love where Syracuse plays, the Carrier Dome. It's a football stadium, but it seats 30,000 people. There might be ice and snow outside, but it's always 70 indoors. It's not intimidating but it's just special to see a place that big with so many people. And I always get the adrenalin flowing when I go down to Rupp Arena where Kentucky plays. There's something about it. As soon as I walk in there I think of all the magical moments that have taken place there over the years.

The success of TV has led to some friction between the electronic and print media. The guys who bang the typewriter sometimes resent the kind of money that's made in TV, in the world of the electronic media, and I can understand that.

But I don't see a war coming on. You see a lot of print media guys making the transfer, being interviewed on TV constantly, involved in the *SportsCenter* shows and the like. I think guys understand there's room for both. I think certain guys do well banging a typewriter and certain guys do well with a microphone. I think there's a mutual respect out there.

Some people believe college basketball has reached the point of over-saturation on TV. For somebody who's a general sports fan, maybe. But for a junkie — like me — there's never enough. But I do have some concerns that the number of games on TV might affect live attendance around the country.

I don't see the major programs being hurt at all. They all sell out. The fans have too much of a love affair with their local teams, and that won't stop. But I worry about hurting the high school kids or Division II and III teams that don't play on television and have trouble drawing fans. I worry that too many fans are choosing to stay home to watch Kentucky-Arkansas or UConn-Syracuse rather than go to a local high school game. I don't want to see the little guy get hurt. It bothers me when there are games on TV on nights that the high schools play. I don't like that at all. But people have choices. They can turn off the tube and go to the local gym.

More and more people, it seems, are attending women's games and watching them on the tube. That's why I was so happy that ESPN and the NCAA signed a contract to televise 23 postseason games beginning in 1996. In the past, CBS did three women's Final Four games on TV. The new seven-year deal will pay the NCAA $19 million and will allow for a day off between the semis and the finals.

ESPN is going to make it super special for those young ladies. The more exposure the women get, the more prime time, the better their game will get. Young kids watching at home will be inspired to go out and play. Having two girls who are athletes at Notre Dame, I've seen the women's sports programs continue to escalate.

I've really come to respect the women's game and many of the players. It's all getting bigger and bigger, and better and better.

It's all basketball, and I love it on every level.

# 9
# Taking a Stand

Don't get me started. I could go on all day about my dislike for Proposition 48, which requires a high school prospect to achieve at least a 2.5 grade point average in 13 core courses and score either 820 on the rescaled SAT or 17 on the ACT to receive an athletic scholarship and be eligible as a freshman.

I can just hear all those who are singing the praises of that amendment saying, "It's great for kids. It makes them get to the library. It makes them study."

Give me a break.

It doesn't. I think it hurts kids rather than helps them. And as I've said many times, all of us involved in college athletics should be in the business of helping kids.

Why should we hold kids hostage to test scores? It should be up to the university. If a school believes that a kid meets its academic requirements and can handle the course load, the student should be given the opportunity. This is America, the land of opportunity, the land of dreams.

Even though the NCAA has changed the rules to allow a partial qualifier in 1996-97 to practice with a team at its home facility and receive an athletic scholarship in his first year at the school, it still takes a year of eligibility away from athletes and brands those who don't meet the academic standard with a scarlet letter.

Who are we to label kids? Donta Bright told me that when he first enrolled at UMass he was embarrassed because he had been labeled a Prop. 48. No kid should have to walk onto a campus with a brand on his back. Everyone knows it when an athlete doesn't qualify, and he has to live with it all through his college career. And every announcer, including yours truly, winds up saying, "Hey, he didn't play last year. He was a Prop. 48."

The same thing happened to Rumeal Robinson. You remember Rumeal. He led the Michigan Wolverines to the national title in 1989. He drilled two free throws in the final three seconds of overtime to beat Seton Hall, my Pirates, in the championship game after he drove the lane and official John Clougherty, one of the best, blew the whistle and sent Robinson to the line. Robinson's game-winning free throws ended the dreams of my alma mater.

Robinson grew up in a tough environment before settling in Cambridge, Mass., where he played ball for Mike Jarvis, now the head coach at George Washington University. Jarvis and Robinson hooked up at Rindge and Latin High School, the same school that produced Patrick Ewing. Robinson was a high school All-America, but he had to sit out his first year at Michigan because he was a Prop. 48. He told me, "I walked onto the campus and everybody knew my SAT scores. Everybody knew I was ineligible."

Robinson showed them. Not only did he graduate from Michigan, but he did it in 3½ years. Then, when he went into the NBA, he began taking graduate courses at Harvard. Why shouldn't a kid like that, who has proven himself in the classroom, be given an opportunity to have an additional year of eligibility?

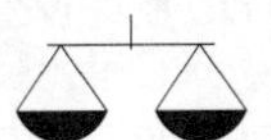

As I've said before, I'm a big believer in making all freshmen ineligible and giving them five years to play four. Put them in a situation where they can grow, go to class, play on a freshman team against local community colleges, and then step up. That would take away some of the stigma.

I believe in academics as much as anyone, but we fail to realize what some of these kids experience growing up. I wish the administrators would listen more to the people they hire. I was out there recruiting. I was in homes. But I know most of the academic administrators who make these decisions have never been made aware of the things coaches learn during the recruiting process. And I wish they would rely on the judgment of the coaches they hire.

Most administrators simply haven't seen firsthand how some kids have to grow up. Some don't have their own bed to sleep in. Maybe Dad is out of the picture and Mom is working two jobs to put food on the table. She doesn't have time to help her kids with their homework or even make sure they stay home at night.

*I get a lot of opportunities to do motivational speaking, which I love. Here I'm talking with people at Chrysler High School in New Castle, Ind. As the sign says, this is the largest high school gym in the world. It holds more than 9,000 people.*

A kid from an environment like that doesn't have the same opportunity as students like my girls, who had all the academic advantages growing up. A kid from an impoverished background doesn't have parents who can afford to write an $800 check for the Princeton Review course or pay a tutor $50 an hour so he can improve his test scores.

Why throw another obstacle at a kid like that by penalizing him for something he can't control?

Many of these kids have so much potential to develop later in life. Put that kid in a more stable environment, with guidance counselors and academic advisers, and maybe he becomes a late bloomer academically. There are some tremendous academic support systems available to kids. Any school that doesn't have one is still in the Dark Ages. Who are we to deny these kids?

If kids prove they can do the work, like a Tony Rice at Notre Dame did, let's salute them. Rice was a Prop. 48 student who had to sit out his freshman year before becoming the starting quarterback and leading the Irish to the national championship in 1988. And because of the guidance and supervision he received, he walked down the aisle with his diploma. That's a beautiful story, and that's what opportunities are all about. Rice took advantage of his chance and made the most of it. He wrote a beautiful ending.

I know, it all comes down to the youngster and how badly he wants his degree. He's got to apply himself. He's not going to get it done sleeping in until noon. Wimp Sanderson, the former coach at Alabama, said it best when asked how many of his players graduate: "All that want to."

There's no question the kid is ultimately responsible for whether or not he gets a degree. But you have to acknowledge that the academic playing fields aren't level.

I've spoken with John Thompson of Georgetown at length about this. He's big on offering kids a chance to better their lives because he remembers what such an opportunity did for him. Thompson was born in southern Maryland and grew up in segregated Washington, D.C., in the late 1950s. His father was a mechanic in a tile factory. His mother had a teaching certificate, but when the family moved to the District she found out she couldn't teach there with a four-year degree and wound up cleaning houses. When the family attended church, John had to sit in the back. He also had to wait until the whites in attendance took Communion before he could.

By the time John was 13 he was already 6 feet, 6½ inches tall and had attracted the attention of coaches at predominately white Archbishop Carroll. They awarded him a scholarship, and he went on to become an All-America at the Catholic League school, which won 55 straight games and two city titles. Thompson was offered a scholarship by Providence College after being scouted by Father Collins, a close friend of Joe Mullaney, at the annual Knights of Columbus Tournament.

He once told me, "If I weren't given an opportunity, if somebody didn't give me a chance to attend Providence and then become a coach, my three kids would have never had a chance. It's a vicious cycle. We only look at the kids who don't make it. What about the kids who do?"

In John's case, one son graduated from Princeton, his daughter graduated from Brown and his other son graduated from Georgetown. Hey, those kids are PTPers, too.

I look at myself. I was an average student at best. I barely got into college, but I later got my master's degree in education. I didn't learn until later how important education was, and I stressed that when I was a coach and a teacher. When I got into teaching I learned the importance of trying to inspire kids, and I took that message home to my daughters. From the moment they entered elementary school, I kept talking to them about the importance of preparation and doing their best academically. Our oldest daughter, Terri, just picked up her master's degree in marketing at Notre Dame. You'd better believe I was proud when she graduated magna cum laude, baby, with a 3.9. I was on Cloud Nine. Her sister, Sherri, is entering her senior year at Notre Dame where she is on a tennis scholarship. Sherri was No. 1 in her high school class, so I'm very fortunate both girls took after Mom and not Dad, both physically and academically.

Thompson has a list of his former players who are successful in the corporate world today. Sometimes we get a little too pure and think, "Aw, this one doesn't belong in college. That one doesn't belong."

Thompson has never done that.

Thompson wields a big stick. He is one of the giants in the profession. He won a national championship in 1984 and took teams to the Final Four in 1982 and 1985. He coached the Olympic team in 1988, and he's produced some great pros like Patrick Ewing, Dikembe Mutombo and Alonzo Mourning. When Alan Iverson's mother was looking for a man to look after her son after he had finished serving four months in jail for his alleged involvement in a bowling alley brawl, she called John Thompson. Iverson, one of the two best prospects in the country, actually recruited Georgetown.

Thompson's track record for graduating players and keeping them in school for four years is impressive.

He has always taken a passionate stand against the college entrance exams, which he believes are culturally biased against blacks, and he doesn't believe they should be used to determine an athlete's eligibility.

In 1989, when the NCAA passed legislation that would have prevented financial aid to any student who did not meet the minimum requirements, Thompson staged a highly publicized walkout before a home game against Boston College. He left a white towel draped across the back of his chair as a reminder that he had been there and left.

That got people's attention, but it didn't stop the NCAA from eventually carrying out its plan to limit athletic scholarship aid to those who had not met specific academic requirements. It was instituted the following year. The NCAA did vote to allow ineligible students to receive financial aid so they could continue their education.

Thompson and John Chaney were like voices crying in the wilderness whenever they spoke up about the subject. In the summer of 1993, they rallied other African-American coaches and formed the Black Coaches Association so they could voice their concerns. When they united, you'd better believe people started listening.

The BCA, which attracted powerful spokesmen — heavyweights like George Raveling and Nolan Richardson and its president, Rudy Washington — made an immediate splash that fall when it opted to boycott a coaches' summit in Charlotte to attend a meeting with the Congressional Black Caucus.

I've known George Raveling for years, and I was sorry to see him get out of coaching. George was involved in a serious automobile accident in the fall of 1994 that left him hospitalized with a broken clavicle and fractured ribs. I know that played a big role in his decision to retire, but he was thinking about doing so anyway. He just got fed up with the problems of coaching and recruiting. He's since gone on to TV, working for CBS. Just what I need, another competitor.

I personally believe George would be an unbelievable administrator. And he is in this because he believes in equal opportunity. Back in 1963, when he was just beginning his career as an assistant at Villanova, he drove down to Washington, D.C., to be part of the Martin Luther King March on the Capitol.

George volunteered to be a marshal and wound up on stage at the Lincoln Memorial, close to Dr. King when he made his *I Have a Dream* speech. When the speech ended, Dr. King gave the notes to George, who had them framed as a reminder that all men are created equal.

I firmly believe we're all in this together. Black, white, it doesn't matter. Protestant, Catholic, Muslim, it doesn't matter. I woke up one day and I was white. I had no say about it. George Raveling woke up one day, and he was black. He had no say about that. But we have a say about what kind of human beings we are. I love people, regardless of race. You treat me well, I treat you well. What I worry about is a separation between the African-American and the white coaches. I hope that doesn't happen. I know Mike Krzyzewski and a lot of other coaches in the National Association of Basketball Coaches are supportive of many of the issues of the BCA.

However, I have great empathy and understanding for the BCA. It wants to address certain issues: admissions policies; rising academic standards they believe adversely affect the chances of minority students to earn scholarships; the need for additional scholarships and job opportunities for African-American coaches. It felt its concerns weren't being heard, so it organized.

In short, the black coaches were tired of being thought of as merely recruiters.

That winter, Richardson, Chaney, Thompson and Raveling led the call for a boycott at midseason after they believed they had been betrayed by the NCAA President's Commission, which had reportedly promised them support for an additional scholarship. There were a lot of rumors about walkouts before the start of games. But I don't think that's the way to solve things, and I think they realized that, too. The boycott never happened, but the BCA established itself as a legitimate lobbying group and a political force.

I think the BCA has been effective. The group has made some inroads, gotten some issues addressed. There's still animosity because some administrators out there don't want to be hit on the head with a hammer. But sometimes you have no other choice.

Black coaching leaders also boycotted 1994's Issues Summit to call attention to what they said was the NCAA's insensitivity to minority issues and the NABC's efforts to sway the NCAA on race-related issues.

They took their concerns to the Rev. Jesse Jackson after the 1994 NCAA Convention. The BCA was upset at the NCAA's refusal to abandon the ACT and SAT as key factors in determining eligibility and that tougher academic standards are scheduled to go into effect in August 1996.

The new legislation calls for a sliding scale to determine eligibility. If I were an African-American, the new legislation would bother me tremendously. If you bump up test standards too high, you're really restricting kids. You're hurting kids who have potential. And I have a problem with that. I have no problem with the core curriculum requirements. I think if a kid wants to go to college, he should be taking the algebra and chemistry classes. If he can't handle them, he shouldn't be in school. But I have a problem with the testing. I really do.

There are some risks involved with classroom credits, however. When the FBI was conducting a probe of academic fraud within Baylor's program, it had serious questions about correspondence credits earned by four Baylor players and a half dozen players at other schools, including Texas, Syracuse and Pan American.

The center of scrutiny was Southeastern College of the Assemblies of God, a Lakeland, Fla., school that offered a correspondence algebra course taken by a number of junior college players in 1993 who were attempting to become eligible at NCAA or NAIA schools. Some of them passed the final exam under unusual circumstances.

The NCAA became concerned about the Florida school because the way it operated in 1993 seemed to invite cheating. Tests varied little from student to student, and just about anyone with a teaching certificate, including a coach, could serve as final-exam proctor. The FBI entered 21 final-exam answer sheets into evidence in the Baylor case to show how they compared with those turned in by the Baylor players. It appears as though the easy credits given by Southeastern could turn out to be a major scandal that involves several programs.

Academics is on everybody's mind these days. Pitt faced an unusual situation in 1994. It signed a great recruiting class, but three of the early signees were academically ineligible. College coaches have to sign kids early, because if they don't someone else will. But I've always promoted this rule: Nobody on the high school level should be allowed to sign until meeting all the existing criteria — the SAT scores and the core courses. If you do this, neither the schools nor the recruits will be embarrassed later if a kid fails to qualify.

There are still some misguided administrators who feel black student athletes can't do the job academically. I'm still in shock over the statements of Rutgers president Francis Lawrence, who said in the fall of 1994 that minorities do not test well because of genetic background.

Rutgers is one of the great state universities in America. It's a school that has always given an opportunity to minorities, given a chance to people who may not have produced the grades in high school but had potential. However, it's mind-boggling to me that any human being — especially an administrator on a college campus — would make such a statement about genetics. What about David Robinson, who had 1400 on his SAT? That, to me, is a slap in the face — not just of blacks, but every fair-minded person.

Some Rutgers students protested by staging a sit-in at midcourt during halftime of a game against UMass. I think they had a legitimate gripe. If I were an African-American, I'd be offended. Hey, I'm a Caucasian, and I'm offended. But I think their protest should have been made in a different forum rather than the one they chose. Their noisy interruption of a game that Rutgers was winning, 31-29, showed little respect for the players, and probably turned more people against them than for them.

The BCA is also concerned about minority hiring. It has taken its gripes to Rev. Jackson, whose Rainbow Coalition is setting up a "fairness index" which will rate NCAA schools in minority hiring of coaches and administrators and in graduation rates of minority athletes. The BCA is threatening to steer African-American athletes from certain schools at the bottom of the list. The game is dominated by the inner city athlete, and I think we have to be more realistic about hiring practices.

That's why I'm so happy that Georgia hired Tubby Smith of Tulsa. It was a great choice, and he deserved it. He has made it to two Sweet 16s and has coached under Rick Pitino at Kentucky. I think Vince Dooley, Georgia's AD, should be saluted for hiring Smith. It's too bad that race should become an issue, but this would not have happened in the past in the deep South. I think it's a step in the right direction that Georgia went out and hired a qualified coach and didn't worry about race. Period.

It's much better, I'm proud to say, in basketball than in football. When you look at the number of African-American football coaches in Division I, it's a joke. Finally, Stanford showed some guts, but when you look at most of the schools that are hiring African-American head coaches, they're all facing an uphill battle. We're talking Temple, Wake Forest, Eastern Michigan, Louisville. They're not exactly perennial top 20 teams.

Most of the established black coaches were not handed the keys to success. They worked hard for them. If you check their backgrounds, they didn't arrive on Easy Street. They grew up with poverty and racism. Take a look at where John Chaney came from in South Philadelphia. His family was so poor that he couldn't even afford a sports jacket to attend a banquet at which he was being presented the Public League Player of the Year Trophy, so he had to borrow his father's old zoot suit.

Chaney was the second-best player in the city in 1952, ranking just behind Tom Gola. He always wanted to go to Temple, but never received an offer, and wound up at Bethune-Cookman, a small NAIA school in Florida. He had NBA ability, but was exiled to the Eastern League because there was still a quota system in the pros at the time.

When he got into coaching, he was mired at Cheyney State, a Division II school, for 10 years before Temple gave him a break in 1983. He has since taken the Owls to the final eight three times and should eventually make the Hall of Fame, just as Thompson should.

Nolan Richardson traveled a similar path. He was raised by his grandmother and grew up in a poor Mexican neighborhood in El Paso. He experienced more than his share of racial taunts as a youngster. When he wanted to go to the movies, he had to travel across the border to Juarez, Mexico. Richardson was the first black student among whites and Mexicans at Bowie High in the early 1960s. He had to put up with all sorts of instances of racism and segregation. But he turned out to be the best athlete in the city and got a break when Don Haskins took him in at Texas Western.

Then he had to wait his turn to get into coaching. Richardson had huge successes in high school and at West Texas Junior College, but he never received a Division I coaching job — at Tulsa — until he was 38 years old. He got his first major college offer in 1986 when he replaced Eddie Sutton at Arkansas. Nolan was the first black coach in the Southwest Conference and there were times when that was a heavy burden.

When you come from nowhere, when you're not part of the inner circle, you've got to claw your way. People are knocking you down, never giving you the same breaks they give to the mainstream guy. You have to give these survivors credit. They have to be tough and they've endured. Is it any wonder they might have small chips on their shoulders?

Richardson's first two years at Arkansas were hell. When his team finished 12-16 his first year, the racists came out of the woodwork, questioning whether he could coach at that level. But even that couldn't compare to the loss of his young daughter, Yvonne, who was in and out of Tulsa hospitals for two years before she died of leukemia. On several occasions I've seen him break down into tears when he thinks of her. As the father of two girls, I can't imagine what it must be like to have to go through that pain. No loss of a basketball game will ever, ever cause him the grief that he faced over his daughter.

All he wants is respect.

Nolan stood up and said African-American coaches don't get any credit for their knowledge of the game, the X's and O's, that they get stereotyped as great motivators and recruiters. "We don't win games; our players win basketball games," Richardson said, paraphrasing the critics. "You hear it all the time. All you've got to do is open your ears and hear it, or open your eyes and read it."

A lot of people out there — writers, fans, sportscasters — get annoyed when they hear people complain, especially when they're at a forum like the Final Four. There was an undercurrent of that when Nolan spoke up before his team won the national championship in 1994. But you know what? He didn't care. He just wanted to get his feelings off his chest. There was no better time for him to do so. He had a perfect vehicle. If you study his comments, you see he was not only speaking on behalf of Nolan Richardson, he was speaking on behalf of his fraternity, his coaches and guys like himself who had to struggle.

I know he was upset when one nationally known sportswriter was asked to pick the winner of the championship game between Arkansas and Duke and said he felt "the more intelligent team" would win. "If you're going to be in a fight," Richardson asked, "would you want a big, tough guy or a smart, little guy?"

It's easy to see why coaches like Thompson, Chaney and Richardson feel so strongly about injustice. It's also easy to see why their programs have become reflections of their personalities.

Look at what Thompson's done at Georgetown. The school won two games the year before he arrived. Now it's one of the great programs in America. John has become so big there that the program's going to take a dip when he leaves — a lot like Marquette did when Al McGuire walked away.

The same with Temple. When you look at its urban campus, it's amazing what's been accomplished there. I think John Chaney has done more with less than any coach in the country.

You develop another John Chaney, another John Thompson, by giving a young coach a chance. That's why I'm so bothered that the NCAA has taken away a coaching position and restricted the number of full-time assistants on a staff to two. When you deny guys the chance to be part of a staff, you don't give programs a chance to develop new blood, to develop new, exciting coaches. And then everybody suffers.

This voluntary, part-time status for coaches blows my mind. Let each head coach have three assistants, the way it used to be. And don't restrict coaches in the amount of money they can make.

Some of the rules are absurd. The rule book is too thick; it's filled with a lot of nonsense. Go after those who are paying athletes. Go after those who are buying athletes. Go after those who are breaking rules, such as by altering transcripts. But let's get away from some of this Mickey Mouse stuff that goes on.

You've got coaches out there who genuinely care about young people. They strive to see that the rules are obeyed. It's unfortunate that some of the rules are not made by the guys who have to work every day with these kids. It's absurd, for example, that a kid goes to college for four years and has long periods of time when he can't work with the coach to develop his game. I find that mind-boggling. If a coach wants to work with a kid one-on-one, why does he just have to allow that kid to go by himself and play? I don't buy that. The kid comes there to be made into a better player, a better student.

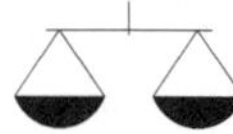

As for scholarships, I have no problem with the 13 the NCAA allows now. I'll bet most schools don't give out a full complement anyway. I know for a fact that the Indianas and the Dukes never used all their scholarships when they were allowed to give out 14 or 15. You really don't need that many players. In fact, it can be dangerous to have too many scholarship players on your roster, because you can only play five at a time.

Some people complain that reducing the number of scholarships by one per team means taking away an opportunity for 302 kids who could be playing in Division I schools. But really, rather than sitting the pine, those kids could be going to a Division II school on a scholarship, playing and starring. I don't like to see schools loading up on players just to take a kid away from another school. And you do have to make some concessions when budgets are such a concern.

Not everybody belongs in college, and basketball should acknowledge this. A lot of professional baseball players didn't go to college. I've gone to minor-league baseball camps and watched kids right out of high school trying to make it as professionals. Why can't basketball do the same thing? I believe the NBA should subsidize a minor-league system for kids coming out of high school who have no desire to go to college. Would there have been such a hullabaloo over Kevin Garnett going professional straight from high school if he were a baseball or hockey player? Think about it. Kids coming out of high school who play baseball and hockey do this all the time, and nobody considers it a big deal.

To me, college is for those who want to further their education. It's a great thing, but there is nothing wrong with those who do not want to go. This country would not exist today without people who practice a trade — without mechanics, heavy machinery operators, carpenters, hairdressers and the like. My only stipulation would be that in order for kids to play in a rookie league, they must learn a vocation, a professional trade. That way, if they don't become professional athletes, they've still learned how to get along in life.

It's a sin for a college to accept a kid who doesn't have the ability to do the work. It's so unfair to the kid — I don't care how good a player he is. You sit him out as a Prop. 48 and you put him in classes where he cannot keep up. That is not a formula for success.

Chris Washburn is a good example. He was America's No. 1 high school player when he signed with N.C. State. But it has since been documented that Chris had less than 500 on his SAT. Was it fair for him to have to walk into a college classroom, trying to handle the academic load he had to face on the collegiate level? It was a nightmare for everyone involved. You had people trying to force-feed him, trying to get him eligible, and that's sad. It's tough for any kid to survive when he doesn't have the necessary background to handle the curriculum he must face.

This wasn't Jim Valvano's fault. He was only guilty of outrecruiting the 100 others in line to take Washburn. It's the system's fault, a system that says you have to have some college experience to move on to the NBA. I wonder where

Chris would be today if he could have played in a minor league and learned a vocation instead of going to college. Nobody would be pointing fingers at him and he would be doing something he loved.

People have to understand that not going to college doesn't make anybody a bad kid.

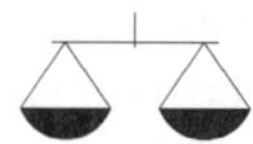

A lot has been written recently about gender equity and the push to put women's sports on equal footing with men's sports in college. The situation at Brown University drew the attention of a U.S. district judge, who ruled recently that even though the university funds 13 varsity sports for women and 12 for men, and even though Brown women engage in athletics at nearly three times the average rate for American colleges, that was not enough to comply with Title IX.

When a shortage of funding forced Brown to drop women's volleyball and gymnastics from varsity to club sports— as it did with men's water polo and golf — it broke the law by failing to provide enough opportunities for women to compete.

Although the Brown women outnumber the men on campus, they make up only 40 percent of the varsity athletes. The judge wanted an equal split.

I don't know all the details in terms of the problems athletic directors have in balancing their budgets, but I do know this: If a young woman qualifies as a student athlete to a Division I school and they're giving out scholarships, she should get the same — the room and board, and the books — as any guy in football or basketball gets. I've seen the time my girls put into tennis. They're putting in as much time as any guy, and they deserve the same opportunity.

I know it's costly and I know it's difficult to balance all those scholarships that are given out in football, but there's a way to bring equal opportunity to college athletics. There has to be, with all the money college athletics bring in. I agree with Notre Dame coach Lou Holtz, who says you don't make your neighborhood better by burning down someone else's house. By that he meant you shouldn't help other sports by taking away from football. After all, football pays most of the bills, and besides, the sport isn't offered to women.

Fairness is all that should be expected.

# 10
# He's Back

I just love the spirit of Chris Berman, ESPN's announcer. He's famous for his call of outfielders running back to catch fly balls at the wall: "Back, back, back, back, back, back, back."

I thought of that in March 1995 when Michael Jordan returned to basketball. When all the details had been worked out, he faxed the Chicago Bulls a short note: "I'm back."

I first heard of Michael Jordan when he was at Howard Garfinkel's Five-Star camp in Honesville, Pa. It was 1979. After watching Jordan scrimmage for 10 minutes, Garf yells out, "Who is that?"

The coaches said, "Michael Jordan."

Garf went nuts. He called up *Street and Smith's*, the people who picked the preseason high school All-America team at the time, and began screaming, "Michael Jordan! First team All-America!"

Hey, Garf, you finally got one right. We won't tell them what you said about Robby West, who went to Duke and disappeared as a player. Garf, please, no phone calls. You know I'm only kidding. But somebody's got to keep you humble, baby.

I was in Cincinnati earlier in the 1994-95 season to watch the unveiling of a statue of Oscar Robertson at Shoemaker

Arena. He's had so many honors, but he was absolutely thrilled by the fact that the school erected this statue of him — in that classic triple-threat position — outside the arena. I was like a little kid, going nuts. He was always my favorite player. I can still remember him coming to Madison Square Garden as a sophomore at Cincinnati. I think that's where he kicked off his real national fame. He scored 56 points against my alma mater, Seton Hall. He outscored the entire Seton Hall team, which scored only 54.

Here I am teasing The Big O, telling him I had followed him from that day on. He was a legend. Try this on for size. They get all excited now when a player has a triple-double. Get out the record book, baby. The Big O averaged that for an entire season one year in the NBA, in scoring, rebounds and assists.

Oscar loves to bust me about the adjectives I use to describe some of the supers playing on the collegiate level. Oscar says, "Dick, you get so excited about some of those guys. What adjectives would you use if I was playing?" Are you kidding? There wouldn't be enough. But it kills me to have to admit it: Michael Jordan, Michael the Magnificent, is the best player of all time, the best ever to lace 'em up. It's not even close. I always thought that Oscar, Magic and Larry Bird were the most complete and versatile guys ever to play. But after watching Mr. Jordan do his thing, nobody does it better.

It didn't take Michael long to prove he could still play the way he had before he tried baseball. Just five games after he announced he was returning to professional basketball, Jordan took his act to Broadway, the Great White Way. And he was a big hit, scoring 55 points as the Chicago Bulls defeated the Knicks, 113-111, at the Garden.

I was watching the game on TV, and it was spellbinding because this wasn't 55 in a 40-point blowout. This was 55 in a two-point game.

When it came down to the last shot, everyone knew who was going to get the ball. All the celebrities in the audience

. . . Connie Chung . . . Phil Donohue . . . Spike Lee . . . Woody Allen . . . Katie Couric. . . . they all knew.

I just about jumped out of my chair when Michael drove the lane, drew the defense, and dished the ball to his teammate, Bill Wennington, for the winning basket. I wish I had been calling that baby. I'd have had every adjective flowing. Michael was truly the "Three-S Man" that night — super, scintillating and sensational. Pat Riley of the Knicks acknowledged afterward that some players just transcend the game, and Michael is one of them.

Jordan's return was so big that he temporarily upstaged the NCAA Tournament in the Nielsen ratings. The Sunday he came back for his first game, in Indiana against the Pacers, NBC's ratings were 13.4 compared to CBS's 5.9 for its second-round tripleheader in the tournament.

Michael was all-world when he played for the Chicago Bulls. He won three rings, then walked away from the game to pursue another dream — playing professional baseball. He gave it his best shot for a year before returning to the NBA. I have great, great respect for him. He was willing to risk failure by trying baseball, a game he hadn't played since high school, simply because he wanted another challenge. I think that's a great lesson for everybody. You can't fear failure if you're going to succeed in life.

Michael's performance in New York brought to mind a conversation I had with him while he was playing baseball. We were sitting around in the White Sox trainer's room. Just me and him. We started talking about basketball and I said, "Michael, you haven't touched a ball in months. If they called you and you had to play tonight — no practice, no nothing — what do you think you could do?"

"Well, I know one thing," he said. "You can put 25 in the book to start with. What's so hard about getting six or seven points each quarter? I can get that just off transition."

He struggled in his first game back against the Pacers, but it didn't take him long to find his old groove. He went out and immediately regained the respect of everybody. He's a special high wire act.

Michael is so magnetic. Scalpers in New York were asking — and getting — $1,600 for a pair of decent seats to Michael's return at the Garden. The scalpers in Chicago did a great business, too, and will for as long as he plays with the Bulls.

Jordan makes millions, more from endorsements than from playing basketball. It's estimated that he makes more than $30 million a year from his endorsements. He makes less than $4 million playing basketball. Some people resent that, but he's worth every penny he earns. He's been an unbelievable bargain for the Bulls. Just think about how much money he's made for that franchise.

Michael has always been easy to get along with, and has always been able to poke fun at himself. But everything he does is placed under the microscope. When Chicago defeated Charlotte, 85-84, to advance to the second round of the playoffs, there was a questionable play at the end of the game. As Hersey Hawkins went up for a last-second shot that might have given Charlotte a victory, Jordan appeared to foul him. But there was no whistle, leading to the old charge that the superstars receive special treatment.

I think they've earned a break. I know people cry about that. But when you're dealing with superstars, they get a break here and there from the officials. Is it deliberate, is it intentional? No way. I don't buy that. It's subconscious.

The Jordans, the Barkleys, the Ewings, the Olajuwons get breaks that lesser known players don't get. The same is true in the entertainment world with big stars like Tom Hanks, Denzel Washington, Tom Cruise and all the people who are on the "A List." They don't have to go out and beg and plead for scripts.

But being a player of Jordan's status can work both ways.

When Orlando beat the Bulls, 94-91, in the first game of the Eastern Conference semifinals, the Chicago papers jumped all over Jordan because he didn't make a shot down the stretch. We're accustomed to seeing him make that shot, so it stood out. I checked out his numbers for the game. They weren't bad — 19 points, five rebounds, three assists. But he turned the ball over eight times, and he didn't make a shot on the last possession. It wasn't a typical Jordan game.

I think people fail to realize how much the Bulls missed Horace Grant, the star power forward who went from Chicago to Orlando. If Grant were in the Bulls' lineup instead of Orlando's, do you think the results might have been different? Don't get all worked up in Houston, but I have a feeling that if Horace Grant were still playing in Chicago, they would still be dancing in the Windy City. Before you take Jordan apart, take a look at his supporting cast. Jordan averaged 31.5 points in the playoffs, but it was not enough to get the Bulls past the Magic.

I first met Michael when he was a freshman at the University of North Carolina. You could just see greatness all over him. The first time I did one of his games, I couldn't help but let the adjectives flow. I was doing the ACC

*I love baseball almost as much as basketball, and I look forward to spring training every year. Lorraine and I really enjoyed watching Michael Jordan when he tried out for the White Sox. For the greatest basketball player of all time to risk failure in another sport because he loved the challenge sent a great message, I thought.*

Tournament one year when a woman yelled out from the stands, "Hey, Dick! Hey, Dick! I just wanted to thank you for all the nice things you say about my son!"

I said, "Who's your son?"

She said, "Michael Jordan." And I got a big kiss from Michael's mom, a beautiful lady. Eat your heart out, Billy Packer; eat your heart out.

But never in my imagination did I think he would reach this level. Nobody in his right mind would have thought that. Michael was cut from his high school team as a sophomore. And Carolina was the only ACC team to scout him during his junior year. Even after a spectacular career with the Heels, he was only the third pick in the NBA draft in 1984, behind Hakeem Olajuwon of Houston and Sam Bowie of Kentucky. Olajuwon went to the Houston Rockets and has become one of the greatest centers of all time. You can't criticize that choice. Bowie went to Portland and has since played for several teams, but has been plagued by injuries. Portland is still catching all kinds of heat for making that choice.

There's only one guy who can stop Michael Jordan and that's Michael Jordan. Oh, wait a minute, there's one other guy: Dean Smith. He was able to stop him when Michael played at Carolina. He ran the passing game. He said, "Michael, TEAM, baby, TEAM! We play as a team."

Hey, I'm only teasing you, Deano. He gets very sensitive about this issue. I teased him about that when I was roasted for the Jimmy V Foundation down in Raleigh. All the ACC coaches gathered to take their best hits at yours truly for a special cause and a special guy, Jimmy V. But take a look at Dean's record and all the guys he's produced for the NBA, and it looks like a Who's Who of basketball. That's why you can't really knock him for what he's done with his players. He puts discipline in their games. He lets them play in transition. They play multiple defenses. He has a way of getting players to play within the team confines. They don't become individuals and you don't read about them becoming a problem to coach.

Michael's sudden return provided a much-needed lift for the NBA because he's such a superb goodwill ambassador. He handles himself so well in interviews. He dresses up, smiles, looks like a million dollars when addressing the press. I think guys like Jordan, David Robinson and Hakeem Olajuwon should give seminars to younger players on responsibility and how to carry themselves, both on and off the court. So many pro athletes today have been pampered. They've been stars at every level and they're never had anybody sit them down and let them know what the real world is all about.

Michael addressed that issue. "A lot of young guys have to understand that although it's nice to earn exorbitant dollars, young kids have a responsibility to carry themselves with a bit of class. We owe it to ourselves and our families," he said.

He also said players should go out and show fans they enjoy playing, rather than carrying a chip on their shoulders. I hope the message was sent loud and clear. The NBA has been hurt by a tidal wave of negative publicity recently, including stories about Derrick Coleman, Dennis Rodman, Rod Strickland, Vernon Maxwell. That's why it was such a big lift for the league when Jordan decided to return.

Grant Hill, the Detroit Pistons rookie, seems too good to be true; there are a lot of guys like Robinson: Jordan, Olajuwon, Karl Malone, John Stockton, Joe Dumars and Dan Majerle fall into that category, too. But some of the players have hurt the league's image with their spoiled attitudes. People don't want to read about guys who are making big dollars and who are always unhappy.

It amazes me how Dennis Rodman can get on the cover of *Sports Illustrated* for acting like a fool. Sure, he can rebound. Sure he plays good defense, but that doesn't justify his behavior. David Robinson plays for the same team and won the NBA's MVP trophy. He does everything the right way. He's class personified. But he's not on the cover of *SI*. What does that say about our thinking process when we make bigger stories out of those who act in an irrational manner as opposed to those who are positive influences?

Rodman just doesn't get it. He has no idea how it makes him look when he's laying there on the floor, with his shoes off and a towel on his head. Or how it makes him look when he's in Never Never Land, staring into space instead of listening in the team huddle during time-outs. The fans must be numb to his antics by now. After he returned from a one-game suspension in the playoffs, he was welcomed back with a standing ovation. Get real. The Spurs' management can really learn from observing what happened in Houston, where the Rockets became a better team by subtraction rather than by addition. Houston suspended Vernon Maxwell and all his antics, and the team united. Maybe the same thing can happen in San Antonio.

You have to have harmony to win in basketball. Remember Charlie Finley's Oakland A's in the early 1970s with Reggie Jackson, Sal Bando, Rollie Fingers, Catfish Hunter and the rest? They used to battle and battle in the locker room and then come out on to the field and get it done. Baseball is a team game, but it's different than basketball. If I'm playing right field and you're playing third base, we might not share one play during a game. But basketball is different. If I'm the point guard directing the offense and I'm coming down with the rock, we have to have rhythm and continuity. We have to play with unity or we're not going to win.

You have to practice hard, too, and this is another thing that separates the winners from the losers. It's tough enough in college, when you practice only three or four days a week. It's really tough in the NBA, when you're traveling and playing all the time. But the great ones play hard in practice. You ask anybody and they'll tell you that Jordan's work habits are unreal. He hates to lose in anything. A lot of the superstar guys don't like to practice, and their teammates know it so they don't gain their respect. They know they can get their 20, so they coast during the workouts.

I always remind kids that the average life span is 75. Even if you're lucky enough to play until you're 30, you still have 45 years left to be a contributor to society. You could have all the money in the world, but if you don't have something to do with your life, you won't be happy. If you're 30 or 35, what are you going to do, sit home every day and stare at the beautiful cars in your driveway? Believe me, you'll get bored quickly, and that boredom can lead to major problems.

Magic Johnson and Michael Jordan have all the money in the world, but they get excited about every day of their lives. Magic has his traveling all-star team and corporate interests. He's opened a beautiful theater in a tough part of Los Angeles to try to help develop that area. He's a great example of how an athlete should stay active with business and community interests. Nobody is going to want you to be part of an organization if you're constantly going around with a chip on your shoulder. It amazes me how some guys get angry about signing autographs and meeting with the public when they're leading a life in Fantasyland. Believe me, Michael and Magic have never been like that.

Living in Florida, I had a lot of chances to visit with Jordan in spring training, to see how thrilled he was. He was like a little kid, carrying the bats and playing table tennis with the young players. All of the kids on the team looked up to him because they had such respect for him. He didn't come in and try to big-time them. He didn't ask for special treatment. He was always out there taking extra batting practice, running extra sprints, taking extra fielding practice.

Michael was having the time of his life. Everybody was impressed by his unbelievable, tenacious, relentless effort. I visited with him in the locker room and he autographed for my girls a motivational book he had written. I would recommend it to everyone. Hey, I want to be Michael's press agent for a minute. I want to get 10 percent of his action.

He opens the book talking about his high school career. Everybody was saying he couldn't play, that he should have gone into the Air Force Academy, that he couldn't play for North Carolina. Maybe the Air Force coaches saw him fly in the sky. Whenever someone doubted him, he took it as a challenge and went out to try and prove that person wrong. "I don't believe in the word 'can't'," he once told me. "I don't believe in the word 'never'."

He got a lot of his philosophy from his father, who told him, "Always try to do your best. If you can look in the mirror and know you've done your best, you're a winner." That's how he always attacked everything, including baseball.

I was rooting like crazy for him. I would hear people ripping him, saying he was wasting his time. I was cheering for him to do well because the guy was so dedicated. He'd show up at the batting cage at 6:30 in the morning. His hands would be calloused and bleeding. And he'd be working with Walt Hriniak, one of the best batting instructors in the game. Believe me, this guy just didn't come out and put in a token appearance. Jordan gave it a tremendous shot. But he was trying to do in two months what other guys have needed 20 years to do.

The White Sox were searching every way they could to get him on the major-league roster as a 25th guy. Not only because of the dollars he could bring in, but because they felt he brought so many positive qualities you can't teach to the players. He brought excitement and optimism wherever he entered the dugout.

Michael hit .202 in 1994 for the Class A Birmingham Barons of the Southern Association. In the end, he wasn't progressing as quickly as he wanted, and he didn't want to be part of a strike. And he still had an itch to play hoops. I hear Michael used to play pickup games against some of his minor-league teammates, and that may have rekindled his interest to play pro basketball again.

So did a trip to his alma mater in mid-January. Michael came back to visit with Dean Smith and work out with the team. He scrimmaged with the second team against the first team. Guess who won? His Airness did his thing. Of course, he could have lined up with Dean, myself, Mike Patrick and John Saunders of ESPN and we'd have had a shot to win — as long as we just got out of his way and let him play. After practice ended, Michael went one-on-one against Jerry Stackhouse and took him to school. I was talking to Jerry about it and he was all excited, telling me that he dunked on Michael. "But," he said, "you should have seen what he did to me."

When the first reports came out that he might return to pro basketball, I thought it was a joke. But I'm happy to see him doing what he does best. He told me one time, "I love basketball, Dick. If I could just do away with the regular season — the grind of the 82 games — and just come in and play the playoffs, that would be ideal."

That's almost what he did when he returned in 1995. He has less than two months to prepare for the playoffs. But he can't do that every year. Now he has to go through an 82-game season again. I think he gets kind of bored during the regular season because it comes so easily to him. Michael thrives on challenges, and the challenges during the regular season don't excite him as much.

At least Jordan earns his money. Everybody should make what he can make, but there should be some adjustment to the NBA salary structure. I dislike the fact that some veteran players don't get the dollars the rookies get. The money belongs to those who have done it. They are entertainers; they're the ones putting people in the stands. They deserve the mega, mega dollars, not the kids coming in out of college. I think a player should prove he can earn his keep before management throws out $60, $70 million dollars to him.

Instant wealth spoils young players and inflates their egos. Some young players even demand their coach be fired. How wacky can this get? Finally, owners, and even some players, are attempting to take a stronger stand against rookies who come in and demand the world. I thought it was hilarious when Herb Kohl of the Milwaukee Bucks said he would like to switch places with Glenn Robinson. He said he'd give the franchise to Robinson and take the millions in salary Robinson's agent was asking for. Glenn had to settle for $65 million. I wonder if he sent any over to Gene Keady and the people at Purdue? But let me tell you, the Big Dog will eventually earn his money. He'll become one of the big-time scorers in the NBA.

If there were a graduated salary structure, based on experience as well as talent, it would reduce the kind of antagonism that exists between the rookies and veterans, not to mention the fans.

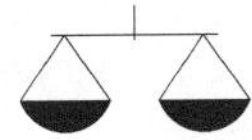

I have to admit, I have a soft spot for the sport Michael left behind. But as much as I love baseball, I don't think I could broadcast it on TV. So relax, Bob Costas, Jon Miller, Al Michaels and all you guys who do a super job talking about the game.

First of all, I have one major problem: I can't follow that little ball very well with only one eye. I'd have to use the monitor all the time. But I just love the environment; there's something about the relaxed atmosphere, the smell of the grass, watching batting practice and seeing all the uniforms that really appeals to me.

Roy Campanella, the Hall of Fame catcher with the old Brooklyn Dodgers, used to say, "We may be men, but when you put on the uniform, we're all little kids." That sums up baseball.

I was 10 years old when I got my first baseball glove. My dad, who worked in a factory, saved some dollars and bought it for me. It was a pitching glove, with long fingers. When I got that, and my Little League uniform, I literally took them to bed with me every night. And I always used to dream about playing at Yankee Stadium with the Yankees, wearing the pinstripes. A boy, a glove, a dream.

I remember sneaking into Yankee Stadium one day, with a buddy of mine when I was about 18. We got into the stadium on an off-day and had a blast, running around the base paths — the bases weren't installed — standing on the pitcher's mound, hanging around outside the locker room.

And I remember the first time I walked into the Yankee locker room and saw the pinstripes hanging up. I wasn't a kid any more, either. I was coaching in college; I was 31, 32 years old. I had become really good friends with Roy White, a former left fielder with the Yankees, and he invited me into the clubhouse. When I walked into that room, I was like a little boy. I couldn't help but be awed. This was a special place where Ruth, DiMaggio, Mantle, Maris, and all those other great players had passed through.

Baseball affects me that way. I really missed it when the players went on strike in August of 1994, especially with Ken Griffey Jr. of the Seattle Mariners and Frank Thomas of the Chicago White Sox putting together such unbelievable years. Those guys might have posted some amazing numbers, but we'll never know.

I got to know Ken Griffey Jr. at the Foot Locker Slam Fest which we televised on ABC. We brought in all kinds of celebrities to demonstrate their dunking ability and other basketball skills. Griffey was special. He had a certain flair when he walked into the arena. People would just flock, and the cameras started to pop. I like his personality and he's only 25 years old. He's the Michael Jordan of the baseball diamond. He was born in Seattle, and he's making the mega dollars there now, as he should.

I would like to see him in a winning environment, with guys who can protect him at the plate. Can you imagine what he'd be like if he played in New York with the Yankees? I heard a lot about him from my former neighbor, Hal McRae,

*Cal Ripken is one of the ultimate PTPers. If I were picking a basketball all-star team of baseball players, he'd be my point guard.*

who played with his dad, Ken Griffey Sr., on the Reds. Ken Griffey Jr. grew up in a major-league environment with Hal's son, Brian, who plays for the Chicago Cubs. He's a great defensive center fielder who also has a great love for college hoops. He even attended the Final Four in Seattle.

Griffey and Barry Bonds are the two best all-around players in baseball. I got to know Barry through spring training when he was with the Pirates. One year I picked Carolina to win a big game against Syracuse in the 1987 regionals when the Tar Heels had J.R. Reid. And they got bumped by Rony Seikaly and company. I came out to watch the Pirates play, and Barry starts jumping all over me. "Man, I listened to you! What do you know?" He was putting me on big-time with his screaming and ranting and raving, when really he's not all that mean. He said, "You're like all those other guys. Carolina — look what they did. What do you know?"

Barry came to my house one time, riding his motorcycle and wearing his leather jacket. We sat down and talked. He's a lot like Deion Sanders. Prime Time has the chain hanging around his neck and the earring dangling and people get a certain image of him. But his bark is worse than his bite, just like Bonds. When you get to know them, they're really nice guys. I like both of them a lot.

One time I got scared out of my mind while I was shooting the breeze with Barry at the batting cage. We were fooling around and he had his face against the screen. The batter hit a line drive into the screen and Barry cut his face and had to go to the hospital for a couple of stitches. I was so scared. They ran highlights on ESPN and I was praying he wasn't seriously injured. Fortunately, he wasn't.

The best pure hitter in baseball is Frank Thomas. I just love his style. He's such a warm person, too. It's hard to believe he's still a few years from reaching 30. He was just like Bo Jackson. He played football at Auburn, too. But he's a tremendous hitter, and probably still a little underrated.

I saw him when he first came down to the Florida State League and, man, you could see the power just by looking at his body. But he has more than that. He has quick hands. And he really takes great pride in what he does. He's working like crazy to develop a better defensive game.

The bottom line is, the guy has won the MVP two years in a row. I don't think a lot of guys realize that because all you ever hear about are Griffey and Bonds. His numbers for the last five years have just been fantastic.

I'm a fanatical fan. I love to hang out at the ballpark during spring training. Fortunately, many of the managers have given me permission. Jimmy Leyland of the Pirates and Gene Lamont of the White Sox are big-time college basketball fans. Leyland can tell you about every team in America, and has a great feel for the stars in the game. He's always asking questions about the Bob Knights, the Nolan Richardsons, the Mike Krzyzewskis and all the other big-time winners.

It's amazing how these guys want to talk hoops. They're such hoops fans, it's unreal. Remember, spring training comes around the same time as the NCAA Tournament, so basketball is on everybody's mind. I remember telling Joe Torre, the Cardinals' manager, to go with Kentucky during the tournament one year. "Torre, you're a paisan," I said. "You've got to go with Pitino. Take them in your office pool." So he did, and the next time he saw me he really let me have it.

Cal Ripken is another big basketball fan. He has a regulation-sized gym in his house. He plays hoops all the time. He's 6-foot-4, big for a shortstop, and he can dunk a basketball. He would be the point guard on my all-star basketball team of baseball players. Frank Thomas, who is the Karl Malone of baseball, would be my power forward. Ken Griffey wants to handle the rock, thinks he's a point guard, but I'm playing him at off-guard. Barry Bonds would be my swing forward, my Scottie Pippen. And Randy Johnson, the 6-10 pitcher for the Mariners, would be my center.

It's hard to keep up with players anymore. With free agency and all the teams "renting" players for their playoff runs, how do you know who's playing where? When I was growing up, I could name every player on the Yankees and his jersey number — Mickey Mantle (7), Roger Maris (9), Yogi Berra (8), Bobby Richardson (1), Tony Kubek (10), Elston Howard (32), Clete Boyer (6), Whitey Ford (16) — I could go on and on. Today, you walk into camp and you don't know who's there. You're thinking Brett Butler is a Dodger, and you find out he's a Met. You turn around and see Marquis Grissom. He was born to be a Montreal Expo, but he's now with the Braves. You turn around again and see Andy Van Slyke, who's been a fixture at center field for the Pirates, playing with the Orioles. And before you know it, he's traded again.

One of the great things about baseball has always been its stability. There's a game almost every day during the summer, and you can always look forward to reading the box score in the newspaper the next day. It used to be that you looked at your favorite team like an extended family. The roster didn't change much, and the players returned every summer. You felt like you got to know them. But that's changed.

Having said that, I have no problem with free agency. A player should have the chance to be able to make his money. I mean, that's a way of life. I wish there was a way to compensate these guys so they stayed with their original teams. But everything is relative. Guys have to go with whatever the market bears. And players want to be with winners. The fans moan and groan, but they would do the same thing if they were in the players' shoes.

I think baseball did tremendous damage to itself with the strike. The owners and players could have solved their dilemma without a work stoppage. They showed no concern for the fans. They could have continued playing while negotiating. They were no further along when the 1995 season started than before the work stoppage.

Now NBA players and owners are battling. I'll still bet my last dollar we won't see a strike. David Stern won't let it happen. The NBA went the entire season without a collective bargaining agreement. They had a no-strike, no-lockout situation, but they kept playing. I might be wrong, but I can't see the NBA players and owners allowing it to reach a point where it becomes a nightmare in the public eye. They have a good thing going, and they know it.

Michael Jordan and Patrick Ewing, with their agent David Falk, have led a move for decertification of the union. But I don't think the league will miss any games. The difference between basketball and the other sports is leadership, and the reason is S-t-e-r-n. That's what baseball lacks: a commissioner. More than that, a commissioner who isn't a puppet.

Sitting on the outside looking in, I think arbitration benefits the players and offers almost nothing to the owners. A player can't lose in arbitration. Basically, if club X offers Joe Jones $500,000 and Joe Jones wants $1 million, both sides go to arbitration. If Joe loses arbitration, he still gets

$500,000. There's no give-and-take, so the players have nothing to lose. It all comes down to the stats.

Ownership has to take part of the responsibility for baseball's mess. They say they want to win, that they don't care about stats, that they care only about production and intangibles. Then, when a player sits down to talk about a new contract, the owners don't want to hear about how he advanced a guy to second base. They don't reward the team players as much as the guys who produce stats.

I think arbitration is something the players have to think about giving back. But then the owners have to turn around and give the players a little more freedom, not force a player to be tied to a team for six years. People outside of professional sports aren't tied to a company for six years. If you get a better offer and you're not under contract, or your contract has expired, you can move on.

I also think the league has to help the smaller markets with revenue-sharing. It's really scary what's happening in places like Kansas City, Montreal and Milwaukee. When the Expos have to get rid of guys like John Wetteland and Marquis Grissom, when Kansas City has to trade David Cone, because they can't afford to pay them their market value, that's a major problem. If those clubs collapse, it affects everybody.

Baseball has a major public relations problem. You have owners and players bad-mouthing each other, and nobody shows the fans enough respect. Why can't the players sit in the stands for awhile before they take batting and fielding practice and sign autographs? When I was a kid, if I could have sat in the stands with a Mickey Mantle and gotten an autograph, I would have gone totally bananas. Are you kidding? To be near a Ted Williams, a Mantle, a Babe? Wow. You could take a Bonds, a Griffey, a Frank Thomas, and put him in the stands with the people for half an hour or so and that would alleviate some of the animosity that exists.

The fans have to do their part, too. I know people want to release the tensions and the frustrations they feel in their own lives, and many of them do it by going to sporting events. Unfortunately, some of them get really carried away and handle themselves poorly.

We've had some embarrassing incidents in professional sports recently. Vernon Maxwell of the Rockets went into the stands after a fan late in the 1994-95 season, and Chili Davis of the Angels did the same thing in July of '95. The players were wrong; you have to ignore the fans. But the fans have to be civil, too. You can't yell things at people on the street or at work, so why should you be able to do it at a sporting event? Hey, the solution is simple. Ushers should immediately warn fans who become antagonistic and violate reasonable behavior standards. Fans who persist should be immediately ejected. And if they still carry on, take them to the clinker. That would really clean this up.

The problems in baseball are so far-reaching, though. I was really disturbed on opening day for the 1995 season. Here I am, a baseball fan — I can't wait for them to throw out the first ball so I could watch the Dodgers go head-to-head with Florida on ESPN. Then I read quotes from Gene Orza of the Players Association. He claims if the owners don't put $48 million into the pension fund by the All-Star Game, the players will walk. Talk about dumb. I don't know Orza from Adam. But I do know a little about marketing and promotion. And what he said on opening day was absolutely dumb. You have people like Tommy Lasorda and Sparky Anderson, two great ambassadors for the game, ready to play ball, and then you have a guy like Gene Orza talking about a strike.

Baseball doesn't need any more Gene Orzas. What it needs is more Michael Jordans — who can hit.

# 11
# March Madness

I still don't know which college football team was the best after the 1994 season. Can somebody tell me?

Nebraska and Penn State both finished 12-0, but they never got a chance to play each other. Because the Big Eight — excuse me, soon to be the Big Twelve; how do we keep up with expansion? — automatically sends its champion to the Orange Bowl, Nebraska had to play there. Penn State, meanwhile, had to play in the Rose Bowl because of the Big Ten's contract. One went East, the other West, and never the twain did meet.

That was a shame because Nebraska was ranked No. 1 going into the bowl games and Penn State was ranked No. 2. Both teams won their bowl games, so the pollsters had to decide the national championship. Nebraska got the call, and I was happy for them. Tom Osborne is a classy guy and his kids don't play with the strut like the Miami guys.

But why couldn't Nebraska and Penn State play each other for the title? Why not settle it on the field rather than in the polls? People talk about the difficulty in putting together a playoff system, but it can't be that tough. People talk about missed class time, but a championship game can be played when most schools are on a semester break. And I really believe if kids want to do the work academically, they'll find a way.

If the NCAA doesn't want a playoff, it's time for the Rose Bowl to change its old way of thinking and allow the champions from the Big Ten and the Pac-10 to play in another bowl game if they're in the running for the national championship.

The title game should have been between Penn State and Nebraska, not Nebraska and Miami. And the game should have been played on a neutral site, not on Miami's home field. That's archaic thinking. I think some of the decision-makers in football better take a hard look at all the success of the NCAA basketball tournament.

I can see it right now. Nebraska kicking off to Penn State. Frazier vs. Kerry Collins. Ki-Jana Carter going up against that big defensive line of the Cornhuskers. Tom Osborne vs. Joe Paterno. Two unbeaten clubs. Are you serious? I'd get on the first plane to go watch that game. That would be Pigskin Heaven. The players would be deciding their own fate.

I felt the same way about my Irish two years ago. My daughters were in school there, so I would go put on a sweatshirt and sit in the stands like any other dad. Florida State won the national title that season with a 12-1 record. Notre Dame had only one loss, too, and they defeated Florida State in a regular season game at South Bend. The Irish were ranked No. 1 for a week, but then they dropped behind the Seminoles after a late-season loss at home to Boston College. Wouldn't it have been great if those two teams could have met again for the championship?

In this respect, college basketball is light years ahead of college football. Come March, 64 teams are going to take the floor for the Big Dance, the NCAA Tournament.

This is Letterman. This is Jay Leno. This is the superstars at their best. This is March Madness, baby. The NCAA Tournament captures the imagination of the entire country for three weeks. Every year, it seems, it gets more exciting and more dramatic. I don't care if I go to spring training, to a gas station, a restaurant, a hotel, everybody's got one question: Who's going to the Final Four? I'm going to start running around with a sign on my back that reads, "I don't know. Help me out, baby."

The tournament has also become a financial bonanza for everyone involved. Just 25 years ago, the NCAA Tournament was a 25-team event worth $1.3 million. It got minimal TV coverage and had a perennial champion in UCLA. Many of the games were played late at night. But it took off after the 1979 national championship game between Michigan State and Indiana State, which featured the head-to-head duel between Magic and Bird. Now it's one of the three biggest prizes in all sports, falling right behind the Super Bowl and the Olympics.

The tournament now makes $114 million on its own and an additional $153 million with its TV contract. CBS has agreed to pay the NCAA $1.75 billion over eight years for the rights. The network sees it as a solid investment. It's the premier sports event, with sponsors paying $500,000 for each 30 seconds of advertising during the championship game.

And every school gets a piece of the action. In the past, individual schools used to keep their full share of tournament appearance money. The money is now awarded to conferences according to a six-year NCAA formula based on the number of times member teams advance in the tournament over that period. Individual conferences then determine how the money is divided. The leading money winner in 1994, for example, was the Atlantic Coast Conference, which earned $4.1 million, thanks in part to the fact that Duke had won two national titles and North Carolina won one over that six-year stretch.

That's a healthy concept because it takes away some of the pressure on the coach to bring in the enormous dollars for the university. There's enough pressure on most coaches just to get into the brackets.

We hear a cry from many critics to change the NCAA's tournament system. They want to eliminate all the politics and let everybody into the tournament. I don't like that concept.

It was really tough a couple of decades ago. Then, only 32 teams would get the call from Wayne Duke, the former Big Ten commissioner who was the head of the tournament selection committee. Detroit went 23-4 in 1978 when Dave Gaines coached the team and was left out of the tournament. It was Heartbreak Hotel for a bunch of kids who deserved to be part of something special.

Now, with 64 teams, everybody has to win six games to win the championship. Nobody gets a bye. I really have no problem with the current setup. In fact, every season we have a little mystery, as someone is always sitting on the bubble. I love it on Selection Sunday, trying to guess who's going to get in the tournament. It seems like every game we do on ESPN in the month of March leading up to that night, we're grabbing the mike during the opening and saying things like, "Hey, they're on the bubble. They'd better win this game, or they're going to be No. 65. They'll be chanting, 'We're No. 65, playing in the NIT.' That's what makes for excitement. It makes the games meaningful at the end of the season.

The tournament selection committee, headed by Bob Fredericks, the athletic director at Kansas, does a solid job. It has sent the message loud and clear that teams that do well over the long haul are going to be rewarded. You get rewarded for playing a challenging schedule, and that's the way it should be.

Bobby Cremins and his players at Georgia Tech were stunned, absolutely shocked, to be left out of the 1995 tournament after finishing 8-8 in the ACC, the toughest league in America. Tech won 18 games and played a tough nonconference schedule. The NCAA is always talking about how it places a huge emphasis on strength of schedule and the strength of a conference, computer rankings and a team's record against Top 50 clubs.

If that's the criteria involved, then Georgia Tech should have been in the tournament. To put it in simple terms, Robert Cremins, you were flat-out robbed. It was an absolute mugging.

If the committee is going to award at-large bids to mid-major teams like Manhattan, which have great regular seasons, that's fine with me. Manhattan won 25 games in the MAAC and got in, even though it lost in the finals of its conference tournament.

All I'm asking for is consistency. Not from referees, but from the committee. The bottom line is, all the coaches want is a consistent evaluation by the committee. If the criteria state that schedule strength is going to be the major factor, then Georgia Tech should have been in the tournament. If a super record is the most important factor, fine, but spell it out and be consistent in making those decisions.

The quickest way to a bid is by winning the conference tournament. That also gives schools that didn't have a great run during the regular season, for whatever reason, one last shot. This silences the critics who say everyone should be let into the tournament because other than the Ivy League, the Big Ten and the Pac-10, everyone has a tournament. And that gives everyone a chance to make the tournament.

That means a team with an average record can get hot and shock the world, the way N.C. State did in 1983. State entered the ACC Tournament with a 17-10 record and was unranked.

If Jimmy V doesn't go on a roll, if he doesn't beat North Carolina with its great club that included Sam Perkins and Jordan, if he doesn't beat the Ralph Sampson club at Virginia, then he doesn't get into the tournament. Jimmy V used to say all the time that was the beauty of college hoops as opposed to college football. In football, one bad game like the Fighting Irish of Notre Dame had against Michigan early in the 1994 season, can end your chances of winning a national title.

Think about the miracle that happened to Florida International in 1995. They won seven games during the regular season. They had a lame duck coach in Bob Weltlich, who had announced his retirement at midseason. But they got on a roll in the TAAC tournament and earned their way into the tournament.

Conference tournaments are not as pressure-packed as they were years ago when the NCAA Tournament field was smaller. For example, in the ACC, it was a war to get that automatic bid. That's pressure, my friend, big-time pressure. You had to win the conference tournament to get the automatic bid for the NCAA Tournament because nobody else in the conference could get one. Now, the major conferences get multiple bids. The Big Ten got six in 1995. The SEC, the Pac-10 and the Big Eight sent five, and the Big East and the ACC sent four. I don't think more than 50 percent of the teams in a conference should get an NCAA Tournament bid. And I'd like to see every conference — even the Ivy League — have a postseason tournament.

I also have a problem with the NCAA giving an at-large bid to any team that has a .500 record or less in conference play. I don't want to hear the cry that the league's tough and competitive. If you can't produce a winning record in your conference, you should stay home.

One team I thought earned serious consideration in 1995 was College of Charleston. It won 21 games and had the longest winning streak in the country — 19 — but got shut out. It was a member of the TransAmerica Athletic Conference, but it was not allowed to participate in the conference tournament and get an automatic bid because it hadn't been in the league long enough.

Charleston was a classic example of a team the big guys dodged. The year before, it got a chance to get some big wins because it played Alabama, Wake Forest and Penn State. But it couldn't get those clubs to play it again, so it couldn't post the big wins that would raise its computer ranking. I felt bad for its coach, John Kresse.

It's great when a Charleston pops up in the tournament and becomes a Cinderella team. That's the beauty of the tournament, when the little guy hooks up against the giant, and at least scares him a little bit. Sure, a 16th-seeded team has never defeated a No. 1 seed. Some people would say I've got a better chance of growing hair. But it could happen eventually. And some No.15 seeds have defeated No. 2 seeds. People love to root for the little guy because they can relate to him. Most of us consider ourselves "little guys" in the bigger scheme of things.

There's all kinds of talk about the power conferences combining to form a super association. I hope it never happens in basketball. I'm a believer in the system where you give the little guy a chance. That epitomizes what America is all about, and it should epitomize what the NCAA is all about — that an Old Dominion can play a Villanova or a Weber State can take on a Michigan State — and have a chance to pull off the upset.

When I arrived at Detroit we got lucky, although I didn't think so at the time. We had Michigan on our schedule and I began to shake in my boots. Back East, you think of the name, "Michigan," and you think of football, Rose Bowls, and all the success it had in basketball with players like Cazzie Russell. In 1973, we had to play against Johnny Orr's outstanding team headed by All-America Campy Russell. But I'll never forget the score that night. We beat them, 70-59, in Calihan Hall. Owen Wells, my 6-foot-7 forward, scored 39 points and we really rattled the Wolverines with our matchup zone defense.

So then I wanted to play them on a regular basis. I begged. I pleaded. I got down on my hands and knees. I told Orr, "We'll play you anywhere. We just want a shot." Well, it never happened until the 1976-77 season when Michigan was the No. 1 team in the nation and returned the nucleus of the team that had gone to the NCAA finals the previous year against the great Indiana team.

Michigan had some great players, such as Phil Hubbard, Rickey Green and Steve Grote. We had a special team, too, led by John Long, Terry Tyler and Terry Deurod. We went 23-4 and won 21 in a row. We even beat Marquette in Milwaukee when Dennis Boyd hit a jumper at the buzzer. It was a good thing, too. My buddy Larry Donald, the publisher of *Basketball Times*, told me he didn't think the committee would invite us if we lost. I couldn't believe he said that, but he was probably right. The next year, the Titans went 23-4 and lost to Marquette and they didn't get a bid. Hey, sometimes the media guys actually know what they're talking about.

Anyway, we couldn't believe it when the NCAA announced the pairings that year. We celebrated like crazy when we found out Michigan was in our half of the regional bracket. That's why I have to laugh when the committee says it doesn't make matchups, that the computer decides everything. Come on. When I see a Georgetown playing an Arkansas in the second round, I see matchups made by people, not a computer.

Our game against Michigan was the last one I ever coached at the University of Detroit. I came walking into Rupp Arena, wearing my maize and blue outfit. Muhammad Ali was fighting Chuck Wepner at the time and I kept screaming at Johnny Orr. "You're Muhammad Ali, baby. You're the champ. I'm Chuck Wepner. I'm going to bleed, and I'm going to get cut, but I'm going to fight. We're the little guy. We're going to fight the majestic Maize and Blue." All the writers and broadcasters in Detroit were picking up on it.

I thought Michigan was the best team in the country that year. We battled them, took them to the last minute. They beat us, but I really believe we cost them a national title. They didn't have anything left for UNC-Charlotte because we had taken so much out of them, physically, emotionally and mentally. They were drained. Less than 48 hours later, they had to play UNC-Charlotte and they got bumped off. Charlotte went on to the Final Four and Michigan went home to Ann Arbor. That Charlotte team, with Cornbread Maxwell, was the last true Cinderella team to advance to the Final Four.

The little guy hardly ever gets to play the big guy on equal terms. I thought it was super when Michigan went down and played Tennessee-Chattanooga in the 1994-95 season. Purdue did it, too. Both Big Ten teams won, but they were willing to take the risk. I did the Michigan game for ESPN, and I went out to breakfast with UTC coach Mack McCarthy the next morning. We were shooting the breeze and I said, "Isn't that great, Michigan coming down here after you went up there last year?" He said, "Yeah, but Dick, we got to go up there 3-for-1. But it doesn't kick in until the year 2,000. By that time, I'll probably be out of here." He was laughing.

But you can't really blame Steve Fisher for that sort of arrangement. He's coaching one of the elite programs in America. He's calling the shots, and he can get away with it. A coach like him takes a big risk playing on UTC's home court.

There are usually only about 12 teams, the Dazzling Dozen I call them, good enough to win six games in a row and win the national championship. The teams from the super conferences should dominate the tournament year in and year out. They have the ability to recruit the great players. They have alumni support, tradition, facilities.

But at least the NCAA Tournament gives the little guy a moment in the sun. We talk about teams getting an equal shot, but realistically not everyone has a chance to win the tournament. Some schools are trying to reach the Final Four. Others are in Jubilation City just to be there, and are hoping to pull off one big upset.

But even if they get blown out, they've been there. Their name was put up in lights for awhile. They received a lot of recognition. There's always a Mount St. Mary's coming along to capture everyone's imagination, a team with a coach like Jimmy Phelan, who is 65 and wearing a trademark bow tie. Phelan has coached at the Mount — a tiny school in Emmitsburg, Md., that plays in the Northeast Conference — for more than 40 years. The school didn't go Division I until 1987. It got its first trip to the NCAA Tournament in 1995, and lost by a bundle to Kentucky. But so what?

Every now and then one of those little teams sneaks up and wins one or two. Upsets are more common than they used to be because of the three-point shot. An underdog can get hot from trifecta range. That's the great equalizer. That's how 12th-seeded Manhattan became an overnight sensation by upsetting fourth-seed Oklahoma, 77-67, in a first-round game in 1995.

"I guess," Manhattan coach Fran Fraschilla said, "the selection committee isn't as dumb as people think."

The tournament can be so unpredictable at times, and that's a reflection of the parity that exists these days. I've never seen college basketball this wide open. Hardly any score shocks me during the regular season anymore. Texas Southern walks into Minnesota's barn, Williams Arena, and wins by 20. Texas-San Antonio goes on the road and beats a good Arizona State team. Coppin goes to LSU and wins.

It happens because this is such an emotional game, and because there are so many good coaches out there. Take good players who are willing to work hard and give them a coach like a Dick Bennett of Wisconsin-Green Bay or Pete Carril of Princeton, a coach who knows how to manage tempo, maximize talent and hide liabilities, and anything can happen. The supposed superstars get a little cocky, the underdogs get a little hot and hit a few three-pointers, and anything can happen.

The reduction of scholarships to 13 also has made a difference. That opens the door for players who used to go to the marquee teams to go to the less established programs. Some of those players blossom late and become better than the players getting scholarships to the big-time programs.

The most monumental upset I ever witnessed in a championship game occurred in 1983 when N.C. State defeated Houston, 54-52, at The Pit in Albuquerque. It was the culmination of nine consecutive wins in the ACC and NCAA tournaments for N.C. State. I didn't think State had a chance against Phi Slamma Jamma. I thought Houston, having gotten by Louisville with those megastars like Clyde Drexler and Olajuwon, was definitely the team that would win it all.

Jimmy V coached a special game that night. And the game had a special ending. With time running out, Dereck Whittenburg took a desperation shot from the top of the key that didn't even hit the rim. But Lorenzo Charles grabbed the ball and slammed it home as time ran out and Jimmy V wound up prancing all over the court, looking for someone to hug.

A lot of people put Villanova's stunning victory over Georgetown in 1985 in the same category. That was the night Rollie Massimino pitched a perfect game, as Ed Pinckney, Harold Pressley and Dwayne McClain led the Wildcats over Patrick Ewing and Georgetown. But Villanova had played Georgetown tough twice that season and at that time the Big East was the premier conference in America. So how shocking was it, really? The bottom line is, Massimino's team was well prepared and played to near perfection to beat a great Georgetown team. However, when you really study how both clubs played during the regular season, it wasn't a total shock, unlike North Carolina State's stunner over Phi Slamma Jamma.

The UCLA teams with Kareem Abdul-Jabbar were the best I ever saw in the tournament. They never had a close call during their three years in the finals from 1967 through 1969. Opponents did everything to stop him, and the NCAA even changed the rules by outlawing the dunk. But you could have surrounded Jabbar with four guys and the Bruins still would have won the title. He was just such a special player.

Kareem was so complete, the most complete offensive player I've ever seen in the post. Do you hear me, Wilt Chamberlain? Don't get mad at me, Wilt. Don't call me in your room for a one-on-oner like you did several years ago when I was at the Foot Locker Slam Fest.

John Saunders and I walked in and Wilt's lying there. He jumped all over my case for saying Kareem was the most complete offensive player. Wilt was the greatest athlete ever to put on a basketball uniform. He could run, he had great hands, and he was so strong and intimidating. But Kareem was the most versatile player ever to play. Bill Russell was the most dominating defender to play in the middle, Kareem was the most complete offensive player, and Wilt was the best athlete. There, is everybody happy?

You throw all the NCAA championship teams in a pot, and I'd have to go with UCLA during the Kareem era to beat any other team in a one-game shot. Any club he was on would have found a way to win, because he was unstoppable, and basketball efficiency, offensively and defensively, starts in the three-second area.

I say this with all due respect to the 1976 Indiana team that finished 32-0. That was the last team to finish undefeated and the best team I've ever seen assembled in terms of everybody complementing each other and understanding his role. They epitomized the word T-E-A-M in every respect. Quinn Buckner knew how to distribute the ball and defend. Scott May, the national Player of the Year, knew how to score and rebound. He averaged 23.5 points and nearly eight rebounds. Bobby Wilkerson was a great defender. Kent Benson could score and rebound.

*I get to meet a lot of great athletes, of all sizes — like Shaquille O'Neal (above) and Calvin Murphy and Wilt Chamberlain (below). Some people believe Murphy is the best little man to play the game and some believe Chamberlain is the best big man of all time. But some believe O'Neal will earn that honor before he retires.*

Forward Tom Abernethy was a perfect complement to the other four, a solid defender and rebounder who could hit open shots. All five starters played at least five years in the NBA. And they had the luxury of being coached by Bob Knight, who came up with great game plans.

Knight coached Indiana to 36 straight wins in the Big Ten in 1975 and 1976. We'll probably never see that again in a major conference. That's like Joe DiMaggio's 56-game hitting streak. I honestly believe that group would have won the 1975 national title if Scott May hadn't broken his arm just before the tournament. May came back for the Kentucky game in the regional finals, but he was extremely limited during a 92-90 loss.

Another team that really impressed me was the 1984 Georgetown team because of its intense defensive pressure. It led the nation in defensive field-goal percentage, holding its opponents to just 39.5 percent. What it did to the Big Blue of Kentucky in the national semifinals was truly amazing. The Hoyas trailed at halftime but harassed the Wildcats into shooting a dismal 3-for-33 in the second half of a 53-40 victory. The five Kentucky starters were 0-for-21. Georgetown went on to dismantle Houston, 84-75, in the finals.

Ewing was selected the tournament's Most Valuable Player, but nobody on that team defended the ball any better than point guard Gene Smith. He got in your face and he just jumped on you. He jumped on me recently, too, when I did the finals of a summer league all-star tournament in New York City for ABC. Gene was playing for the Washington, D.C., team. He came over to me and said, "I read your book. I can't believe I wasn't picked on your all-time All-Defensive team. You picked Tommy Amaker over me. Are you serious?" And, you know what? He was right. I picked Amaker because of his overall skills, but for pure defense, nobody played point guard better than Mr. Smith.

I also loved watching UCLA during the Walton era, the 1982 North Carolina team with James Worthy, Sam Perkins and that Jordan guy, the Doctors of Dunk at Louisville in 1980 and the Duke team that upset UNLV in the 1991 semifinals. That UNLV team, with Stacey Augmon, Larry Johnson and Greg Anthony, had won a championship the previous year and people might have sung its praises as one of the all-time great clubs if it had repeated.

The 1995 tournament was headed toward controversy if Kansas made it to the Final Four. The Jayhawks had a great regular season but didn't win the Big Eight Tournament. Still, when the bids came out, they received the first seed in the Midwest Regionals. If they had won their first two games they would have advanced to Kemper Arena in Kansas City, their backyard.

I remember when Lou Henson, Lou Do, had to take his Illinois team to Kentucky to play for the right to go to the Final Four in 1984. They had to beat Kentucky at Rupp Arena. You're just not likely to walk into Rupp and beat Kentucky in a big game on that floor, and Illinois didn't. I'm not taking anything away from Kentucky; it had a quality basketball team. But it wasn't fair. Purdue also fell victim to homecourt horrors in the tournament. It lost to Memphis State on the Tigers' homecourt in 1984, and lost to LSU on those Tigers' homecourt in 1986. The committee was smart to disallow homecourt advantages in the tournament.

In 1995, the tournament committee claimed Kansas had no advantage playing in Kemper because it had played only one regular season game there. But it had played two games there in the Big Eight Tournament, and the facility was within driving distance of its campus. Obviously, Kansas was going to have most of the fan support.

The downside of that is that it would have put a lot of pressure on coach Roy Williams. If he had his way, I really believe he would have rather played somewhere else. He was going from press conference to press conference, answering questions about playing in Kansas City. After awhile, Roy got a little upset, and I don't blame him. He was trying to prepare his team and he kept hearing that his team had an advantage. As it turned out, Virginia knocked off Kansas with a strong defense in the Sweet 16 before the Kemper issue could become a major issue.

The tournament is too classy now, too big, too successful to allow any team a homecourt advantage. Fairness should be the prevailing theme. The games are still going to sell out. The ticket revenue will always be there.

Gambling also has become a major issue in the tournament. Roxy Roxborough, the Las Vegas oddsmaker, said he projected $2.5 billion would be gambled illegally on the 1995 tournament, plus an additional $50 million legally in Nevada. Only the Super Bowl does more business. The tournament includes 63 games that can be wagered on, and it's a gold mine.

It's a frightening scenario, because it can lead to a point-shaving scandal. The last one allegedly occurred in 1985 with Tulane, and prompted the school president, Eamon Kelly, to discontinue the program until 1989 when Perry Clark was brought in to rejuvenate it. Clark, one of Bobby Cremins' assistants at Georgia Tech, had to start from scratch, but he now has Tulane headed back in the right direction. And he's doing it the right way.

Just two years ago, bookmakers in Nevada stopped taking action on a game between Arizona State and Washington after three men bet $250,000 at various books — all on Washington to beat the spread. As it turns out, Arizona State won by a substantial margin. That created a nightmare for Bill Frieder. His phone was ringing off the hook.

It's naive to think that a lot of heavy betting on college basketball doesn't take place, especially in the postseason. It occurs not only in office pools across America, but in huge wagers, both legal and illegal. Gambling is becoming a national obsession, and it's bound to reach college basketball.

I hate the fact betting odds are published in the newspapers. I don't look at them; I don't care about them; I don't even want to know about them. That's something I've never gotten into. Last fall, the NCAA Tournament had a proposal in the works that would have denied Final Four credentials to any newspaper that published point spreads. But the media responded with some First Amendment concerns and the matter was dropped. Expect the arguments to continue.

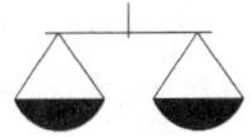

The NCAA Tournament isn't the only game in town during postseason play. The National Invitation Tournament, which used to be a bigger event than the NCAA Tournament, continues to do business. People always complain that the NIT is unnecessary and meaningless, but I don't buy that. Jack Powers and his gang run a first-class tournament. The NIT gives an opportunity to 32 more teams to continue playing. It's a great opportunity for young teams to improve and take a positive step into the off-season. And I like the fact the games are played on college campuses until only four remain, and they're brought to New York City to play in Madison Square Garden. In this case, the homecourt advantage makes sense.

While some coaches more accustomed to playing in the NCAA Tournament have turned down NIT bids in recent years, many others still have a great love for it. Bob Knight, who took his Army teams to the NIT when he was a young coach, has always been a big supporter. His Indiana team won it in 1979, beating Purdue on a last-second shot, and finished second to UCLA in 1985.

A great story took place in 1995. St. Bonaventure won 18 games, but was eliminated in the quarterfinals of the Atlantic 10 tournament. Its coach, Jimmy Baron, got into his car and drove to New York to personally give the selection committee a personal letter, asking to be considered for a bid. Baron had played on St. Bonnie's 1977 NIT championship team, and he said the greatest thrill of his college career was standing at midcourt at the Garden and having his name called out at the ceremony after the game.

"I hope I can give that moment to my kids," he wrote. "Please consider us because there are coaches out there for whom the NIT means so much."

Virginia Tech won the 1995 NIT, defeating Marquette in the finals. That should help Tech heading into the 1995-96 season. It was a club on the verge of an NCAA berth in '95, and it has everybody back. Bill Foster, Virginia Tech's coach, knows how to put a team together, and the NIT was a great springboard for his club.

A lot of teams have benefited from the NIT that way. Villanova, Michigan, Minnesota, Massachusetts ... you can go right down the line. Hey, isn't it better to play a few games in the NIT than lose in the first round of the NCAA Tournament, or not play in a postseason tournament at all? Players want to play, the NIT offers another chance to play, and the competition is good.

I just wish Georgia Tech had participated in the '95 NIT. After it was snubbed by the NCAA Tournament, it in turn snubbed the NIT. I thought that was an emotional reaction. Bobby Cremins is one of the great guys in basketball. He was just so hurt. I thought it was automatic Tech would be part of the 64.

But I really think Bobby made a mistake. It would have been a great experience for a lot of his young kids and it would have given his team a chance to battle adversity. You can't have everything you want all the time, but this would have been a chance for them to regroup. It's still a tournament and you're still playing in a competitive situation. And it would have given Bobby a chance to go back to New York City, where he grew up.

If he had another 24 hours to think about the situation, I think he would have made a different decision. But I really feel for him. I know how hurt he was, how upset he was that James Forrest and Travis Best didn't have a chance to play in the Big Dance their senior year.

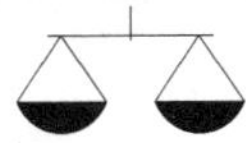

The NCAA women's tournament has also found its niche. Connecticut's women's team found its way into the history books in '95 when it completed a 35-0 season by defeating Tennessee 70-64 before a sellout crowd of 18,038 fans at the Minneapolis Target Center for the national championship.

This was one team that captured the heart of an entire state. I couldn't believe the amount of publicity and notoriety it received. I could see it anytime I'd travel to Bristol, Conn., to work in the ESPN studios. Those players had me running for the newspapers, looking at the scores, seeing what Connecticut was doing. It reached a point where I was absolutely concerned about what they were doing and I was rooting for them down deep.

The women's game is in the early stages of an explosion. The college teams are getting more and more visibility and there has been a spin-off to the lower levels. Girls start playing as early as the boys do now, and they're putting more and more time into developing their skills. The coaching is getting better, too, at all levels. All this is only going to help the college game in the years ahead.

Keep watching. You'll be amazed by what you see.

# 12 Repeat Performances

You should see the palace where Arkansas plays, the Bud Walton Arena.

John Saunders and I were there to do a 1994-95 preseason special featuring the defending national champions. When we walked into the lobby of that 20,000-seat building, I just could not believe it. It was like a living history museum.

The arena includes a Hall of Champions, with a Nolan Richardson theater. Press a button and here comes its NCAA championship victory over Duke. Hit another button and here comes Sidney Moncrief. I could have stayed there all day, pushing buttons, having a blast.

Oh, did Bud Walton do it right. You remember the name Walton? Yes, he was part of the family that built the Wal-Mart chain. You walk around and see a blown-up picture of *Sports Illustrated's* cover shot of Corliss Williamson, Arkansas' All-America forward. There's the gigantic color slide of Scotty Thurman knocking down the J to beat Duke. Yes, Coach K, they've got that in there.

Thurman made the biggest shot in Arkansas' history when he hit a three-point goal in the last 50 seconds that gave the Hogs the lead for good in their 76-72 victory over Duke in the 1994 NCAA Championship game at Charlotte.

He has a video of that game, but he says he doesn't like to watch it. He doesn't want to live in the past, doesn't want to be defined by that one game.

I'm sure Thurman thought he would have another videotape not to watch from the 1995 tournament. Arkansas was ranked No. 1 in every preseason poll but one. I have to give *Sports Illustrated* credit. It went with UCLA. I don't know how you could have picked the Bruins in the preseason. The editors must have owned a crystal ball.

Arkansas was the first defending champ since UCLA in 1968 to return all five starters. That was when the Bruins had Lucius Allen, Michael Warren, Lynn Shackelford, Kenny Heitz and Lew Alcindor. The Hogs had both balance and depth. Aside from Thurman and Williamson, they had senior point guard Corey Beck, who was one of the most underrated players in America, along with bangers like Darnell Robinson, Lee Wilson and Dwight Stewart to patrol the paint, and Clint McDaniel to key the transition game. They also had Al Dillard, who could dial long distance with the best of them beyond the three-point line. Six of their guys had a chance to play at the next level. No wonder so many people thought they would be cutting down the nets again.

It almost happened. Arkansas reached the Final Four for the third time in the past six years, but it lost to UCLA, 89-78, in the championship game in Seattle.

A great season, right? Well, a lot of people jumped on Nolan Richardson and his players for coming up short.

Are you serious?

Arkansas won 32 games and had another great tournament run. It outperformed every team in America but one. It was a phenomenal year.

Arkansas found out why it's so difficult for champions at any level to repeat. It became a victim of its own success. It found out right away, too, when it was trounced by UMass, 104-80, in its season-opening game in the Tipoff Classic.

I was surprised by the margin of victory, but not so much by the fact UMass won. UMass had outstanding personnel and genuine NBA talent in Marcus Camby and Lou Roe.

Roe had a story pasted to his locker where Williamson, just kidding around, said Arkansas' second team could beat Massachusetts. John Calipari had T-shirts printed with "We're the underdog" on them and had Springfield Civic Center totally psyched. John Calipari had a much easier job motivating his players than Nolan Richardson did.

That's the way it goes for defending champions. Everybody plays at a higher level against certain teams, and Arkansas' players had targets on the backs of their jerseys all season. Opponents didn't just see Arkansas, they saw "defending national champions" on those jerseys. Arkansas' players were household names all over the country, and every opponent they faced wanted to make a name for itself by beating them.

Arkansas showed great character by coming back 36 hours after its loss to UMass and beating Georgetown on CBS. The real Hogs showed up that day. Then they went on an 11-game winning streak. That's why Richardson has to be one of the Rolls Royce coaches in the country today. He can adjust to a halfcourt game. He can adjust defenses. He knows how to go full court. He knows how to win.

But Richardson spent most of the season in a pressure cooker. Arkansas was on the bulletin board of every opponent it faced. Whenever it lost, the other school reacted as if it had won a national championship. The players and the fans were dancing in the streets. "It's been a whole year of tournaments for us," Richardson said. "I've never seen so many nets cut down and fans storm the floor."

Auburn was averaging 3,619 fans at home before Arkansas visited. That night, it had a capacity crowd of 11,000 and it put on a show, making 69.8 percent of its shots in a 104-90 victory. It outrebounded Arkansas 43-34 and led by 24 points at one stretch.

The Dow Joneser performances of Richardson's players during the regular season took a toll on him. Many of their wins were struggles and Richardson knew why. "Don't even say you can repeat because you've got the same players," he said. "The reason teams don't repeat is that those people have different agendas. Guys go home over the summer and start thinking, What's in it for me? Is my average down? We've got a couple of guys people are talking about as lottery picks. There are so many distractions — that's got to be part of it. You get other things in your head."

Repeating is hard, if not impossible, these days. A national champion gets so much publicity, it's bound to go to the players' heads. They get around their friends and they're instant heroes. Everybody tells them how great they are. It takes a lot of maturity to maintain the work ethic that got them to the top in the first place. It's only human nature to want to coast when things are going well.

---

*Who says I can't shoot the rock, baby? This one was NBN — nothing but nylon.*

The two biggest dynasties in the history of basketball are the Boston Celtics and UCLA. But I don't think we'll ever see anything like either one again. To me, Celtics coach Red Auerbach epitomized the NBA. He won eight straight titles. He was my idol. I loved it when he used to light that victory cigar.

He got me interested in coaching. I used to watch his teams play, and I'd think, "What's so difficult about that? Run, press and shoot." What I didn't appreciate at the time was that when the ball went on the glass, Red had No. 6, Bill Russell, the original Windex man, to clear it. Russell would kick it out to Bob Cousy, who was unbelievable with the rock in his hands. Cousy would come down, look to his right and see Bill Sharman, and he'd say, "Take me out for dinner and I'll give you the rock, baby." And Sharman would go, bingo, with that jumper of his. The next night Cousy would say, "Heck with you, Sharman, you didn't take me out for steak; I'm going to get the ball to Sam Jones." And Sam would bank it off the glass. It was a great run for the Celtics under Auerbach, who coached for 16 years before retiring in 1966.

The architect of UCLA's dynasty was John Wooden. UCLA won 10 national championships during the Wooden era, from 1964 through 1975. They had great players, such as Alcindor and Walton — Bill, not Bud, — but Wooden won championships in so many different ways.

Kids used to get excited by the mere mention of the name UCLA. But that kind of dynasty will never happen again for several reasons — reduced number of scholarships, the fact more players are available, and all the TV exposure that has given kids a chance to analyze where they fit in best and where they're going to get PT. So we've seen more and more parity. In the 1980s, 10 different teams won the NCAA Tournament. Duke, which made it to the Final Four seven times in a nine-year stretch, is the only team since UCLA to win back-to-back national championships.

So it's amazing what Arkansas did in 1994 and '95. The same thing applies to Michigan, which reached the final game two years in a row, and UNLV, which won a title in 1990 and made it to the Final Four the following year.

It's incredibly difficult to win six games in a row and win a national title once. To do it twice in a row, with everyone chasing you, is next to impossible. And don't forget the impact of the three-point shot. It can turn a game in the blink of an eye.

But all these factors that make it more difficult for teams to win two years in a row, let alone build a dynasty, are good for the game. It's more exciting for the fans when several teams have a chance.

I know there's the argument, and John Madden uses it all the time, that you're better off having the super, super team and everybody else chasing that team. I agree to a point. It makes for a clear-cut chase, and fans can take sides more easily. But I'd rather have the balance. I'd rather have the unknown. I'd rather have the Seton Halls, the Mississippi States coming out of nowhere to make a run. That's healthy for everybody, rather than one team dominating, dominating, dominating.

Arkansas has won more games than any college program over the last five years and has consistently appeared in the Top 10. That's special because it means you're in the running for the championship. If you've done that, you've done one heck of a job. But to expect a team to go back-to-back and knock down a national title two years in a row isn't reasonable. It's been done, but it's not to be expected.

When Arkansas won the 1994 title, everything just fell into place, especially for Williamson, who was selected the Most Outstanding Player. When Williamson returned to Russellville, Ark., 75 miles from Little Rock, they renamed his hometown "Corlissville" for a day. He was the mayor, baby.

Williamson has always been big down there. When he was an eighth-grader, he caused a stir around the state when he shattered a backboard in an AAU tournament. His AAU coach started calling him "Big Nasty," and the nickname stuck.

It's appropriate. The guy's a force. He would work out with weights 15 minutes before a game, then go out and dominate. Williamson reportedly always wanted to play for Georgetown, but Richardson wasn't going to let him leave the state of Arkansas. No way. Williamson was a breakthrough recruit for Richardson and one of only two McDonald's All-Americas on the Hogs' roster their championship season, the other being Robinson. Williamson used to have a pet snake, a python that he called "Little Nasty." I don't know who was more dangerous. I visited with Corliss, and I felt a lot safer when Scotty Thurman, his roommate, told me the snake was out of there.

Williamson suffered a broken bone in his hand in the 1994 championship game. He played nine minutes of the final with a broken thumb, then waited a month before he had the injury X-rayed. Doctors put a cast on his hand and told him no basketball over the summer. Williamson ballooned up to 283 pounds, and it took him half a season to get back into shape.

That was typical of Arkansas' season. The entire team was hit hard by injuries in '95. Center Dwight Stewart had arthroscopic knee surgery. Thurman, McDaniel and Wilson all had ankle injuries. And Davor Rimac had surgery to remove a kidney stone. Arkansas also was limited by the new handchecking rules, which took some of the juice out of its full-court pressure defense. It took the Hogs awhile before they understood the significance of defending the three-point shot and proper ball movement. And they never conquered their rebounding problems. It was as if each guy was waiting for the next guy to carry him.

"It seemed much harder the second time around," Williamson said.

Human nature.

To their credit, the Hogs regrouped in March and survived three cardiac games in the opening rounds of the tournament. I thought they were dead on several occasions. Texas Southern, which had lost to the Hogs by 66 points the previous season, had them on the ropes in the opening round and had the lead most of the game. But Arkansas finally escaped with a 79-78 victory. Then they needed Syracuse guard Lawrence Moten to call a time-out the team didn't have in Round 2 to escape with a 96-94 victory. They also needed Thurman to come up big in overtime after Williamson fouled out with 2:29 left in regulation. Thurman scored 27 points and carried the team in O.T., hitting a three-point shot, a two-point basket and a free throw in the final 2:07.

A lot of people think Richardson has players waiting in line to play for him, that he has no problem recruiting. But he and his top aide, Mike Anderson, have discovered a lot of their players in out-of-the-way places. They found three-point specialist Al Dillard in night school. They found Thurman in Ruston, La., and signed him late. As a high school senior, Thurman dreamed of making the McDonald's All-America game. "I think that's every kid's dream," he said. "But not many of the so-called experts are going to come to Ruston, La., when they can go to the big cities like New York and California, places like that. That's just not going to happen. No one ever came to Ruston to see me play."

Arkansas survived a lot of scares in the '95 tournament, including an overtime victory over Memphis in the second round that drove Memphis coach Larry Finch nuts because of what he thought was a touch foul at a crucial moment. But you've got to give the Hogs credit. They were 11-1 in games decided by three points or less; they almost always found a way to win. Isn't that the sign of a champion? They survived even though they were playing what John Thompson, Richardson's good friend, described as ugly basketball. “He called me and said all the coaches who play pretty basketball are at home,” Richardson said. “The ugly coaches are still playing. So, stay ugly.”

Teams tend to get a little conservative in the tournament. Coaches play fewer players. We always hear about the importance of depth, but it comes into play less at tourney time. Starters get more minutes. That’s the one thing I liked about Arkansas in ’94. The personality didn’t really change. The players picked it up a notch right out of the gate. They were shooting the threes, playing with reckless abandon, playing with defensive intensity that led to offensive scores.

Nolan Richardson likes to call his defensive pressure “40 minutes of hell.” His team’s offense starts with its man-to-man defense. We always hear the argument about Nolan being a coach who can only motivate and recruit, but he can make adjustments on the sidelines. Against Duke in the ’94 championship game, I watched him change tempos and utilize zone and matchup defenses on occasion. Arkansas can absolutely take you out of your rhythm.

The two best defensive teams I’ve seen in the tournament are Georgetown in 1984 and UNLV in 1991. But I’ve seen in Arkansas some of the same intensity and pressure defense those teams showed. The Hogs held North Carolina without a field goal for a 12-minute stretch in the second half in the ’95 tournament. They completely locked up Rasheed Wallace, who got off only one shot in the second half.

When Arkansas finally succumbed to UCLA, Nolan handled the loss with such class and dignity. He said, “Hey, they were a better team tonight and I salute them. They came to play and they got it done.”

After the game, Williamson and Thurman both decided to declare for the NBA, and there were rumors Richardson might join them as the coach of the expansion Toronto Raptors. You can forget that. Nolan Richardson is staying in Fayetteville. He and Mike Anderson have worked too hard to assemble one of the nation’s top programs. They are recruiting better and better. They signed six players for the fall of '95, and will continue to challenge for a championship in the years ahead.

Arkansas has helped make the Southeastern Conference one of the best basketball conferences in the nation. It entered the league in 1992 and has become a major player in a conference that used to be Kentucky and a bunch of football schools. Now it's Kentucky and schools like Alabama, Mississippi State and Florida that have arrived as basketball powers. Two more, Tennessee and South Carolina, are headed in that direction. And LSU will be back if its great guard, Randy Livingston, is healthy again and can play in the same backcourt as Ronnie Henderson.

Would you believe Richardson almost lost his job during his second year at Arkansas? Some people say he might have gotten the ziggy if the Hogs hadn't rallied from 17 down to defeat Arkansas State in an NIT game. I doubt Frank Broyles, Arkansas' athletic director, would go after a guy in his second year, but the fans were so used to winning under the previous coach, Eddie Sutton, that it was causing problems for Richardson.

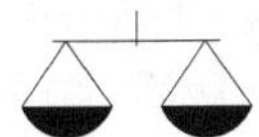

In many ways, Nolan has made Arkansas fans forget about Sutton, or at least realize Sutton isn't the only coach who can win there. Sutton got things rolling in Arkansas back in the late 1970s, when he took that team with the Triplets — Sidney Moncrief, Ron Brewer and Marvin Delph — to the Final Four in 1978. Purdue's Gene Keady was an assistant coach on that team.

Sutton is 59, and he's made an incredible comeback in his coaching career. He knew the '95 tournament might be his best and last chance to get back to the Final Four. When he did, Arkansas fans were dreaming of a Nolan vs. Eddie final, but it didn't happen.

If it had, it might have put President Clinton in a quandary about who to root for in the championship game. Sutton and Clinton first met in 1974, when Clinton was teaching at the University of Arkansas Law School. Sutton got him interested in basketball. When Clinton ran for governor, Sutton's wife and sons worked on his campaign and the two became good friends.

Oklahoma State was one of my Cinderella clubs in the '95 tournament. I told that to Jimmy Leyland of the Pirates and he was quoted in Rudy Martzke's TV column in *USA Today* saying, "My guy, Dickie V, told us watch out for the Cowboys. But he didn't have the guts to say it on the air." Thanks, Mr. Martzke. By the way, I have a question: Did you ever donate some of the megadollars you make to your alma mater, Wisconsin? Give 'em some cash, Rudy.

Oklahoma State had all the essentials for tournament success. It had a player in the lane who provides offensive and defensive efficiency. The Cowboys had that in Bryant "Big Country" Reeves. It had a player who was a threat from the perimeter, a guy who could knock down the three-pointer, in Randy Rutherford. It played great defense and on offense protected the basketball, not making a lot of turnovers. It also had a guy on the sidelines who was a steadying influence. Those are the essential ingredients of any championship contender, so it shouldn't have been a big shock that Oklahoma State made it as far as it did.

Sutton has coached four different teams — Creighton, Arkansas, Kentucky and Oklahoma State — to the tournament. I've done some clinics with him, and he has a great feel and understanding for the game. He knows how it is meant to be played.

Most of the great players come from the urban areas because the game is dominated by the African-American player. However, there are exceptions. You can build a strong team if you get the right kind of people and have a little success in recruiting. Oklahoma State's team included a bunch of small-town kids like Reeves, Rutherford and Scott Pierce, who come from Gans, Okla., Broken Bow, Okla. and Euliss, Tex. — places that aren't going to be mistaken for New York City.

Sutton might be one of the most storied figures in the game if not for what happened when he coached at Kentucky. The NCAA put the Cats on a three-year probation in 1988 for allegedly sending $1,000 to a prospect by overnight mail. Another allegation charged that someone else took the SAT for a prospect. Sutton denied any involvement, but he lost his job. His reputation was seriously damaged and some thought he would be blackballed from coaching. He sat out a year, but Oklahoma State, his alma mater, gave him a second chance after Leonard Hamilton took the job at Miami.

You find out what people are made of when their backs are against the wall, and Eddie Sutton came through like a champion. He didn't complain; he didn't rip people. He just rolled up his sleeves and went back to work like a man. He went to a program that faced a lot of obstacles in becoming one of the top 15 or 20 programs in America today, but he got it done. Gallagher-Iba Arena is rocking again — 6,000 strong — because of his faith and effort.

Today he feels like a million bucks, and he should. If you can battle back from adversity, if you can make adjustments as you get older, that's a sign of great maturity. Sutton deserves every bit of his success.

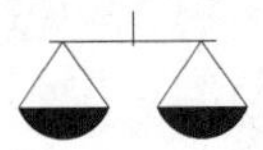

I can't emphasize enough the job Sutton did with Reeves. Big Country got his nickname from Rutherford, because he was from such a tiny town. Gans, near the Oklahoma-Arkansas border, has a population of about 280. It has a post office, a general store, a school and a maze of country roads, and not much more.

Reeves has come a long way since he played for the Gans Grizzlies, a Class B power in the state's smallest school classification. His team had only seven players, so scrimmaging was out of the question. Practice for Reeves used to be some layup drills, a couple of three-man weaves and some shooting. Then he would call it a day after a half-hour or so and take off for his favorite fishing hole. He had seven different coaches, and the last of those, Gerald Ellis, had to split his time with boys' and girls' basketball and girls' volleyball. So it wasn't like Reeves had the best of all possible preparation for major college basketball.

Reeves played in a tiny gym next to a schoolhouse that was built in 1939, and he was able to dominate games merely because of his size. He was recruited by Indiana and Louisville, but signed with OSU because he wanted to play for Sutton.

Sutton thought of Reeves as a project. They still tell the classic story about OSU assistant Bill Self telling Reeves he had to start playing in big cities to improve his game by playing against better competition.

"Coach," Reeves said. "I've been doing that."

"Where?" Self asked. "Oklahoma City? Tulsa?"

"Sallisaw," Reeves answered.

Reeves didn't know what a big city was until he visited New York City at the beginning of his freshman year. I will never forget the moment. Reeves was fresh out of Gans at the time, and Oklahoma State was playing in the preseason NIT at Madison Square Garden. Here he is, a small-town diaper dandy in the big city. He had just flown on an airplane for the first time. We were walking back from practice at the Garden and he was so overwhelmed by what he was seeing that he had to run to a pay phone and tell his mother about all the skyscrapers.

Reeves didn't have to tell his mother about the backboard he shattered at the '95 Final Four, though. She was there to see it, along with 29,000 fans who attended the Friday afternoon shoot-around at the Kingdome.

That moment seemed to serve as Reeves' declaration that he had arrived. I don't think Big Country Reeves really believed he was a star until the Final Four his senior season. I think he was a little shocked by the success he had experienced. I'll bet he pinches himself occasionally, just like I do. Hey, I can relate to this kid. We both live in Fantasyland because of all the great things that have happened in our lives because of the round ball. Big Country didn't fit the mold of a polished, high school superstar who

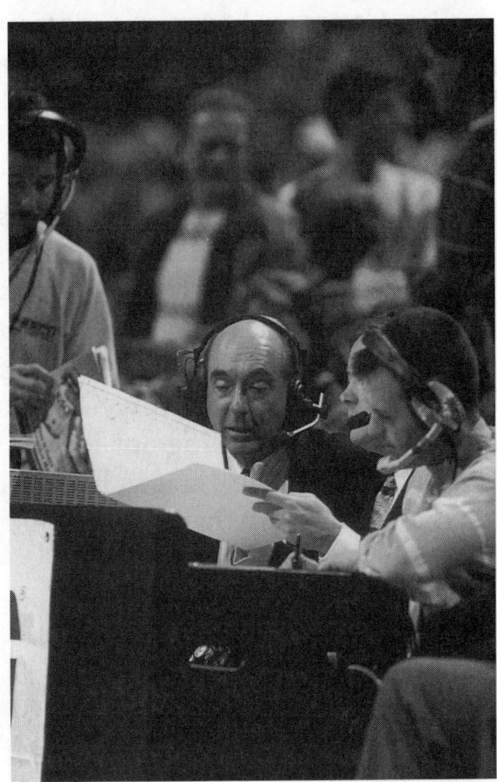

*I'm always searching for a little more information before we go on the air.*

comes in and takes over in college, just like I didn't fit the announcer's mold of a good-looking, athletic guy with nice hair.

ESPN played a major part in Reeves becoming a star. Sutton had been trying to get me to come to Stillwater for a game. I finally made it down for Oklahoma State-Kansas. I call Gallagher-Iba "Cameron Indoor Stadium West" because it reminds me of Duke's arena. The students are right on top of you, along the baselines and the sidelines, and it really rocks. Kansas came in ranked No. 2 in America; the Jayhawks were just blowing people out — Connecticut by 29 and Iowa State by 23. They were on a roll.

Reeves, in front of all the scouts, came through with the biggest game of his career: 33 points and 20 rebounds. He had guys hanging onto him. Kansas coach Roy Williams said it was one of the great individual performances he had ever witnessed.

Big Country became a national icon as the season progressed. I can't tell you how many times I would walk through an airport and hear people shout, "Hey, Dick, do you think Big Country can play in the NBA?"

After watching him hold his own against Antonio McDyess, Tim Duncan and Marcus Camby during the '95 tournament, I have no doubt that he can.

Reeves dominated Camby in the regional finals, scoring 24 points and grabbing 10 rebounds as Oklahoma State defeated UMass, 68-54, to earn its first trip back to the Final Four since 1951. Camby had just six points and four rebounds before fouling out late in the game.

It was fitting he did it in East Rutherford, in the shadow of New York City, where he got his big-time baptism.

# 13

# Paradise Regained: The Lesson of Coach Harrick

When you think of Hollywood, you think of people like Tom Hanks, Tom Cruise, Kevin Costner, Denzel Washington, Jack Nicholson and Whoopi Goldberg.

But let me tell you, the real star of Tinseltown these days is UCLA coach Jim Harrick. He attended the Academy Awards. He was on the Jay Leno show. He can go anywhere he wants now, from the Bel Air Hotel to Rodeo Drive, and be applauded.

This is your time, Mr. Harrick. Enjoy it. Because you, more than anyone, know how quickly things can change.

Harrick nearly lost his job a few years ago after a down season. And when UCLA was eliminated in the first round of the 1994 tournament by Tulsa, the talk shows were screaming for his head again. But one year later, his team was the national champion after defeating Arkansas 89-78, and he was on top of the world.

I'll admit, I didn't pick UCLA to beat Arkansas in the final game. I've got the letters to prove it. The UCLA fans came out of the woodwork to remind me. They were all over me and Digger Phelps, who also picked Arkansas.

But let me tell you something: We weren't alone. And if Arkansas played UCLA again and I knew Bruins point guard Tyus Edney wouldn't be playing, I'd have to pick Arkansas again.

Television viewers get so carried away by what they hear. If we, as analysts, say we think a team is going to win a game, the fans of the other team take it to heart. Picking Arkansas doesn't necessarily mean we're down on UCLA. I just happened to think Arkansas would win that game. But the great thing about athletics is you never know for sure. I agree with Billy Packer, who says we shouldn't get involved in predictions. But the people at ESPN want us to make an analysis and prediction before games. Unfortunately, some fans think we're insulting their programs when we do that.

Edney was the story of the '95 tournament. He's only 5-foot-9, but when the ball's in his hands he plays like he's 6-9. He was on the floor for less three than minutes in the championship game because he had sprained his right wrist in UCLA's semifinal victory over Oklahoma State, and he couldn't dribble the ball.

But anything can happen in a one-game matchup. That's the beauty of the NCAA Tournament. The NBA is the best of seven games. In college, it's Russian Roulette. You've got to make it happen that night or the party's over.

I was reminded of that at halftime of the UCLA-Arkansas game. Norm Nixon, the former Lakers star, was sitting in front of me and we talked. He said the game reminded him of the 1980 NBA Finals when the Lakers went to Philadelphia for the deciding game without Kareem. Nobody gave them a shot. But Magic Johnson, a mere rookie at the time, scored 42 points and the Lakers won.

Nixon told me there's an automatic psychological lift for a team that has to play without a key player. Everybody knows he has to raise the level of his game to make up for the loss. Everybody says, "Tonight I've got to play my best game." That's what happened for UCLA against Arkansas. Just about every guy had the game of his life. Nobody had a bad game. They functioned perfectly as a unit.

It all started with the captain, Ed O'Bannon, UCLA's All-America forward. Eddie O had a phenomenal game, scoring 30 points and grabbing 17 rebounds. He was a huge inspiration. And it was an appropriate way for him to finish his career. When the game ended, O'Bannon had tears in his eyes. His mother, Madeline, said the last time she had seen her son cry like that was five years earlier after he had torn up his knee playing in a pickup game at Pauley Pavilion.

Ed O'Bannon was the best prospect in the country when he was a senior at Lakewood High in Artesia, Calif. I remember doing the McDonald's All-America game that year and he was the best player on the floor. That game was filled with great talent, including Grant Hill, Shawn Bradley, Eric Montross and Indiana's hometown favorite, Damon Bailey. But the star of stars that day was O'Bannon.

O'Bannon and Shon Tarver, another high school star from Southern California, both verbally committed to Nevada-Las Vegas. But the Rebels were hit with NCAA probation before they enrolled, so they chose UCLA on the rebound. It was a great break for the Bruins, and further proof that you need a little luck to win a championship. Maybe UCLA should cut off a piece of its championship trophy and send it to Jerry Tarkanian because if everything had gone smoothly in Vegas, Ed O'Bannon never would have put on a UCLA uniform.

Harrick immediately penciled O'Bannon into a starting front line with Tracy Murray and Don MacLean, but O'Bannon didn't get to play his first season because of the

*UCLA's Jim Harrick had the last laugh in the 1995 NCAA Tournament. Play No. 2 must have been for Ed O'Bannon.*

injury. He had to work hard to rehabilitate his knee and regain his status, and it didn't come quickly. He averaged just three points as a freshman and still was favoring his leg as a sophomore. He started to come on as a junior, and UCLA was ranked No. 1 in the country in January that season. But the season ended with the first-round loss to Tulsa in the tournament. Tulsa had the Bruins down 29 points at halftime and cruised to the victory. But if that game did a great deal of harm to Harrick at the time, it provided a great boost for Tulsa's coach, Tubby Smith. Somebody wins and somebody loses, but that game should prove that losing doesn't make somebody a loser.

O'Bannon was especially motivated during UCLA's championship run. Not only was he playing with his younger brother, Charles, the other starting forward, but he was playing for his newborn son, Aaron. O'Bannon introduced his son and his girlfriend, Rosa Bravo, to the fans at Pauley Pavilion during Senior Night.

He gave them all, and his parents, something to remember all season. Harrick has always been Ed's biggest supporter. I remember being at UCLA in February to do its game with Duke. Harrick came over and jumped all over my case because I had just picked Shawn Respert of Michigan State as my midseason Player of the Year.

He was acting like Ed's campaign manager. He wanted equal time. Let me tell you, there's nothing like a coach fighting for his player. It's like a mother bear protecting her cub. But Harrick had good arguments: Like the five-game stretch against Arizona, Arizona State, Cal, Stanford and Duke. O'Bannon starred in each one, averaging 27 points and nine rebounds overall. He was just dominating. He made seven three-pointers in a game at Cal. To me, that was his breakthrough. From that point on, he was my Player of the Year.

I announced my PTP Awards from Seattle and he was my choice for the Rolls Royce Player of the Year. It wasn't just his statistics; it was everything else he brought to the table. He was a true inspiration.

He couldn't have closed out his career any better. He had one of the great performances in the history of the tournament, right up there with Bill Walton's 21-for-22 shooting performance against Memphis in 1973, Danny Manning's performance against Oklahoma in the 1988 finals, and Jack Givens' 42 points against Duke in the 1978 championship game. It wasn't just the 30 points and 17 rebounds. It was his leadership.

O'Bannon showed why he was such a great leader when he picked up his Most Valuable Player award. He gave credit to Edney, and acknowledged that the Bruins wouldn't have made it to the championship game without him.

Edney belongs in the NBA. But when he was a 17-year-old prospect making his official visit to Westwood, Harrick wasn't sure he belonged in a UCLA uniform. Harrick thought the kid looked like he was 12 years old, and should be playing CYO ball somewhere. But once he saw him perform, he knew he was capable of handling UCLA's explosive transition game.

Harrick had just finished coaching Pooh Richardson, who was the 10th player taken in the first round of the 1989 draft by Minnesota, and he did not know if Edney could fill those shoes. He had to be convinced by Edney's high school coach, Ron Palmer, who said Tyus was the best guard he had ever coached, including the Gwynn brothers — Tony and Chris. Tony went on to become a great guard at San Diego State and is now a future baseball Hall of Famer.

Harrick took a gamble and won big. I remember a big game against Arizona early in the year, when Edney was really fired up. He scored the first two times he touched the rock, taking it right to Damon Stoudamire. It was almost like he was saying to Damon, "I'm the star tonight. I'm the best point guard in America. Move over, Damon. I know Dickie V is at courtside singing your praises as the best point guard in the land. But tonight the show belongs to me."

Edney dominated the game, leading UCLA to a big victory in Tucson, where Arizona never loses. Two nights later, UCLA beat Arizona State in Tempe. That showed the Bruins were for real.

Edney was named after the great Olympic sprinter Wilimena Tyus. That was appropriate when he made a mad dash down the floor to score the winning field goal as UCLA defeated Missouri, 75-74, to advance to the Sweet 16.

I didn't know if UCLA would get that far. I had questions. I felt the weight of its tournament track record would catch up with it psychologically. The tournament mystique John Wooden had built had long since disappeared. And I didn't know if UCLA shot the three-pointer well enough, despite

Ed O'Bannon's hot hand at the end of the season. I thought someone might sneak up on the Bruins in an early-round game, the way Tulsa had the previous year. I thought that someone might be Indiana. Bob Knight's team put the big hurt on them in the 1992 Final Eight and I thought Indiana was the one team UCLA didn't want to play. But I also thought if UCLA could survive that round, the Bruins would be tough to deal with in the regional — and they were.

It took only one small miracle — the one from Edney — to get them over the hump. Missouri led UCLA 74-73 with just 4.8 seconds left in their Sunday afternoon game in Boise, but Edney weaved his way through Missouri's defense like a New York City cab driver in rush hour traffic and hit a driving shot over 6-9 Derek Grimm at the buzzer. It saved UCLA's season and saved Harrick from hearing the same refrains that had been drifting through L.A. ever since John Wooden retired in 1975.

The NCAA Tournament has been witness to a lot of big shots, like Christian Laettner's turnaround jumper from the top of the key to give Duke a one-point, double-overtime victory over Kentucky in 1992, U.S. Reed's half-court bomb that gave Arkansas a victory over LSU, and Danny Ainge's coast-to-coast driving layup to knock Notre Dame out of the tournament in 1980.

I was sitting with Digger when Edney made his shot, and I was saying "Danny Ainge, baby! You remember that, Digger? Deja vu. BYU. Danny Ainge, baby!" That's one of those plays you'll always remember if you're a college basketball fan. But this was even more miraculous because it wasn't a layup. Edney had to make an acrobatic shot over a 6-9 guy who had his arms outstretched. Grimm played it perfectly. But Edney went in and converted.

Edney became a giant on campus after making that shot. The little guy was as big as Kareem Abdul-Jabbar. From that moment on, UCLA felt the tournament was in its hands. Sometimes a championship team needs that kind of moment to make it feel like a team of destiny. Edney's shot no doubt gave the Bruins a lot of confidence and optimism about the rest of the tournament.

It took 20 years, but Jim Harrick became the first UCLA coach to escape the giant shadow that John Wooden, the Wizard, had cast over the program. Wooden retired in 1975 with those 10 titles. Gene Bartow, Gary Cunningham, Larry Brown, Larry Farmer, and Walt Hazzard all took turns as the Bruins' head coach, and all had success. But none of them could bring a national championship back to Westwood until Harrick did it.

When I was coaching at East Rutherford High School in New Jersey, I used to admire the late Vince Lombardi, who got his start at nearby St. Cecilia's. He won in both football and basketball there, long before he went to the Packers and started piling up NFL championships. Sometimes, whenever I wanted to feel good, I would drive over there and walk the hallways and look in the trophy case and think, "Wow, this is where coach Lombardi got his start." It gave me inspiration.

Lombardi was a legend, along with coaches such as Red Auerbach, Casey Stengel and Knute Rockne. But nobody has accomplished what John Wooden achieved at UCLA.

He won 10 NCAA championships from 1964 through 1975.

He won 38 consecutive tournament games.

He won 88 straight games over four seasons.

He coached four undefeated teams.

He was 149-2 in Pauley Pavilion.

Remember, in the NBA you can lose 11 games in the playoffs and still be the world champs. The first series is best three-out-of-five and the next three are four-out-of-seven. I didn't go to Harvard, but I know 3+3+3+2 is 11, and you can still cut down the nets and walk away with the title. But in college ball it just takes one bad night, one little misfortune, and you're done.

Some people look back on Bartow, Cunningham, Brown, Farmer and Hazzard as not having been particularly successful, but they were. They had very impressive numbers.

Bartow was 52-9 from 1975-77 and reached the Final Four.

Cunningham was 50-8 from 1977-79.

Brown was 42-17 from 1979-81 and reached the championship game.

Farmer was 61-23 from 1981-84.

Hazzard was 77-47 from 1984-88 and won the NIT over Indiana in 1985.

But none lasted in the job longer than four seasons.

Wooden's accomplishments had raised the expectations to an unreasonable level, and it was nearly impossible to live up to them. Wooden himself was a victim of that. His team lost to N.C. State in double-overtime in 1974, breaking a string of seven straight titles. After it beat Kentucky in 1975 to win the championship again, a fan approached Wooden and said something like, "Congratulations, coach. You let us down last year, but this helps make up for it."

Unbelievable.

People forget that Wooden was at UCLA for 15 seasons before he won his first championship. Harrick actually did more in his first six years at UCLA than Wooden. He averaged more than 20 wins a season and reached the NCAA Tournament each year. But he still hadn't reached the Final Four, and that's all some fans care about.

That is an unfortunate element of college basketball today, particularly for the high-profile programs. If you don't win the title, people think you really haven't done anything. You're measured by what happens in March. People forget about the rest of the year.

It's an NBA mentality that's crept into college. In 1994, for example, the Seattle SuperSonics won 63 games but lost to Denver in the first round of the playoffs. I went to Seattle to give a speech at a convention and I thought George Karl, their coach, had gone 30-52 or something. I thought he had done what I did, go 30-52 with the Pistons before getting the ziggy early the following year.

The bottom line was, he hadn't done anything in the playoffs, so people were saying he was a failure. Hey, the guy was 63-19. That's a great record in the big leagues, where everybody's got players. But people were trying to bury him, and it looked as though he might get fired.

UCLA is one of the storied programs in college basketball, but I don't think it's a plum job. There's enormous pressure to win there, and win big. And it doesn't pay that much relative to other less publicized places like UMass, Cincinnati, Texas and Utah. Wooden made only about $32,000 a year when he retired in 1975. That was typical of what top coaches made in that era, but it's still amazing to think about. And when Harrick complained publicly about his salary a few years ago, he was thought to be out of line. Harrick doesn't have a TV show. He doesn't have the camps and clinics like a lot of coaches have. And UCLA is just part of what's going on in the L.A. area, along with the Lakers, the Dodgers, Hollywood and everything else out there. It's not like at most major programs, where the college teams are about the only show in town.

Harrick was called a lot of things by many of the talk show callers, people Wooden refers to as "kooks." But he took the hits. The talk shows have become powerful. They stimulate negative conversation among the fans, and it can get pretty tough to survive because it all filters down to your players and your support system. The fans love their moment in the sun, and if it's taken away from them they go on the attack.

I was on a number of talk shows the last couple of years, defending Harrick like crazy. I said, "Wait a minute, this guy is a winner. He's won at Pepperdine. He's won at UCLA. He represents what coaching is supposed to be about. He

*Here I get a dance with the UCLA Bruins' mascot. She was dancing plenty in Seattle when UCLA won the national championship.*

---

coached at junior high, high school, and was an assistant at UCLA before moving up the ladder. You're looking at only one thing — national titles."

Don't tell me people like that deserve to be fired.

Even Bill Walton, the former Bruin great who was broadcasting their games on Prime TV, buried the program. I know for a fact that Harrick was livid about that. Just before the 1993 tournament, Walton said something to the effect that the Bruins peak against the Sisters of Mercy and then don't produce against the better teams. And he thought some players were leaving the program worse than when they came in.

Those statements angered even Wooden. He was unbelievably disappointed. Walton later apologized, but three days later came the Tulsa disaster in the first round. At that time, a lot of people were agreeing with Walton.

You have to remember that Walton was a perfectionist as a player. That's one of the reasons he was so great. I think he has a problem with anybody who doesn't approach the game the way he did. Believe me, there aren't too many Bill Waltons out there. Harrick had a meeting with Walton and shared his feelings with him. He had Walton come back to campus and speak to the team in preseason and they bridged that gap. But that shows you how bad it had gotten in L.A. — Harrick's own people were pounding him.

The only way Harrick could have survived, could have been viewed as a success, was to win a national title. And he did it. He deserves a lot of respect. He always handled himself with class. He didn't publicly lash out at the media or the fans; he just kept working.

Harrick never hid from the UCLA tradition, either. If anything, he embraced it. He made coach Wooden a part of the program again. He invited him to practice, visited him at home. Others in the program did the same. Steve Lavin, one of UCLA's assistants, has become particularly close to Wooden. None of Harrick's predecessors excluded Wooden from the program, but Harrick really brought him into it. He had always been close to Wooden; he even visited John's wife, Nell, for 100 straight days in the hospital when she took sick.

The Bruins' championship team was one Wooden would have been proud to coach. They had great togetherness, all the right stuff.

UCLA had more than Ed O'Bannon and Edney going for it, though. Center George Zidek came from the Czech Republic, where he had been involved in anti-Communist protests as a teenager before the Iron Curtain finally fell in 1989. The 7-footer has great bloodlines. His father, Jiri, was Czechoslovakia's best player ever and had coached the country's national team.

Zidek's is an amazing story. UCLA coaches didn't really recruit him. They went after another player, Julius Michalik. They went to Europe to see Michalik and found out he didn't want them. He wanted to play at Iowa State. They saw Zidek, however, and were able to sign him, although P.J. Carlesimo was trying to get him to Seton Hall. What did I say about championship teams having a little luck?

Zidek is one of the hardest workers you'll ever see. And he was a great student. His stock kept rising during the tournament. Commentators keep talking about a player's stock going up or down during the tournament, but Zidek's stock just kept going up.

Charles O'Bannon followed his brother to UCLA because they had always talked about playing together, but it wasn't automatic. He thought about going to Kentucky. Rick Pitino even spoke at his postseason banquet. But, in the end, family ties were too strong.

Charles had a solid year. He thought he could come in as a freshman and just dazzle them, but he found out it wasn't that easy. He made some adjustments. He understood his role, and had some special moments in transition.

Harrick got Cameron Dollar late. N.C. State turned him down, which turned out to be a mistake. Dollar started out at Douglass High School in Atlanta, playing for his father. When Donald Dollar stopped coaching, Cameron transferred to a private school in Maryland, nationally ranked St. John's of Prospect Hall. UCLA got him after he played in the Capital Classic.

Harrick got his two diaper dandies — versatile 6-9 J.R. Henderson and guard Toby Bailey — early. Bailey grew up in Los Angeles. His father, John, a parole officer, is a UCLA grad and Toby knew all about UCLA's history. John always wanted his son to go to UCLA and Toby always wanted to play there. He developed into one of the two best high school guards in Southern California, along with his childhood friend, Jelani Gardner. Bailey committed to the Bruins early in his senior year at Loyola High School. "I had choices," he said, "but it was ingrained."

Henderson came from Bakersfield, Calif., where his father was one of his high school coaches. Going into his senior year in high school, Henderson was generally acknowledged as the best prospect in the state. But his stock dropped after he injured an ankle and had a lackluster performance at the Nike camp that summer. Henderson came up big in the state tournament, though, leading East Bakersfield to the Division II title. He has elevated his play even higher since joining the program, and should have a great career.

Henderson and Bailey were able to come in and blend in. They had great talent around them, and didn't have to be the go-to guys. If Bailey had a bad night, it didn't matter because Ed O'Bannon was there to carry the team. That was an advantage they had over other marquee freshmen such as Felipe Lopez of St. John's, whose team usually lost if he didn't play well.

J.R. Henderson won respect immediately when he nailed eight straight free throws, including two at the end of the game, to beat Kentucky in the Wooden Classic on national TV. But Bailey scored only one point in that game and pouted afterwards. Ed O'Bannon had to take him aside and tell him the facts of life.

Bailey must have listened. He came back to have monster games off the bench. I made him my John Havlicek. I called him the best sixth man in the college game because of his enthusiasm and emotion, which were contagious.

Bailey became a star in the tournament. He scored 26 points and grabbed nine rebounds as UCLA defeated UConn, 102-96, in the finals of the Western Regionals at Oakland. Henderson came up big, too, contributing 18 points on 9-of-12 shooting.

Some coaches believe you shouldn't talk about championships, that you put too much pressure on the players. But Harrick made it a point to keep his team focused on that. UCLA went to the Final Four with a different attitude than some teams. Harrick had put up a big poster of the Kingdome in the team's locker room as a reminder. And when UCLA went to Seattle to play the University of Washington in February, Harrick took them on a tour of the Kingdome to help keep them focused, to help them see what they were working for.

The Hollywood stars came out for UCLA in the Final Four. People like Tom Hanks, Kevin Costner and Jack Nicholson were there. They were all big UCLA fans. There were celebrities everywhere. I was sitting with my wife, Lorraine, and who do I spot, sitting next to me? Gil Garcetti, the Los Angeles District Attorney who was directing the prosecution at the O.J. Simpson trial. He was a UCLA fan, too.

My wife was saying to me, "Don't you dare start talking to him about the case."

Are you kidding me? I couldn't wait. I started talking a little hoops, then I started asking him about the case. He didn't get into any specifics, but he reiterated to me what he has said on the air: That he felt very confident that they had a strong case, that he thought his people were doing a strong job, and when it was all said and done, the jurors would bring in an honest verdict.

Hopefully, the jury's no longer out on Harrick. The criticism should be history now.

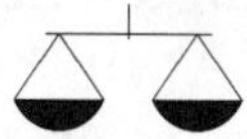

I had one of the great thrills of my life in 1991 when I was the guest speaker at a banquet in honor of Wooden during the Final Four in Indianapolis. In my speech, I said, "You can't understand what a thrill it is for me, a guy who was a sixth-grade teacher in 1970 writing letters to great coaches like John Wooden and getting back a letter from him with the Pyramid of Success enclosed."

Now, here I was, 20 years later, standing there honoring the greatest coach of all time. To go 50-0 in the tournament in 10 seasons is amazing. We can talk about how things were different then; how the regional out West wasn't that tough; how a team didn't have to win six games to win a title then. You can make all the excuses you want. He got it done like nobody else did. Sure, he had great players, but he got them to understand their roles and he got them to play as a team.

I loved the fact John Wooden went to Seattle to see the Bruins win it all. He flew in on the day of the game from St. Louis, where he was attending the McDonald's High School All-America game. Some people thought his presence would steal some of the glory from the Bruins, but I thought it was beautiful. Harrick wanted him there.

Wooden isn't the type to attract attention to himself. As much success as he's had, he has no ego hang-ups. He sat there in the second row and watched. You could see how proud he was, how good he felt. I thought it was a touching, beautiful moment. UCLA's coaches talked about him speaking to the team before the game, but he refused. He didn't want to crash somebody else's party. When it was over, Wooden headed outside to a waiting limousine and was gone.

Now Harrick is not just another guy who succeeded Wooden. After you win the national title, the monkey is gone. I think Jim will be there for a long time. His recruiting will only get better, and UCLA will be on top for a long time. But let's not put the pressure on them to win back-to-back titles.

UCLA fans have savored the moment from the '95 championship, though, and some of it has been at my expense. Just a few weeks after UCLA's title I attended George Foreman's heavyweight championship fight in Las Vegas. I wandered over to the weigh-in at the MGM Grand, and Bob Arum, the promoter, called me up to this big stage to say a few words before they introduced the fighters. I got up there and talked about how it was my first heavyweight fight and it was going to be awesome, baby. I don't know anything about boxing, but I was telling people that from what I heard from all the experts like Charlie Steiner and Al Bernstein, we were looking at a UCLA-Oglethorpe matchup. Blowout City.

A lot of UCLA fans started getting on me, since I had picked the Bruins to lose to Arkansas. They were yelling, "Hey George. You're in trouble if Dickie V's picking you to win."

They were right, I guess. I thought Axel Schultz won the fight. I was sitting next to some fans from Germany and they were going bananas after the decision was announced.

George wound up with the W. There's nothing like the homecourt advantage, huh?

# 14
## Facing the Future

The Olympics come to Atlanta in the summer of '96. It's going to be a great show, and once again the NBA is planning to send its ultimate team.

It might not be Dream Team I. Nothing can match that group. But the USA will still be a heavy favorite with the likes of David Robinson, Hakeem Olajuwon, Shaquille O'Neal, Karl Malone, Scottie Pippen, John Stockton, Anfernee Hardaway, Reggie Miller, Grant Hill and Glenn Robinson.

I used to be in favor of college players representing our country in the Olympics. I thought they could always be competitive. I thought it would be better to risk losing with college kids than always winning with pros.

But I've changed my mind. It tore my heart out in 1988 when the players representing the Soviet Union were running around with gold medals around their necks and we had to settle for bronze. The Soviets thought they were the best in the world then, that the best basketball was being played in their country. But they were using professionals who were older and played all year long.

I decided if other countries are going to use their best, we have to do the same. Let's face reality. The Olympics are not amateur sporting events anymore, in any way, shape or form. So let's bring on the Jordans, the Magics, the Birds, the very best we've got, and show them. My American pride got the best of me. That's the way I feel about it.

Dream Team I was so special in 1992. Larry Bird, Magic Johnson and Michael Jordan — those guys transcended the sport and epitomized how the game is meant to be played. You talk about ambassadors. Everywhere they went in Barcelona, they were heroes. In Michael, you had the greatest ever to play the game. Magic and Bird flat-out knew how to get everybody involved and were genuine, big-time winners. That was one special team. It was like having one huge gold Rolls Royce out there.

Michael, Magic and Bird teamed with Patrick Ewing, Charles Barkley, Chris Mullin, Clyde Drexler, Karl Malone, John Stockton, Christian Laettner, David Robinson, Scottie Pippen and coach Chuck Daly to make history. They didn't have much competition. The Soviet Union had collapsed by then and didn't have a representative team. The Americans blew out everybody, even Croatia in the finals. But you know what? The opposing players didn't mind. They were honored to play against the U.S. team. They were in awe, asking for autographs afterward.

All sorts of politicians, kings, queens and movie stars flocked to the '92 Olympics. But the fans all wanted to see the Dream Team. I will never forget going to the gymnastics competition with my wife, daughters and their friends. The place was packed. We're sitting there, and it's absolutely quiet. Five minutes into the action, who comes walking in but Earvin Johnson. And he gets a standing ovation. People were going out of their minds because Magic had arrived. Everywhere the Dream Teamers went, they were the toast of Barcelona. They couldn't walk down the street without being mobbed.

In 1994, we sent a group of NBA stars to play in the World Championships in Toronto. Dream Team II didn't have the same pizazz as the first group — how could it? — but you had guys who could get it done.

The rest of the world used the 1992 Olympics as a measuring stick for where it wants to go. That team set the standard. There's a lot more age-group basketball being played around the world, and more and more international players are raising the level of their game and surfacing on NBA rosters. Manute Bol is from the Sudan; Dikembe Mutombo of Denver is from Zaire; Rik Smits of the Pacers is from Holland; Carl Herrera of Houston is from Venezuela; Chicago center Luc Longley is fromAustralia; Bulls forward Toni Kukoc, Celtics forward Dino Radja, and Lakers center Vlade Divac were born in the former Yugoslavia; Seattle guard Sarunas Marciulionis is from Lithuania; SuperSonics guard Detlef Schrempf is from Germany; and Golden State center Rony Seikaly is from Greece.

And now Ardyvis Sabonis, the 7-foot-3 center from Lithuania who was the European player of the year while leading Real Madrid to the European club championship, says he intends to sign with the Portland Trail Blazers. During the 1994-95 season in the Spanish League, the 30-year-old Sabonis averaged 22.8 points, 13.2 rebounds, 2.6 blocked shots and 2.4 assists per game.

When NBA commissioner David Stern announced Sabonis as the draft's 24th overall pick in 1986, it drew a surprised murmur from those in attendance. Since then the Blazers have had a long, often frustrating courtship with the man generally considered to be the best player in Europe.

There have been concerns about Sabonis' durability and mobility. He's had several serious injuries, including a ruptured Achilles tendon in the late 1980s. But the Trail Blazers consider him a very skilled player for someone his size.

Basketball is becoming a global sport. And I think the NBA has done a great job marketing itself internationally. That's why David Stern is the No. 1 commissioner in all of sports. He had a vision and he followed it. The NBA has expanded to Canada now with Toronto and Vancouver. I don't think we'll have an NBA franchise located outside North

America, but I think we'll have more and more games being played around the world. We've already seen regular-season games played in Japan. And Stern brought an international flavor to the game with the McDonald's Classic.

In my mind, basketball is the most popular sport in the world. I know how big soccer is in other countries, but forget it. I can't relate to it. I tried hard as a fan to sit there and watch the final of the World Cup and get excited. When it comes to soccer and hockey, I just don't understand all the rules. That puck is flying all over the place. Red line, blue line, green line, white lines.

I really respect the athletic ability. It's obvious soccer is very demanding. Anybody who's been around sports can see that the demands on those athletes and the physical intensity are incredible. The hand-eye coordination of the goalie, the ability to control that ball on your foot, your head ... it just blows my mind.

But it comes down to a lack of scoring. American sports fans like action and scoring. The fan who's not competing can relate when the scoreboard lights up. That's what excites people.

Basketball has always captured my imagination. The game is such a thing of beauty. I remember when I was a kid, Bob Cousy was my hero. I used to take the rock and go to the playground by myself. The rim didn't even have a net. The backboard was half-broken. But I'd be dribbling and shooting and dreaming of being No. 14. A boy, a ball, a dream. That's a motto I stole from a buddy of mine back in New Jersey, Stacy Cirignano of Passaic High School. He used it one time. But I get all the credit for it now.

You don't need five guys; you just go out by yourself and get the thrill of stroking that jumper, getting nothing but nylon, and imagining it's Magic vs. Michael. The hoop scene is so special. There's nothing like it.

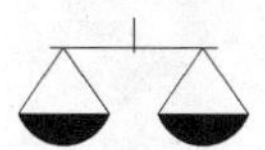

There should be a growing number of opportunities for all athletes with all this expansion in pro sports. Sports have become so popular and such big business, and a lot of communities believe they can support clubs. I know we're excited as heck about major-league baseball expanding into the Tampa Bay area, with my buddy, Vince Namoli, getting the Devil Rays. I'm going to become a big Devil Ray fan. I can see it right now. I've got my four season tickets. Devil Rays vs. Yankees. It doesn't sound right. But it will because they will support it. The fans are going out of their minds.

As long as expansion's done within reason and it doesn't get carried away, I have no problem with it. But all the professional sports are in danger of going too far with it. I wonder if there are enough players to make teams competitive. That takes a while. You hate to see teams embarrassed and humiliated.

That's why it's imperative for pro sports to keep the draft. It creates balance. I know some people say you'll ultimately have balance if you have free agency for the athletes coming out of college, but I don't believe that. If everybody were a free agent, the New Yorks and the L.A.'s of the world would totally dominate the scene, while franchises like SanAntonio and Indiana would not be able to compete. And the poor expansion franchises, like Vancouver and Toronto, probably wouldn't have a chance. They need a draft to divide the top collegiate players. The draft is the ultimate equalizer.

I don't know how the NBA, with all this expansion, is going to come up with 30 centers who can take the pounding in the low post. Pro basketball is becoming so physical. For a while it was getting out of hand.

The game should be Michael Jordan floating through the air; Charles Barkley, with the body of a tight end, taking that ball and going the length of the court and jamming that sucker.

It used to drive me nuts watching three guys holding an opponent's arms down, pounding on him physically, beating on him. Something had to be done, because that wasn't good for the game.

The NBA made a positive move when it eliminated handchecking and all the unnecessary physical contact. People want to see more offense. They want to watch players play defense with their heads and their feet, beating people with quickness instead of their fists.

I'd like to see college basketball make some rule changes, too. First of all, move the three-point line. Right now it's 19 feet, 9 inches. I was talking to Hank Nichols, the supervisor of officials in the NCAA, about it, and I told him the number of three-point attempts by clubs have almost doubled from the time when it was initiated.

What's happening now is teams are just running guys to the three-point line in their initial phase of transition rather than going for the layup. I've done plenty of games where teams fall behind by 10, 11 or 12 points late and just start launching the three, baby. Let it fly. Because of the inflated value of the shot, coaches are recruiting guys who can shoot the standstill three and do little else.

The shot is too easy for the points it earns. I'd like to see the line moved out to the international distance — 20 feet, 6 inches. Those extra nine inches make a difference. Only the quality shooters will be able to knock it down consistently.

I'd also like to see the NCAA open the lane to the international trapezoid. That would take the two post players out of the paint and allow for more dribble penetration. It also would allow the offensive team to attack the basket and generally create more motion on offense.

I have no problem with the shot clock at 35 seconds. The main thing is to have a clock. When teams didn't have to shoot the ball within a given period, it created so many farces, like the one that occurred in the 1982 ACC final between North Carolina and Ralph Sampson's Virginia team. The Tar Heels led, 44-43, with 7:30 remaining when Dean Smith ordered his team to hold the ball in an effort to draw Ralph Sampson away from the basket. Virginia opted not to chase, and six minutes ran off the clock.

Finally, with two minutes left to play, Virginia was forced to foul, and committed five personals in less than a minute until North Carolina was in the bonus. The Tar Heels held on for a 47-45 win, but the game added momentum for the crusade to incorporate a shot clock. Nobody wanted to watch great players like Sampson and Jordan just standing around.

Some people want to lower the clock to 30 seconds, like the women's game, but I like it where it is.

I'd like to see the NCAA bring back the five-second closely guarded rule. I don't think a ball handler should be able to pound the ball and pound the ball. If a team plays tight defense on a ball handler and he doesn't advance the ball, it should be rewarded with a turnover.

Ultimately, though, everything comes down to the officials. They have to enforce whatever rules are in effect. I think officials are underpaid on every level, both college and pro. With all the money on the line, those guys blowing the whistle deserve better compensation. That would lead to more full-time officials and even better officiating. The games have become too big to be managed by part-timers.

You aren't going to get full-time officials, however, unless you pay them six figures, like they do in the NBA. The college refs are teachers, lawyers, professionals. They're not going to give up their regular jobs unless somebody can make it financially rewarding for them.

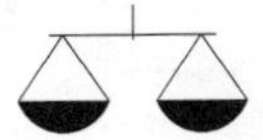

I worry so much about the drug scene. I worry like any other father. I have two girls who are as vulnerable as anybody else. I've been lucky, knock wood. I've given speeches across the country about the drug scene and it's so heartbreaking when I receive letters from people telling me how their lives and those of their families have been ruined.

The NCAA conducts random tests after tournament games, but I don't know if that's the answer. It's too easy for kids to play games with the bottles for the urine tests. The NCAA is worried about privacy, so they leave the kids alone when they provide the samples. That opens the door for dishonesty.

I don't have the solution. I tell young kids across the country, with all the education that's there, they have to make their own decisions. They've got to look in the mirror and know right from wrong. You can guide kids, direct them, but you can't be with them every moment.

That's why I have a problem with professional teams when guys get four, five, six, seven shots, and just keep coming back. How many other people out there get that many chances? You're Johnny Jones, working in an ordinary environment and you've been nailed for drugs two, three, four times. Do you think you're still keeping your job? No way, baby.

We have guys who are suspended for a lifetime. That's become a joke. They're back in 30 days. They come back and they're saying, "I'll be ready; all my problems are behind me." Right. I just don't think that it's fair to the athlete; it's not fair to the club; it's not fair to everyone involved when a guy like that can come back to standing ovations, write a book, give lectures and, all of a sudden, he becomes a hero.

You're only kidding yourself. The guy who's the great athlete and gets caught, he's thinking to himself, You know what? If I can shoot the jumper ... if I can swing the bat ... if I can run with the football ... they're going to find a way to get me in uniform.

If an athlete breaks down, the system should take care of him. It should try to rehabilitate him. I'd like to see everybody get a second chance, because we all make mistakes in life. But you have to draw the line somewhere. As far as I'm concerned, the second time an athlete tests positive, his playing career should be terminated. Simple as that. Maybe that would send a message loud and clear to college athletes and to young kids. Maybe they would think twice about messing with drugs and damaging their lives and the lives of people who love them. I don't know much about the legal aspects, but I hope something can be done to end the farce that a player can be banned for life and then get chance after chance. It's an absolute joke. If you're in the business world and you keep testing positive for drugs, do you think you'll be coming back to standing ovations?

John Lucas, the coach of the Philadelphia 76ers, is trying with his drug and alcohol rehab center in Houston. Lucas had a drug problem himself, but he showed you can come back and succeed and be a positive influence. I salute him.

Hey, the game is going to go on. The Dwight Goodens and Darryl Strawberrys all learn that. The same with the NBA. The people in the hierarchy just have to learn they don't have to put up with this nonsense.

I once read a quote from Giants linebacker, Lawrence Taylor. He had gotten involved in drugs at one point during his career and he said, "My advice is very simple to any young person out there: There's only one way to beat this drug scene — don't start."

I say amen to that.

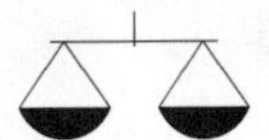

It's sad, but the average sports fan is getting squeezed out of pro events. I hope it doesn't happen in college sports, too. Whenever I'm in New York and have a day off, I try to watch the Knicks play. Hey, I told you I'm a hoops junkie.

You walk into the employees' entrance at Madison Square Garden to pick up your credential and there are always a lot of kids there, screaming for a ticket, dying to get in. The vast majority are African-American youngsters. It really bothers me because the game is dominated by the African-American athlete, but when you look in the stands, it's all corporate America, paying the megadollars for the tickets. It's out of whack.

The little guy who really, really supports the team, who dreams about playing, who can tell you all the stats, who thinks it's really special to see a game rarely gets the chance because he can't afford the ticket, and it bothers me. It should bother the players, too. I know some of them have gone out of their way to try to buy tickets and make them available to kids' groups and so forth, but we need more. The NBA should do something. You have to nurture your future fans.

Families are getting priced out of live events, too. If a dad wants to take his son to a game in New York, even if he can get tickets at a legitimate price, you're talking about more than $100 when you include parking and getting something to eat. That's too much for an average family.

I remember as a kid, my dad and mom worked in a factory and I'd go out and hustle every dime I could make to be able to see the Knicks and the Yankees. I'd pay for a grandstand seat at Yankee Stadium, then try to sneak down into the box seats.

We can't shut out the average fan.

Speaking of that, I can only imagine the rush for tickets to the 1996 Final Four at the Meadowlands in East Rutherford. After the schools, coaches, NCAA officials and VIPs get their ticket allotment, only about 1,000 seats are left for the fan on the street.

The demand is going to be incredible. The scalpers are going to be in heaven. But you know what? I get to go for free. That's why I have the greatest job in the world. And the game is right in my backyard. I used to teach at Franklin Elementary School, just five to ten minutes away from the Meadowlands. It'll be a homecoming for me — right back where it all began for a one-eyed, bald-headed basketball whacko whose passion for the game started on the streets of East Rutherford.

Let's hope the Prez and Hillary will be there, too.

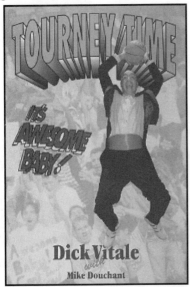